LOVE WITH N

This book is dedicated to

Ntombentile Protasia Khoti
Mark James Themba
Simon Anthony Sipho

LOVE WITH NO REGRETS

From the Catholic Priesthood to an African Marriage

by

TONY TORKINGTON

SPENNITHORNE PUBLICATIONS

If I have all the eloquence of Man or of Angels, but speak without love, I am simply a gong booming or a cymbal clashing . . . And if I have faith in all it's fullness, to move mountains, but without love, then I am nothing at all.

1 Corinithians

First Published in 1988 by:
Spennithorne Publications
Spennithorne House
1 Bourton House
Hunts Cross
Liverpool, L25 0PB

Copyright © Spennithorne Publications 1988

British Library Cataloguing in Publication Data
Torkington, Percy Anthony Thomas, 1931 – 1985
  Love With No Regrets.
  1. Great Britain, Social life – Biographies
  I. Title
  941.085 8 0924

Cover Design by:
Sister Paula Margaret OP
Monastery of Catherine of Siena
Chord Road
Drogheda, Ireland

ISBN 0 9512805 1 1

Typesetting by Graphic Communications Ltd., Liverpool
Printed by Cox Rockliff Ltd., Aintree, Liverpool

Chapter One

"Why did you marry a black woman Dad?" Mark asked as we made our way out of the church.

"Because he's colour blind, of course", said Pro interrupting.

"Surely you know that; it was three months before he realised what he'd done, but by then it was too late, so he had to keep me."

Mark looked at his mother only momentarily satisfied by her answer.

"Then why did you marry a white man mum, you're not colour blind." Mark's sharp little mind struck back.

"Well that's different, you see where I come from a girl had no choice once the bride price had been settled."

"How much did Dad have to pay for you?" Mark demanded.

"One cow, one sheep and one goat" said Pro.

"Never " said Mark with a wicked little grin, "It was daylight robbery."

"Come here you little devil", said Pro "I'll give you daylight robbery".

But before Pro could grab him Mark had made off at speed to join his younger brother Simon to take part in the ritual game of hide and seek that always followed Sunday morning mass at least when the weather permitted, and it did permit that particular June morning. It was a scorcher, and it made Liverpool feel like the tropics.

After the subdued light of the Church, the sudden brightness blinded me to my surroundings. I was taken back to other churches, fifteen, twenty years ago, bathed in the light and heat of an African sun. I smiled to myself as I remembered greeting and being greeted; wiping my face and the back of my neck with a handkerchief, feeling my hair plastered down with sweat and hating the stickiness. The greetings, though formal, were exchanged with nods and smiles. There was laughter always.

The pictures and memories reappeared with ease and clarity. I was surprised at the facility with which it all flashed through my mind, though it was hardly the first time I had remembered events from my years in South Africa. The memories would build up on each other until I recalled the naivity and simplicity with which we, young priests, first began our lives in that country of contrasts and contradictions.

****

It was only a couple of months before I finished my theological studies that I was invited to go to South Africa. I had known there were priests and brothers of my Franciscan Order in Natal and Transvaal but I had never seriously considered offering my services in that area. It had been suggested, rather belatedly, that I should sit the entrance examination for Cambridge. So belatedly that I did not get offered a place, or so I comforted myself. Thus with only weeks to go before I finished my priestly studies I had no intimation of what I might be asked to do next. I was surprised when the request came and I asked for a couple of days to think about it. However, given that I had no idea of what else I might be drafted into and could not really think of any sound reasons for refusing, I accepted.

With final exams upon me, I had no time to inform myself about South Africa. I had spent six years in the sheltered confines of a religious house with minimal contact with the outside world; I was scarcely even aware of what was going on in the world, apart from radio news bulletins and occasionally reading the newspaper. At twenty-eight I was, as I look back now, very innocent and ignorant of all but the theological studies I had been immersed in for several years. I had little interest in politics, and even less comprehension. If this was true of British politics, my knowledge of South African politics was almost totally non-existent. An old aunt of my mother had lived there for many years and comments from her had, from time to time, been related at home. However, these had left me with only the most nebulous notions of what South Africa was like, apart from a vague awareness that black/white tensions existed. The kindest way of describing my approach to South Africa would be to call it open-minded, though empty headed would have been a more accurate description. As my departure approached I was undoubtedly filled with zeal for apostolic endeavour. I was conscious of the efforts of great missionaries of the past and fantasised about my own future inspired by their lives. The Church had been my world – from my early days in a staunchly Catholic family living on the outskirts of Manchester to my attendance at Catholic schools, and then theological college. Everything else seemed peripheral and therefore of secondary importance and interest. In this state of comprehensive ignorance I approached what was certainly to me, a dark continent. There are those who believe the ideal way to learn to swim is to be pushed in at the deep end. I learnt about Africa the same way.

****

I started my life in South Africa at Ermelo, a small town parish in south eastern Transvaal. There I was supposed to acclimatise myself and prepare for whatever lay ahead. My immediate task was to be assistant priest to Fr. Cormac, an old hand who had been in South Africa for twelve years. I spent the first week passing from one out-station to another with Fr. Cormac, adjusting my mind to a new concept of a parish. To me the word meant a church in an urban area surrounded by houses from which the parishoners walked or drove to the church in a matter of minutes. Rural African parishes were usually huge, sparsely populated areas. Here it was the priest who went to the people gathered in local centres once or twice a month. When the priest was not there an official church representative would be the catechist, or lacking a catechist, a local teacher might lead the services. The catechist would be a paid worker, whereas the teacher or other leader was an unpaid volunteer. It was not only my concept of a parish and its staff that needed adjustment. Many things were different – the variety of ethnic groups, the sounds and smells of the countryside, the small isolated towns separated by thirty, forty, fifty miles of open rolling veldt.

At Ermelo the priests' house was next to the church. Both were set on rising ground at the eastern edge of the town, about three quarters of a mile from the town centre. The house lay in a coppice of pine trees on the hillside overlooking a dirt road. My abiding memory of my first few weeks is the slightly suffocating smell of the pines wafting into my room and the strange cry of an unfamiliar bird perched among the trees chanting a two-note lament in a minor key. The scent of the pines was accentuated by the increasing heat of the early summer days. I experienced a feeling of sickly languor about 11.00 each morning for the first two or three weeks. I worried I had caught some fatal tropical disease. I even began to hear the doleful chant of the bird as presaging an unhappy ending to my new life in a strange land. In fact the languor was merely caused by the rarefied air found at five thousand feet. I was still acclimatising. The same air was frequently thick with red dust. It rose up in clouds every time a vehicle passed along the road in front of the house. The tables were constantly coated with grit, it was necessary to dust the top of a desk several times a day in summer when all the windows were open.

The white population lived in the town itself. Their houses were usually bungalows surrounded by spacious gardens. These were invariably beautifully kept with lawns made green by water-sprinklers, hedges neatly trimmed and an abundance of richly-coloured flowers, revelling in the almost continual sunshine which was broken but briefly by the summer rains. The only danger to the gardens was the occasional hail storm in summer. The hail stones were quite commonly the size of marbles and often larger. They brought devastation to many unsheltered, manicured flower beds and more worryingly to windows and asbestos roofing. A person caught in such a storm could suffer small cuts to unprotected face and arms. This picture of small town suburbia portrayed a population even more garden-proud than their English counterparts. Admittedly the climate invited interest in the outdoors and a great deal of time was spent in the garden during summer. There was however another factor. In most gardens I visited I saw a building which, at first, I took to be some sort of domestic outbuilding like a laundry or workshop. Maybe they went in for brick-built garden sheds? They were, in reality, the quarters of

9

the 'native' servant or servants.

It was soon apparent that the white South Africans generally enjoyed a very high standard of living. Part of that high standard was the possession of servants. We often visited parishioners at night, perhaps for a meal. Unobtrusively sliding in and out would be an African servant working in the kitchen, even at that time of the evening. Although interest in the upkeep of the garden was genuine enough, the chores of weeding, lawn-mowing and digging were in the hands of the 'garden boy'. Some households also employed a black 'nanny' to look after the children. Where two to three servants were being employed I guessed that either the white man was earning a great deal of money or servants came cheap in South Africa. I discovered fairly quickly the latter was the case. Africans in general, and in domestic service in particular, were paid very low wages indeed. Their family lives were a constant battle for survival. Those in domestic service fared better only in that they were assured of regular meals from the white man's kitchen, their wages enabled them to buy only the barest necessities of life for their families.

The majority of Africans who worked in the towns lived in areas set aside for their use called 'locations'. In urban areas the locations were built by the town council outside the town limits. The houses were small, concrete, four-roomed bungalows. The tiny rooms were hot in summer and cold in the frosty high-veldt winters. Mains drainage and electricity were virtually unheard of. In small towns the roads were unmade. They became deeply rutted and the surfaces were washed away by the summer rains. In these depressing conditions a few made a brave effort to fence off a small garden and grow vegetables. During the first few weeks I visited various locations and mine compounds. The best housing was in these municipal locations, the worst was often found in mine compounds: corrugated iron sheds for single men working their contracts with the mines. Even the very best of this housing was worlds apart from the housing enjoyed by the white man. The contrast was so stark it made the concept of mixed housing areas outside the realms of possibility.

Fr. Cormac watched my reactions as we went from one place to another, from one society to another. He knew what I was thinking, because he had lived with this for twelve years. He knew that the solutions were not easy and still a long way off given the racist nature of the government. The one thing that saved me from total despair was the sunshine. I could imagine in the drabness of a dirty Lancashire town, on a miserable, chilly November day, the same human condition would have loaded me with the weight of despair more rapidly. At least the African sunshine shed a golden light which allowed much of life to be lived outdoors, not in the cheerless, cramped interiors of inadequate accommodation. But the real sunshine shone in the laughter and noise of a location street. Perhaps I was looking for some relief, some ameliorating factor to grasp. Amid the squalor and poverty of the African residential areas I found a gaiety and camaraderie, doubtless born of fellowship in suffering, which did something to relieve my despondency.

After a fortnight's introduction to all these facets of South African life, I was left gasping a little at the complexity of it all. I wondered if I would ever take it all in my stride as Fr. Cormac seemed to do. In retrospect my confusion was exacerbated by Fr. Cormac's very individual style of induction. He moved suddenly and apparently impetuously announcing visits to people or places with little or no prior warning. He marched around the town leaving me struggling to keep up with him. He seemed to know so many people though he later admitted he had never met many of those he engaged in conversation. As the need demanded Cormac switched from English to Zulu to Afrikaans, greeting all with vigorous handshakes and hearty laughter. He was an exhausting man; a man of changing moods and attitudes. I don't mean that he was a moody man in the usual sense; Cormac's moods were only too predictable. The beginning of the day was still ruled by the practices he had learned as a student in a religious community; so there was a prayerful start to the day. After rising quietly, time was spent in prayer before and after mass. He was serious; his head bowed as he moved from house to church, from church to convent, avoiding contact with others while he concentrated on his communion with God. We concluded morning devotions with some formal prayers together. Then as we left church a huge beam of greeting would cover his face and he would wish me, and whoever else happened to be present, the heartiest of good mornings, commenting on the beauty of the new day. The greeting was as invariable as the sunshine. Such was the gusto of his "Good morning" that even passers by on the road would feel embraced by it. Indeed if they chanced to look across, curious about the disturbance behind the hedge, they too would be caught up in this morning greeting by an expansive, sweeping gesture of his arms, with accompanying peals of laughter. We breakfasted at the convent in a small dining room set aside for our use. In the confined space, Cormac moderated his morning euphoria, except when giving an effusive welcome to the Sister who brought our breakfast. On one occasion a Sister from another convent brought in the feed. She shied like a startled horse at the robust greeting, put down the tray and made her exit hurriedly with a puzzled smile. She was apparently quite unnerved by the experience. Cormac was well aware of the effect on the young, impressionable nun and could not restrain himself from producing a loud guffaw which must have been audible not only to the retreating Sister, but to most of the convent.

Cormac's driving, I decided after a couple of weeks, was not actually dangerous or reckless, it just looked as if it was. Most of the unease and anxiety in his passengers was caused not by narrow escapes from disaster but rather from the impression created by Cormac's manner that disaster was imminent. He would crouch his large body

11

over the wheel, sometimes even contorting himself to peer through it. From time to time, he would cast sidelong glances through the windows or at his passengers, behaving like a paranoiac, constantly vigilant against impending attack. At other times, he would adopt the role of a tour guide pointing out features of interest to right and to left as we drove along in a voice loud enough to carry to the back of a touring coach. In the small 'beetle' Volkswagen such stentorian announcements set the head buzzing.

Beneath this superficially aggressive bonhomie, Cormac was deeply religious and firmly attached to the simple and traditional faith of his Irish ancestors. His clowning, a cover for shyness, got him a richly deserved reputation for eccentricity. For those few who knew him well this was no bar to an appreciation of his sincerity and goodness. Anybody in need or with a problem immediately won his whole-hearted attention. A tramp at the door would cheerfully be given Cormac's shorts, or indeed mine once when all his were at the laundry. He knew that I would not mind, he said later, amid conciliatory laughter.

Cormac's simple approach to life ruled out subterfuge or subtlety. After I had been with him for a month, Bishop Ulyatt telephoned and spoke to him for some time. Cormac appeared at my open door, beaming at me with a half-mocking, half-pitying smile.

"The Bishop says I have to break this to you gently over the next day or two". He cocked his head on one side, as if deciding how to prepare me for the news from the Bishop. The task was performed in just three seconds.

"You're going to Besters". The exercise in diplomacy over, he burst out laughing. Cormac knew perfectly well that no such tact was necessary. I had come to South Africa with no preconceptions or preferences and was quite ready to go anywhere at all. Anyway, I could hardly have formed any lasting attachment to a place in four weeks.

"When?" I asked, as a matter of interest.

"He's probably coming to see you in a couple of days and will arrange everything then; but pretty soon, I understand."

The Bishop arrived to see me two days later. Cormac was out when the Bishop arrived, so there was no chance for consultation as to how I had taken the fateful news.

"Hello, old boy," he greeted me, and dropped his slightly podgy frame into a chair. "How are you settling down?"

"Wonderfully," I told him, "I really like this place. You know, I have never, unlike many brothers at home, had any itch to travel, see the world, and yet here I am six thousand miles from my own country. Anyway I tend to settle very easily. I have really taken to this place now that I have looked around a bit. As far as I am concerned I wouldn't mind staying here for the rest of my days. There's plenty of work to be done, plenty to challenge me."

My little speech evidently caused him some unease and he shifted about in his chair.

"Yes," he mused, obviously convinced that Cormac's subtle approach had not yet got through to me. He looked out of the window for a moment.

"Where's Cormac, do you know?" he asked.

"He went into town as far as I know."

"Back soon?" he asked hopefully.

"I really don't know, Monsignor," I replied.

"Mmm," he murmured, apparently searching for words. "Well, I stayed here for a couple of years once, but you get a bit tired of one place after a while and a move is a good thing really."

As I got to know the Bishop, as the years went by, I learnt how he hated being the bearer of bad news. He tied himself up in knots every time he had to tick someone off or move someone who really didn't want to be moved. I could keep my face straight no longer and burst out laughing.

He was taken aback at the sudden outburst.

"I'm sorry," I apologised, "but I do know about the intended move."

The Bishop's enormous relief was very apparent, though he tried to appear nonchalant.

"Oh, Cormac did mention it, did he? I asked him to break it gently to you."

"Oh, he did," I said, "It took all of three seconds after he had come off the phone."

"Yes," the Bishop replied, "Cormac's a dear chap, but a bit unsubtle." And a chuckle started, slowly like a hiccough but gradually building to a continuous chortle. Cormac and the Bishop had known each other many years; there was a great deal of mutual affection, but no illusions about each other.

"Yes, that's Cormac alright", he said as the chuckle subsided. He looked weary no longer and sat up in his chair, ready to set aside casual small talk and get down to business.

"Well, what do you think? Do you mind moving so much?"

"Not in the least. I will go where you want me to, I really don't know enough to know where I would be best used or even to have a preference yet. What is Besters anyway?"

"Well," he started slowly. The Bishop's 'well' was long drawn-out. He lingered on the last 'L', buying himself time to decide what to say next. "Well, Besters is one of the farm missions our order is just taking over from the Durban Archdiocese. It's quite near Ladysmith, – I shall ask the Fathers there to give you all the help they can, of course – and it's all African. How's your Zulu coming on, by the way?".

"Slowly," I replied.

"Yes, well I am afraid it takes time." And after a moment's thought, "In fact, it's taking me a long, long time. I don't really suppose that at my age I shall ever be proficient at it. But you must get down and work hard at it, while you still have time. Once you start getting involved with work, you will find it harder and harder to find time to study. Anyway, the job I want you to do at Besters is very special -that's why I have chosen you." He favoured me with a smile which signified he had recognised my sterling qualities and was about to give them a worthy task. Then getting nearer to the truth he added:

"Actually, Old Lambert is there at the moment, but it is too much for him. All the out- stations are situated along country roads which are a bit bumpy for a man of his age. Anyway he's never going to learn the language now." Old Lambert was only just over sixty but I suppose that a life lived in an English urban parish was not good preparation for missionary activity in the bundu of South Africa. Apart from the physical rigours, the culture shock must have been tremendous.

At this point Cormac returned.

"Monsignor", he boomed, "You are welcome. Did the boy" – he meant me – "get you a cup of tea?"

"No, but we have been talking; it doesn't matter."

"Sam," Cormac looked over to me, "this won't do. Our hospitality is renowned throughout the south eastern Transvaal. You have failed. I'm afraid you will have to go". He laughed heartily, knowing very well that we were discussing my departure.

"You broke it gently to him I hear, Cormac," said the Bishop.

"Broke it gently?" said Cormac scornfully. "Well, I told him, if that's what you mean." He went out and broke into song in the corridor.

"I shall miss all that, of course," I told the Bishop.

"Yes," said the Bishop thoughtfully, and then after a pause, "It can become a little tedious after a time, you know." He pulled his thoughts together again. "The special job I want you to do is to open a minor seminary for me. We must start the job of getting African priests for Africa, you know. We are only here to facilitate things, that's all. So what do you think?"

He knew he had dropped a bombshell. The Franciscan Order in South Africa had never before attempted to train African priests. He obviously expected me to both assimilate the idea and have opinions about it immediately. He viewed me with expectation, eager to hear my reaction.

"I have no experience of setting up minor seminaries."

"Well of course you haven't, dear boy, nobody else has either. But it's got to be done." And seeing that I wasn't immediately up in arms about the idea, or my involvement in it, he launched into his sales pitch.

"The future is in the hands of young men like you, dear boy. Old Lambert, Cormac and the rest of us who have been here some years have got into a way of doing things, it's very hard for us to change or branch out. But you young fellows are the ones who are going to change the face of the Church in Africa. We look to you, we need you and we

14

have the confidence that you can and will meet the challenge, d'you see? What?" His rhetorical exhortations expected no reply, they were designed to bring total acceptance, preferably immediately.

"So I'll come and fetch you on Monday." It was Thursday, but then I had hardly unpacked.

"There may just be one or two points to discuss..." I began.

"Oh, yes, yes, yes, yes," he brushed me aside with mock irritation,

"we shall discuss all that down there on Monday." He bounded up out of his chair and went to the sitting-room door. "Cormac," he bellowed, "Are you going to give us lunch?"

"Of course, Monsignor", Cormac replied, from the other end of the house, "our hospitality, as you know..."

"Yes, yes, yes, old boy, I know." The Bishop was in high good humour, the negotiations had gone well with me and all was arranged for Monday.

Cormac must have spread the word that I was leaving, for a couple of the Sisters at the convent mentioned politely that they were sorry I was not staying, just as they were getting used to me. They had known Cormac for a long time. I fancy their regret was that Cormac was not getting the young, active help that he needed. Old Lambert was swapping places with me but I suppose they thought his age was against him. The possibility of his setting the southern Transvaal alight with his magnetic presentation of the word was remote.

On Saturday I was surrounded by a group of girls from the convent school as I left lunch. Cormac had gone off to visit an out-station, leaving me alone to hear any confessions during the afternoon. The girls had heard that I was leaving soon and expressed their dismay. Happy in the knowledge that I had no say in the decision, I courteously pretended regret that I should be deprived of the sound of their happy voices both in church and in the playground. They had clustered round me and without appearing to be rude I could not push my way through. There was a certain amount of giggling and whispering, until a tall, shapely, blonde girl blurted out her confession – I was her pin-up. Having steeled herself for this admission, urged on by her class-mates, she then fished down into her gym-slip and produced a small leaflet. This turned out to be a copy of the local diocesan magazine from a couple of months back. It was opened and folded over at a page which contained a full-page photo of myself, captioned "Fr Samuel – soon to join the South African Mission". She blurted out how handsome she found me and how desolated she was to hear of my departure, soon after congratulating herself on my posting to their parish. She emphasised the depth of her feelings by pressing the limp magazine against her bosom, closing her eyes in quiet adoration. It was difficult to know quite what to say. Living in a religious house does not exactly prepare young clerics for such outspoken, not to say public protestations of affection and devotion. There flashed through my mind several possible replies while she

15

enjoyed her moment of ecstasy. A stern rebuke perhaps, about speaking thus to a man of the cloth, who has eschewed all carnal contact with the opposite sex. One might then add a brief review of the good and solid theological reasons for the vow of celibacy and wind up with an admonition that it was incumbent upon good Catholics to help their clergy to keep to this shining way. I doubted whether any of it would have gone down too well. So I laughed – a little hoarsely and with a great deal of embarrassment - in an attempt to keep the whole thing from getting out of hand. I was not used to school girl crushes and felt acutely uncomfortable. I escaped eventually and went up to the house, wiping my sweaty brow and thanking God I was moving on Monday.

The Bishop arrived on Sunday evening, so that we could make an early start next morning, he said. He was at his busiest and best when executing plans, rather than in the, for him, tortuous process of making them. Seen writing a difficult letter or a directive to his clergy, he would be seated at his desk, surrounded by sheets of crumpled paper, a cigarette in one podgy hand which he applied to his mouth between nervous and irritated bites at his knuckles. But the execution of a plan produced the hustling organiser, urging people on like a team captain, communicating the need for haste.

The Bishop followed me around, asking if I had got everything. Anything left in the wash? – don't pinch their towels – is this your book? - have you looked through all the drawers? He asked, doing it himself anyway. And suddenly I was sitting in the car.

"Bye, old boy", the Bishop called to Cormac, and we sped away amid a cloud of dust, which momentarily hid Cormac, but not his laugh which followed us in gusts.

The Bishop smoked Piccadilly cigarettes from a yellow tin. When he was not smoking, he whistled, usually from one of the Brandenburg Concertos, but his tastes in music were catholic and on occasion we would be treated to the latest pop hits. As ideas about the future seminary came to his mind, he would share them with me, promptly demanding my opinion. Putting his thoughts together, what he had in mind was something essentially African, – whatever that might mean in terms of the imported idea of a seminary – with a dash of his own public school thrown in.

"I don't want a Dotheboys Hall, d'you see, Sam, my boy?"

"Indeed not", I reassured him. "But is there anything to work with?"

"Well, not very much, dear boy", he said rather sadly, "But that is where your drive and energy will be tested, and I am confident, nay, assured in my mind with no glimmer of doubt, that you will succeed in this venture". He lapsed on occasions, when he thought it would ignite enthusiasm for difficult jobs, into an almost Churchillian rhetorical style. He looked at me with eyes aglow. "What?" he fired at me, and chuckled, pleased with himself and his oratory.

16

"I think that we should have a board of governors." Another idea was popping out. "You will be on it, of course. And who else...? Well, we can think about that."

"When do we plan to open?" It was now towards the end of November and I had assumed that the following September or even October would be the earliest possible time for starting.

"Well, I thought January, dear boy, when the schools re-open after the summer break."

"Good grief! That doesn't give us a lot of time."

"Well, no, but the matter is so desperately urgent, don't you see, old boy? Time is of the essence, absolutely of the essence. There is a mission school and the boys can attend that. You can add whatever subjects you think fit – bit of Latin, Plain Chant and things, you know. But these are just the details. The thing is to get started."

A bit of Bach brought a brief intermission for me to think about what the Bishop had said. He worked on his next idea.

"I'm leaving Brother Martin to help you", he said breaking off whistling for a moment. "There is plenty of room for a spot of building. I thought of a big rondavel with a thatched roof – cool in summer and warm in winter, you know, – and of course it's African. I've asked Jack about using his travelling builder".

"Will there be room for him to stay at the mission, as well as the boys?" I asked.

"Oh, Jack won't stay, though he would have been a help, he's always away building something".

"No, I meant his travelling builder."

"Well, Martin will use that." I thought it a bit impersonal to refer to the poor man as 'that' and said so.

"Dear boy, a travelling builder is a piece of machinery which makes building blocks".

"Oh", I said lamely.

"Cigarette?" he invited, grabbing for his yellow box.

On our arrival at Besters, Old Lambert greeted us with immense enthusiasm. As I say, he was not really old at all and there was plenty of twinkle left in his eyes. I had feared a difficult take-over with Old Lambert a bit cast down at having to admit he could not cope with the rigours of the terrain, the problems of the language or the thought of being a school master again. But no, Old Lambert was jubilant to see me and told me so with undisguised relief.

"Sooner you than me", he said, with a frankly unreligious spirit, "I couldn't take any more of this lot. But you'll probably like it". He added the last bit by way of some hopeful encouragement, slapped me on the back and walked briskly into the house. I turned to unload my cases. I had scarcely got a handful of bags and books out before Old Lambert was beside me again, bearing his baggage and eager to load it into the car.

"You leaving today Lambert?" I asked in some surprise. I had supposed we would spend the rest of the day discussing the take-over and that he and the Bishop would depart the next day.

"If at all possible, Sammy boy. No offence to you but I am keen to move".

I began to suspect I had been asked to take over a leper colony or, at the very least, that I would be under siege by unfriendly local tribesmen. I also naively supposed that the Bishop would spend a little time with us in policy discussions about the seminary.

"Oh, really", I said, "Is it that bad? I had hoped to have a run-down on the organisation of the place and its out-stations."

"Sam, I have only been here for a month and it's all a bit hazy. I have been driven around by Martin to this place and that. I have said mass at different houses and little churches, but don't ask me to tell you where they were, or what was said by anyone about anything, because I don't know. Martin knows all about it and he will guide you around the area."

Old Lambert really did seem to have had enough in his short stay. He passed on a few friendly warnings with a hint of relish in his voice.

"There is a lot to do sorting out the paperwork left by our predecessors. When I arrived the place looked as if they had all fled from an unexpected earthquake. I have got a little order into things but there is still plenty to do. Oh, and did his Lordship tell you that we have no money? Try that on your vow of poverty. He goes stone-deaf when you tell him about the money situation. Anyway, as I say, good luck to you. I am sure that you will conquer, whereas a strategic retreat is the order of the day for me".

I asked the Bishop about his immediate plans and he confirmed, a little surprised himself, that Old Lambert rather expected to leave within the hour. We did manage to hold him long enough to have some lunch before he pressured his episcopal chauffeur to drive him away from Besters. The Bishop promised to return within a few days.

"just giving you a little time to settle in," he said. "And set Martin to building", he bellowed from the car, "All the best, you chaps," he waved and made his usual brisk exist.

****

18

Chapter Two

I dared to read my first sermon in Zulu a month after my arrival. It was painful for me but must have been agony for my listeners. I wrote it in English and had it translated by one of the Zulu sisters at the convent. I sweated through the tongue-twisters the sister had written down in translation. I gave it out not word by word but syllable by syllable, at what must have been dictation speed. A handkerchief was barely adequate to absorb the wetness running down my head and neck, my shirt was saturated. It was only a month short of Christmas and the summer was starting in earnest.

"Baba Sam," a female voice said.

"Hello, yes?" I replied, looking for the owner of the voice in the crowd of about three hundred people outside the church.

"Ufuna ukuphuza itiye na?" It was Doris, a Zulu woman who lived on the mission farm, she was house servant at the priests' house. She was also my translator and interpreter. She spoke English, but pursuing her policy of making sure I did not use her as interpreter for too long she said everything to me first in Zulu, at least twice. On my failing to understand she repeated what she was saying in English.

I had heard that sentence twice a day for the past month and knew she was asking me if I would like a cup of tea.

"Yebo, ngiyabonga", I replied, "Yes, and thank you," – I was making progress. A pint of ice cold beer would have been more welcome, but I was desperate for liquid replacement.

I looked at the groups of black-skinned people, talking and laughing animatedly outside the church and at the hilly terrain around the mission station. It was mostly green now, the first rains had started the new season's growth a month ago. However, deep clefts in the land stood out brown and sandy. The rushing waters of the summer rains eroded the top soil and vegetation struggled for survival in the ruts, creating a striped landscape. The high hill behind the priests' house was completely bare and rocky – in a moment of enthusiasm I had climbed it a few days before and almost trodden on a snake. Yes, it was another world – even the birds made different noises.

"Nanti itiye, Baba." Doris was back from the convent with a tray of tea and biscuits. The people were drifting away and I went into the house.

The house was some fifty years old and built out of ironstone, a flinty blue-grey colour. The ironstone outcropped all over the mission farm and was said to attract the lightning of the stupendous electric storms during the rainy season, one of which had already put more fear into me than many a hell-fire sermon. The house was a single-storied building with two wings at either end, about half the length of the main block. All one side of the house was shaded by a wide verandah. In England the aspect would have been sombre and forbidding; it was dark, solid and not inviting. In this climate its interior provided a welcome contrast to the heat and the glare of the sun.

The light was quite dim in the sitting room, the windows were covered with a fine-mesh netting to keep out the flies. The main farm buildings were to the back and side of the house, about fifty yards away, but the calf-pens were between the house and the dirt road. Flies bred in profusion. They constantly tried to invade the house and to adhere to my sweaty head and arms.

"Uthi uSister uzokudla ngasikhathi sini?"

Another linguistic puzzle. I knew that the -kudla bit meant food and told Doris I had isolated that important item from her statement, or maybe it was a question? She repeated it gazing at me not too hopefully, like a patient teacher with a retarded child. Doris was small, in her mid-thirties and, hardly credibly, the mother of four growing well- built boys, all now at the mission school at the top of the hill. She was tolerant of the mutilation I inflicted upon her language, and respectful -I was a white man and a priest. However every so often the strain was too much and she gurgled with laughter at my attempts at Zulu, hid her face in her hands for a second and then reappeared under some control, but still with a twinkle of amusement in her eyes. She controlled the regime of the house by gentle persuasion, admonition, or just persistence. I was vulnerable, adrift in an alien culture, hence an easy prey; her suggestions for the running of the house were as law. But when she wanted something for herself or her family, she became coy and bashful. She would bite her knuckles and hold her breath while the great man made a decision about the possibility of her taking that old log of wood from behind the house or the bucket that had sprung a leak.

"Tell Sister that I shall not want any lunch today, thank you." It was too hot to eat or even to walk across to the convent in the middle of the day. It was a daunting fifty yards away. Of course I could always take the truck.

The mission was situated in the northern part of Natal, about twenty miles south-west of Ladysmith. The nearest village was the little railway halt of Besters which was about five miles from a large African tribal reserve. The mission was set in the middle of a farm, about five thousand acres of rolling veldt. The farm was one of many such in the area, all of similar size, for it needs a large acreage to feed cattle in the winter when there is no rain to turn the grass green. All were owned by white men. There was about fifty Zulu families living on our farm. It was argued by unfriendly white neighbours that such a large number of blacks could not be claimed as farm workers; they should be sent to their own tribal area. The law allowed only farm workers to live on white farms, so that places like the mission farms, were known as 'Black Spots' and the Africans scheduled for clearance.

The mission had been started about fifty years previously, first as an occasional calling place for a priest travelling on horseback but as people settled on the land, some as farm workers and some as new church members from the tribal area, a resident priest began to stay in the old stone house. Some ten years later in the late 'thirties the Bishop decided to build a church there. The war slowed down building progress as cement was hard to come by; the shortage resulted in an edifice of sand which was a crumbling, mock-Baroque incongruity.

On the Monday morning following my first public attempts at Zulu I had a visit from one of our next door neighbours. We had two close neighbours; this one was Jim Marais. His name was Afrikaner, but fortunately he was one of the few of his countrymen in Natal who spoke English. In this respect he differed markedly from our other near neighbour, Mr. Van der Merwe, who was from the Free State and unmistakably Afrikaner, speaking English poorly. Mr. Marais had heard of my arrival and was making a neighbourly call to introduce himself. He said he was sorry he had not called before, but he had been in hospital for a week after a cobra spat venom into his eyes. The snake had strayed into his house and they had come face to face in the living room to their mutual suprise. Infuriated by the snake attack, Jack had grabbed a decorative antique sword and cut off the snake's head before dashing off to the hospital to get some serum antidote. They had kept him there for a week in a darkened room, but happily his eyes were not damaged. This story and the memory of my own meeting with a snake, increased my fears. I mentally made all sorts of resolutions about keeping doors closed and looking carefully under the bed before retiring at night.

Jim Marais was a heavily built man, tanned and weather beaten, with immense muscles on his forearms. He was slow spoken and slow to smile, but not, I felt, slow-witted. His farm bordered ours and there were bound to be matters of mutual interest from time to time, even if only fencing. I hoped these could be more amicably settled if we were on friendly terms. His family had dealt with the mission for many years and he was making himself known to the present priest in charge out of courtesy. Most of his dealings would be with the farm manager.

We sat down on the verandah with a cup of tea. Jim asked me how long I had been in South Africa, and what I thought of it. I favoured him with my first impressions, explaining how very different it was from my damp, pocket-sized home country.

"You know, Father," Jim said, after a short pause, "Scientists have proved that the size of the native's brain is smaller than the white man's."

I had been sent out to South Africa at a very short notice by my superiors, but even if I had been given several months advance warning, I doubt if I should have gone very deeply into such anatomical details. I had no idea whether what he said was true or false, but I doubted if he had thrown out the remark merely as a snippet of fascinating information.

21

"Oh, really," I replied, raising the eyebrows in polite and non-committal interest, and waited for more.

Jim thought about it all for a minute.

"Yes, they are like children in many ways. Sometimes you need to be firm with them."

I remained silent.

"Not trying to tell you your job, man, you know, but as you are so new here, I thought I might offer a bit of advice. You don't have to get too close to them, or let them get too close to you. And they're not always very honest." He was breaking it to me as gently as possible. "You see, we live with them and we know them."

A longish pause indicated that Jim had finished for the time being. Some sort of reply was expected from me. I chose to be non-committal, telling him I had come with an open mind. (In view of the suddenness of my decision, it would have been more accurate to say I had arrived in deep ignorance). I thanked him for his neighbourly call and his offers of help and advice. After giving me another few minutes to prolong the discussion and seeing no prospect of my either openly agreeing or disagreeing with him, Jim gathered up his battered and sweat-marked hat, thanked me for the tea and went.

Graham Crossley, the farm-manager, came in about an hour later. I told him that I had been honoured by a visit from Jim Marais.

"Good chap, Jim", Graham said, "A good chap. Been a great help to me, I can tell you, man."

Graham had preceded me by about three months at the mission. He was tall and thin, quick and cheerful and made a great contrast to Jim. I wondered how well the two really got on, they seemed so different. Graham was three years younger than me at twenty-five, Jim must have been in his mid-thirties. Graham's past was a little mysterious and he seemed loth to talk about his life except in odd anecdotes, mainly to do with his drinking or womanising. His qualification for being our farm-manager appeared to be experience of working on a chicken farm, near where he lived originally, on the north coast of Natal.

"Just had contact with your other neighbour, Van der Merwe," said Graham. "Not himself, but he sent one of his 'boys' across to complain about dogs from the mission harassing his sheep. The boy said the baas had shot one of them."

"Oh, dear, what do we do about that?" I asked.

"Nothing. Van der Merwe would quite like a fight with the 'Roman danger', as he calls you, so we keep well clear. He is within his legal rights to shoot a dog which is worrying his sheep."

"Do you know him? Have you ever met him?"

"Once," sad Graham. "He looks like one of his sheep and bleats like one – and judging by the argument we had, he has a brain like one as well. He tried to tell me that our natives had broken down his fences. His one piece of evidence was that he had found broken wires.

To him that was proof. We went round in circles, he saying he was going to call the police and me asking on what evidence. I told him if he wasn't satisfied complaining to me, to come and see the Father at the mission. He looked at me for a minute and then said 'He's not my father; I don't want to see him.' So I waved a despairing hand at him and walked away."

Graham spoke Afrikaans, as well as he spoke English and Zulu. The conversation with Van der Merwe had taken place in Afrikaans. Graham said he knew that Van der Merwe would need a very good reason before he would ever appear at the mission, first because he disliked the Catholics and second because of his poor English.

I joined Graham in another cup of tea and told him about Jim's encounter with the cobra. Graham had heard about it already, he'd been helping out a bit on their farm, while Jim was in hospital. It appeared that they did get on well.

Over mid-morning tea Graham invariably became expansive about the possibilities of making the farm a thriving, money-making concern. His enthusiasm would have been infectious, were it not that his schemes, which all had the virtue of sound common sense and were argued with flawless logic, demanded capital investment and we had no capital. The mission farm had suffered from frequent changes of management over the past thirty years. The priests in charge had possessed varying amounts of enthusiasm for farming and had rarely been appointed for their agricultural ability. My predecessor had some knowledge of motor mechanics and had contrived to keep the tractors running. I had none, fortunately Graham did. But old machines can only be kept going for so long. If Graham was all enthusiasm at morning tea-time, by mid-afternoon he generally appeared disspirited, dishevelled, his ginger hair dirty with engine grease and oil. Always his logic would be perfect. If we don't get this, (usually expensive), part for the tractor – or the harrow, or the plough, – we would not be able to plough or to sow, and hence nothing to reap in the autumn, no winter feed for the cattle.... Perhaps if you asked the Bishop.

I had already. I had assessed the situation and looked at the books.... No, not 'the books', the bits of paper. (I had decided to start the accounts afresh, I really had no option). So armed to the teeth with a profundity of ignorance about farm management, or any kind of management for that matter, but aware that we needed money in the spring in order to reap some profit in the autumn, I decided to speak to the Bishop. I had arrived to take over an empty bank account and a farm manager and workers to be paid each month. I approached the Bishop. He filled me with confidence; he had a giant investment of trust in me, he had heard such reports ... that was why he had placed me at that mission....difficult? Indeed, yes; but he knew he had the man for the job. "Dear boy", he had said, "it's a challenge; d'you see, a challenge, eh? We've just taken over this area and we have to show what we are made of...simple to pour in money." I brightened. "Not that I have any", he said, jumping in and dashing my hopes of easy solutions, "But anyway I am looking to you, Sam. You are one of my young men", he intoned with great emphasis on each word. The Bishop could move remarkably fast for a man of well over 50 with a physique that was becoming distinctly chubby – when the need arose. "Must go; leave it with you. All the best, old boy." He shot out, whistling a Brandenburg Concerto. He left me elated and vaguely hopeful and – well, challenged. It was when I got down to the immediate needs and actual demand for cash with Graham that the elation subsided and the challenge seemed as unyielding as the wall of the ironstone house.

"No Graham; you know I have tried the Bish on that. His idea, which conveniently suits his own lack of funds, is that we make ourselves self-sufficient through the farm."

"You must get something in collections in church; perhaps a little loan..."

"Certainly", I said, "ten shillings and four pence from here and the two out-stations last Sunday."

Silence for three minutes as we readjusted to the scale of the challenge.

"I'll go and chat up Roy at the garage again and see if he has any second-hand spares from old tractors."

By the following morning Graham would have another dazzling scheme.

The sound of rattling scrap metal bespoke the return of my colleague, Father Cosmas, who had joined me a few days earlier. Cosmas looked as dishevelled as usual. His brown hair was ill-kempt and disreputably long. It hung lankly either side of his wide forehead below which his blue eyes peered through his glasses. I would tease him that even in his twenties his thin body looked ravaged by years of alcohol abuse. Occasionally I was more charitable and put this down to his asthma which was aggravated by one of his other vices, continual pipe smoking. Cosmas and myself had been students together, we had arrived in Africa at about the same time and were both in the same process of learning by trial and error. We had come straight from college, without the apprenticeship of being curates or assistant priests under the eye of an experienced parish priest. The change from being members of a large community to being our own bosses, many miles from possible supervision, was pleasant in its novelty. We were priests: we said mass; married young couples; baptised infants; buried the dead; visited the sick – what further guidelines did we need? Perhaps we saw the rest of our lives mapped out through the provision of these services. We should be able to do it all so much better when we spoke the language, but apart from that what did we need? "My dear Boys, what you are doing is spreading the word, d'you see?", the Bishop had said. We had supposed that we knew what that cliche meant. Given the Bible and the accumulated traditions and teaching of the Church

24

which we had been studying for the past six to seven years, we felt we were fully armed to meet the challenge of bringing the word to Africa.

Cos lived at the mission, though the area he served and worked in was about twelve miles distant at its nearest point. It was designated a 'native area' and it was illegal for him to live there. As it was part of the original parish of St. Mary's in Besters, we had decided to split the area and work the two parts as separate entities.

"It's very hot", said Cosmas, collapsing into an easy chair, I agreed. We both wore full-length religious habits, made of heavy serge material. This clothing seemed to trap the heat within its folds. It was like sitting in a closed tent on a hot summer day. But we had decided that we ought to be professional about our calling and wear our habits for all to see. Thus we would demonstrate the evidence of dedication to a higher order of things, which was the call of the Gospel to all men. Which might have been very high-minded, but it was also sweat-producing and pompous. As the first summer wore on, practical doubts did begin to creep up on us, perhaps clothing designed for northern Europe might not be totally suitable in South Africa.

Cosmas looked over his glasses at me.

"I went to see a man yesterday evening about the possibility of his marrying the woman he is living with. I thought it very important, as they have several children already, but he said he couldn't talk to me until he had eaten some food. Even when I went back two hours later he did not appear to see how important it was to rectify their sinful state. I thought that they would be only too glad that I was offering them the opportunity to put everything right in the sight of God. Apparently, his first concern was how to put everything right in the eyes of his father- in-law. He still owes him five head of cattle and according to the Zulu way of doing things he cannot be considered to be fully married until all the bride-price has been paid." We had not learned how to cope with such dilemmas in our courses of theology. Rather, we had learnt the single approach to all problems was to bring them to conformity with Church law and thereby solve them. If the problems proved intractable, then the persons involved could not be considered as full and participating members of the Church. Cultures were expected to bend to the law of the Church. This wasn't really what we had conceived as The Bringing of Good News of the Gospel. But the law did not yield.

"So" I said, "Do we inveigh against the practice of living together and having children before marriage, when the custom seems to be so widespread and entrenched?"

"Other missionaries don't seem to have been noticably successful in the past, do they? Anyway, it's all tied up with their economic situation. How can a man earning ten pounds a month give several cattle, or the equivalent in cash, to his prospective father-in-law all at one go? If we try to insist that they don't live together until all the bride price is paid, the woman would be beyond child-bearing age. But that is purely academic, because no one is going to listen to us, anyway," snorted Cos.

"You could be right there, Reverend. So what do we do about it all? Change the system, the whole political and economic structure? When you see a solution in those terms we haven't a chance, have we? But that couple are still living in sin and they know that. They've been taught that for years and probably won't go to the sacraments while they are in that state. So what do you do about that?"

"How about nothing at all?" replied Cosmas.

"I am sure that you are right, we are not going to be able to change things without a massive overhaul of the whole system and way of life and we can't expect to achieve that. So apart from periodic exhortations and reaffirmation of the basic moral principles of the Church, there isn't a lot you can do. The trouble about the total system is that it does not allow for much flexibility. For the idealistic enforcer a large measure of frustration causes a worrying, gnawing tension between the recommended compassion for the sinner and hatred for the sin. The frustration and the hatred tend to backlash upon the individual sinner and even be justified as righteous disgust.

I gave a girl a lift to the village the other day; she must have been in her late teens or very early twenties. She was slim and wore a very pretty dress."

"You mean," interrupted Cosmas, "that she was very pretty and the dress she was wearing was quite nice too". He put his pipe back between his lips which were pursed into a smug grin.

"You know I don't notice these things; I am all spirit. Anyway she spoke a little English and we chatted. Seemed a pleasant, if rather shy girl. Said she hadn't got a job but helped about the home and hoped to get married in due course. I asked her if she had thought of joining the convent at the mission. She dropped her eyes coyly and said 'No'. Anyway, yesterday her mother came with her to see me and reported her daughter was pregnant by a local boy on the mission. She had brought her to Father to report this enormity. I was most embarrassed as it was evident that I was expected to launch in with a hearty denunciation and a very strong lecture to the errant girl."

Cosmas found this highly amusing. "So did you?"

"Did I what?"

"Weigh in with the heavy lecture?"

"Well, I did a bit but I was taken off my guard. I had to make a quick decision what to do. I hadn't been placed in such a position before. I need a policy about such events for the future. Hey, half past eleven," I jumped up. "I am supposed to be starting my Zulu lesson even now." I fled, running down to the convent. There were about forty sisters in the convent, most of them Zulu, though the founders and present superiors were French. The reason for the large number of sisters was that the convent contained the postulancy and novitiate of the congregation. Two of the Zulu Sisters taught at the mission school and they accompanied me to the different out-stations within a thirty mile radius of the central mission and took Sunday school or catechism classes for the children and adults after mass. The priests of the mission had meals at the convent and were catered for by a French sister who looked on it as her prime vocation in the religious life to overwhelm us with both quantity and choice of food. She could not be dissuaded from providing enough food for five or six and remained smilingly obdurate in the face of our entreaties that she prepared just one dish as we could not cope with all the food offered. Indeed we felt embarrassed at the amount of food on our table when so much poverty and hunger were evident around us. In Sister Denise's mind our embarrassment at the amount of food which was presented to us was glorious evidence of our virtue, self-sacrifice and religious spirit. For that very reason it was all the greater necessity for her to make sure that we did not, in holy unselfishness, neglect ourselves totally in favour of others. Protesting at the gross exaggeration of this line of thought, merely increased her appreciation of our saintly modest and humility

Sister Denise appeared as I arrived panting at the convent. I pulled up courteously to greet her.

"Good morning, Father," she said in her heavy French accent, and beamed with smiling admiration at the holy man of God.

"Good morning, Sister; and how are you?"

"Oh, Father, I am very well. But you, you are always rushing; it is not so good."

"Yes, well, I am late for my Zulu lesson, Sister, I must go." Then I made a mistake. "Oh, Sister," as I moved away, "we shall not be coming for lunch today, thank you."

The beaming smile disappeared to be replaced by a concerned frown and a disapproving look in the eyes. Usually we asked Doris to slip down and tell Sister that we should not be down for a meal, in order to avoid a lecture on taking care of ourselves as a strict duty both to God and the people over whom He (personally, of course) had set us.

"Actually," I attempted to forestall her, "we have some cheeses that friends left us and we are having that today at the house."

It was not strictly true. In fact it was not true at all but it obviated the threatened admonition from Sister Denise and I was already quite late. Sister Denise looked doubtful but she could hardly accuse the holy man of lying. I waved at her and grinned reassuringly.

The convent was made up of a collection of buildings, single-storied and all painted white. They gleamed cheerfully in the blazing sunshine. I think they also did something for my attitude towards the inmates. In Europe convents often are grim, several-storied buildings, large and featureless and, surrounded by an equally grim and forbidding high brick wall. Here the effect was light and cheerful – of

27

course, the climate helped – and the Zulu sisters went about their tasks singing and laughing together. I walked onto the verandah of the main building and along to a small room at one end of the verandah which we used as our dining room. There was a small Zulu sister seated at the table. From day to day I did not know which Sister would give me a lesson, although I did not have more than three or four different teachers. Many of the Zulu sisters spoke good English, but I was usually taught by one of those who had qualified as school teachers. Today, it was Sister Martina. She was small, inclining to plumpness with a round face and huge brown eyes which always appeared soft and pleading when her face was in repose, but which sparkled when she laughed.

"Good morning, Father," she greeted me in her usual gentle voice, inaudible when there was extraneous noise.

"Morning, Sister, sorry I am late; have you been waiting long?"

"Oh, no, Father, not at all."

"Right", I said in a business-like manner. I pulled a chair to the table, sat down clumsily and my knees cannoned against Sister Martina's knees.

"Oh, sorry, Sister," I apologised briefly. But poor Sister Martina was unable to dismiss the incident so lightly. Her eyes fell to the table and she kept them down for perhaps a full minute, while it dawned on me it was possible that I had set all sorts of emotions jangling. She had been taught to eschew all physical contact with men because of the danger such contact constituted in the keeping of her vow of chastity. Here she was alone in a room with a man and he had touched her. It didn't need to be deliberate, the accidental contact was enough. After a minute that seemed an age of embarrassment to me, her eyes came bravely up and she prepared to start the lesson. But I was unnerved and there was a certain constraint until we had an argument about the irregularity of a particular declension. I thought that the whole language ought to change to fit in with what I imagined as some general and unchangable rule. I was indignant that such an irregularlity should make my grasp of the language so much more difficult to attain and my reluctance to accept Sister Martina's explanation "that is how we say it, Father," brought laughter from her as my exasperation grew. She gave me another exercise to do and the lesson ended.

On the next Sunday, as I set out to say the third mass of the day at an out-station some twelve miles distant, there appeared on the horizon over the hills a suggestion of a build-up of clouds. The catechist at the out-station when I arrived said he hoped we should have rain later, the fields needed it badly. During the mass it grew darker in the small hut we used and I hastened outside afterwards to see that huge, threatening black clouds had spread over most of the sky at impressive speed. The catechist thought we should go at once, as the road might become impassable. I had given no thought to this possibility though I had been told of the problems of travel in the

28

middle of a South African storm. It was difficult to leave at great speed for the family who owned the hut had prepared a cup of tea and some home-baked bread. It would have been impolite to rush away merely because a little storm was imminent. They could hardly share my newly-acquired anxiety about the possible impassibility of the road, they travelled on foot and knew none of the hazards of driving a truck.

We took our leave – myself and two teenage boys from the mission - as thunder sounded an ominous warning over the hills. Almost immediately against the dark clouds there appeared impressive flashes of jagged lightning followed by a louder rumble of thunder. One or two massive drops of rain hit the roof of the truck with resonant plops and then no more. The gathering storm had given its warning and we heeded it. We had only struggled half a mile over a rutted cart-track to the road before the real rain came in earnest. The din in the cab of the truck was deafening, so that we could barely hear the thunder above the beating of the rain on the metal roof. The screen-wipers were barely coping with the amount of water that was falling and, as I had to drive slowly enough to see the road, our progress was limited. The road was not tarmac, but dirt. Under the deluge of the storm the surface soon became tricky to negotiate whenever I deviated from a straight course. It felt like driving on an icy road. The deterioration increased as the dirt of the road soaked up more and more rain-water, until the drag of the wet red earth on the tyres slowed us down even more than the need for visibility. After another mile of frantic manipulation of the steering wheel, as I vainly attempted to control the arbitrary movements of the truck, the vehicle slowly slid sideways off the camber of the road into the bank. There the matter rested. The wheels would not pull the truck out of the rushing stream which had appeared along the side of the road; the front wheels were jammed completely and the back wheels merely spun round in the mud.

I turned off the useless engine and sat in thought. It was early evening and should not be dark for at least another hour by the clock, but it was already like night. There appeared to be no break in the cloud, the torrents of rain were unrelenting and thunder and lightning were all round us. All we could make out were rolling acres of farmland, but not a farmhouse in sight. We must still have been eight to nine miles from the mission and even I in my inexperience could guess that the road would not be dry enough that night for us to be able to drive the truck out. One thing was in our favour, we were stuck on a downward incline. The boys agreed that we should try to push the truck down onto the centre of the road.

I was dressed in my religious habit, the boys in shirts and trousers - we had no overcoats of any sort between us. We looked at each other.

"Well, let's go," I said. We plunged out of separate doors, within

29

seconds we were wet through. The rain was an unbelievable deluge. We slopped about in the mud and the newly-made stream at the side of the road, trying to find foot-holds enough to push the truck. We slithered and slid, eventually I lost my grip and fell on to my hands and knees. Through all this the truck remained unmoved. After a very few minutes we were compelled to admit the impossibility of getting the truck out of the mud and water. We started towards the vehicle but then paused and looked at each other. In non- verbal conference we all came to the same conclusion about getting back into the cab in our saturated and filthy state. Moving about in that condition is bad, but sitting like that with no immediate or even medium- term of hope of relief was not acceptable.

"Shall we walk then, boys?" I asked. They merely nodded. 'Walk' is the wrong word. Feet sank into the road three to four inches every step and progress was tiringly and painfully slow. My own fears of the encircling firework display of lightning gradually faded with the need to concentrate all my attention on staying upright and keeping on the road. Indeed in the middle of nowhere we were totally dependent on the lightning in order to see our way at all. In the darkness, the mud of the road merged with the surrounding veldt and we could very easily have wandered off the road and been lost until morning.

After walking for about an hour, covering what cannot have been more than two miles, we saw the lights of a farm-house. For the last ten minutes the going had become increasingly difficult. The centre of the storm was passing and the lightning becoming infrequent and more distant, giving us less and less visibility. The driveway up to the farm-house was stony and made walking easier. I didn't really care whether we should be welcome or not at the farm. A dog within started to bark and a face appeared at one of the windows which showed a light. I had the feeling of arriving in the middle of night and possibly waking up the household but it was only a few minutes after seven. The door opened before we reached it. A white man I recognised stood at the open door. I had seen him pass almost daily along the road which passed the mission and we had exchanged waves. So at least I was on friendly ground. He was astonished at the sight we presented and called back over his shoulder, "It's the Father from the mission". And then to us, "Come in, come in all of you."

We stepped into a large porch area and dripped on to the mats which covered the floor. I apologised for the pools of water we were creating and asked if we could use the phone to call the mission. He brushed aside the apologies; he was a farmer and frequently brought dust or mud into the house on his boots. They just put up with such things. He introduced himself as Hugh Wells. He turned to a servant who was hovering in the background and asked her to make some tea and to look after the boys. Mr. Wells said that the phone had been making crackling noises during the evening as a result of the storm and it might not be working, but if it was I was most welcome to use it. It

30

was just beside us in the porch.

I feared the mission might be getting very worried about us by this time. I wanted to relieve their minds and also to ask if they could get out to the Wells farm with the farm truck to pick us up. After several attempts, by which time I had almost decided that the lines were out of order, I did get through to Graham. He seemed harassed and did not give me the impression that they had been sitting deep in worry over our whereabouts and predicament. When I wondered if they could possibly get out to us with transport, he said he doubted if they could just at that time because they were busy fighting a fire in the convent chapel caused by lightning hitting the thatched roof of the large rondavel. However, as soon as they could, they would see if the road was passable. I left him to get on with fire-fighting.

A large mug of very hot tea awaited me. Now that I was standing - I declined to sit on any of their easy chairs, it would have taken a week to dry out after I had saturated it -and no longer battling through the rain and wet road, I began to feel very cold, in spite of a fire in the Wells' living room. I thought perhaps that it might be as well to start off again and to meet any coming transport en route. My colleagues at the mission would have a better chance of getting to us if we could get to the cross-roads about a quarter of a mile away to meet them. I went through to the kitchen and suggested this to the boys, who were sitting on stools by a warm stove, with large mugs of tea in their hands. They looked at each other and then at me.

"Lisana, Baba", one of them said. He spoke English, but retreated into Zulu I suspected because he was politely disagreeing with me. He was merely stating that it was still raining. The implication was that they had had enough. The Wells also urged me to stay, at least for a short time, as the storm might well slacken off or pass altogether soon. It was certainly not raining as torrentially as it had been when we had arrived at the farm.

Half an hour later the heavy revving of a struggling truck could be heard on the road. I called the boys, thanked the Wells and we dashed for the vehicle whose headlights we could see at the end of the driveway to the farm. It was Graham, swearing a good deal, but in high spirits. After the day's unexpected and sudden rush of events the effect of coming through them reasonably unscathed caused a little light-headedness and we were all in good humour as we slithered our way back to the mission. Graham was much more experienced than I at negotiating wet dirt roads, so that though we did skid about at times, he remained quite unruffled and steered the truck with ease and confidence.

We dropped the boys off as we passed near to their homes and made our way back to the mission-house. I took off my habit and threw around me an old heavy raincoat which hung on a hook in the toilets for common use. A thin wisp of smoke was rising from the partly collapsed roof of the chapel. Cosmas was viewing it musingly, as the Sisters were salvaging the church furnishings which were standing in two or three inches of water. No one seemed to be using a hose-pipe and no buckets were visible.

"Doesn't the smoke indicate that there might still be fire in the roof?", I asked Cosmas. His blue eyes flashed, almost scornfully. After a second he said, "Yes".

"Well, don't you think, we should try to do something about it?"

"What exactly would you suggest?" asked Cosmas.

He turned slowly towards me. "You may not have noticed", he said, speaking slowly and clearly, as if to a dim-witted child, "but it has been raining very heavily; it is still raining quite heavily. I don't really think that we could compete with that. And anyway, the fire is in the middle of that very thick thatch, which I understand is made very thick precisely so that it will be water resistant. So all we can do is to hope that it will get wet enough from the rain and eventually smoulder out."

"Yes, well, that about covers it, I suppose", I replied, abashed. "In that case I think that I shall go and get some dry clothes on, since there appears to be nothing practical to be done."

"I think I shall join you. You had better tell Sister Superior that you are back, so that they can start prayers of thanksgiving in place of their prayers for your safety," he suggested, grinning wickedly.

I found Sister Superior supervising the heaping up of church furniture in the refectory. She laughed heartily at the soaking I had suffered. She did not give the impression that she had been beside herself with worry about my plight. I expressed my regrets about the burnt chapel roof.

"Oh, Father", she said, with her engaging French accent, "all the time things happen in this place. Now, I do not worry myself any more."

Graham had a half bottle of local brandy, which was rough but warming. I slept well.

Chapter Three

Father Marius, our religious superior, used to come over to Besters each Tuesday afternoon and stay overnight. In theory this was to help us out with any teething problems, but, we suspected, it was also to keep an eye on two young, inexperienced priests. Marius drove a three-quarter ton truck, the back of which was fitted with a metal framework covered with heavy canvas. Ideally the canvas was intended to be fairly rigid when properly tied down, but the condition of the roads meant that the ropes, nuts and bolts, holding the canvas in place were constantly being loosened. To anyone unused to seeing the truck in full flight under the frenetic hand of Marius, the first sighting at a distance was strangely evocative and even fantastic. Could it be a gigantic bird striving to achieve flight? Such fantasies were dispelled as, out of the cloud of dust, the "wings" were revealed as flapping canvas accompanied by the sound of rattling metal urged to the limit by the paroxysmal driver. He was not an unfeeling man, but a car or a truck brought no compassion from him. It was made to get you from one place to another as quickly as possible. To be a passenger in his truck was a salutary experience, turning the mind from trivial mundane worries to more basic anxieties of life and death. There was always much over-gay laughter, full of bubbling relief, from his passengers as they giddily set foot on solid ground at the end of a lift from Marius. He would lazily get out of the cab of the truck and shamble forward towards his dismounting passengers. He was very tall with a shock of greying, black hair, and moved so much like a lanky cowboy that one expected to hear the clink of spurs. He smiled a slow, lop-sided smile and always made some remark that brought more laughter. His passengers would depart with happy smiles. Maybe they were just thankful still to be alive.

Marius claims that he taught me to drive. We practised on the tarmac of the National Road some few miles away towards Ladysmith. My previous experience had been driving a farm tractor – in England, not at Besters – and this Marius regarded as quite insufficient for taking a driving test in South Africa. The difficulty about learning to drive on our vehicles was that they were all very individualistic and idiosyncratic and, in some cases, downright dangerous. However, I did drive for several months in our remote area without the benefit of a licence, nor fortunately much chance of meeting traffic police. One Wednesday, I asked Marius if I could borrow his truck and go up to the station to fetch the post. He agreed, saying he would not accompany me as he had a lot of work to get through. He admonished me to drive carefully, and slowly as there was no great rush, and hence no need to drive the vehicle hard. I had various bits and pieces to collect at the small store near the station and I had these purchases on the seat beside me as I drove back down the hill. The effect of the corrugated dirt road on the letters and the shopping was to jolt them on to the dirty floor of the truck. In an attempt to prevent them all falling off I put out one hand protectively. I must have taken my eye off the road for a moment; I certainly lost all sense of direction. The next thing I was conscious of was the whole truck violently bouncing up and down. Unfortunately, the truck and myself were not bouncing in unison, with the result that my head was repeatedly making none-too-gentle contact with the roof. I clung to the wheel. I looked wildly about for some clue as to my whereabouts. All I could see ahead of me was a barbed-wire fence that should not have been there. Happily the bouncing about had dislodged my foot from the accelerator and I did not hit the fence. Unhappily the last bounce brought the truck down on top of a large boulder dislodging one of the front wheels. The driver's door had sprung open at some time during this episode and hung a trifle strangely. I got out, my head ringing. The off- side front wheel was lying on the ground beside the truck and it was immediately evident that some expertise would be needed to make the truck road-worthy again. At that point I became anxious to remove myself from the scene of the accident; I had no driving licence and no idea what the penalities for this crime were in South Africa. I started to walk home. After half an hour I arrived, hot and sweaty and not a little anxious as to how to tell Father Marius about the state of his truck.

Cos was there on the verandah, grinning at me.

"What's the matter, what are you grinning about?" I asked him.

"The matter?", he said, "Me, grinning?"

"Where's Marius?"

"Oh, Marius's gone off on the back of the tractor with Graham."

"What on earth for"? Had he taken to farming? However, it appeared that a Sister, who was a nurse, had driven by the truck and returned to the mission to report its unfortunate condition. She must have missed me as I took a short cut across the fields of the mission farm. Marius and Graham had set out straightaway to retrieve the vehicle.

"Was Marius hopping mad?" I asked Cos.

"Not really; more matter of fact and let's-see-the-extent-of-the-damage attitude".

I was not relieved. The difficult interview for which I had prepared myself was now postponed. It was about an hour later when I had eventually given up pacing the verandah that the sound of scrap metal coming up the roadway announced the return of the battered truck being towed in by the tractor. Graham drove it well up into the farm-yard, about thirty yards from the house. I hastened out to meet Marius. He was examining the door on the driver's side which very obviously was sprained and slightly twisted.

"Think that door needs a drop of oil", he remarked as I approached.

"Aren't you hopping mad"? I asked, beginning to feel some relief that either he had worked himself out of his first fury, or that his Christian charity was well above average.

"Well, it won't help much getting mad, will it; the damage has been done. But it does raise problems about getting it repaired."

"Oh, of course, we shall have to bear the costs of that."

"Very true", he agreed.

"But how will you manage to get home this afternoon?" I asked.

"Oh, that's not a problem", he said, brightening, "I'll take your truck". He beamed and ambled off, looking like Gary Cooper.

Transport remained a problem, to a large extent because we had inherited such old vehicles from our predecessors at the missions in north Natal. In actual years they were of fairly recent acquisition, but they were battered and weary. We were lucky that Graham knew something about the workings of engines but we also patronised a newly opened garage about ten miles away. The Dutch garage owner was grateful for our custom and became friendly and very helpful to us. He was even tolerant of my idiot inquiries, such as the time when the truck did not seem to have much power. He suggested, after the briefest look at the engine, that perhaps if I replaced the disconnected plug lead....

It was not always my embarrassing ignorance that was the problem. I remember a later occasion. As our first Easter approached Cos and myself made great plans to present our new and first parishioners, both at Besters and at his churches, with a liturgical tour de force. We were naively convinced our services would inevitably hit them all with the impact of a revelation, changing their whole way of life. We were still very attached to the austere beauty of the celebrations in a religious house during Holy Week. We lacked the personnel of a religious community, but we should try to add solemnity to the whole complex of services with both of us officiating in all the churches. Organisation and timing would need to be carefully planned; a lot of practice would need to be given to the explanations and sermons in Zulu. We elaborated, over-elaborated and laboured long over it all.

After the services on Maundy Thursday, we sat down in the evening to a little quiet self-congratulation. We even dared to hope we had got some sort of message across – and we applied the acid test – attendances had been very good. There was a low rumble of thunder outside. Perhaps a good rain before the summer finished would be a bonus, we thought. It rained heavily, for several hours through the night.

Good Friday was clear and clean and sparkling after the rain. We set out for the out-station church soon after eleven. The roads were only wet in odd patches and presented no great hazard to hardened and experienced drivers (I even had a licence by this time). We arrived at the ford in the river near Cos's main church. It was impossible to pick out the line of the crossing. The rains of the previous night were now draining down from the hills producing a great swirling muddy river. The river we planned to cross was usually a gentle affair, with clear water trickling through stones and outcrops of rock – except when swelled by the summer rains. The storm we had heard through the night had been a pretty ordinary one, but it must have been more impressive up in the hills and mountains towards the Free State.

We viewed the spectacle for some moments in silence.

"That's interesting", said Cos.

"Yes", I agreed. And after a pause: "What do you think of the prospects of fording the river today?"

"Well, from my vast experience of about six months, I would say there are two possibilities. Either the water level will rise or it will fall. Now that depends on how much rain they had up there in the mountains. And that we don't know. We might just make it across at the moment, but even that is dubious".

"I must admit I should be extremely doubtful about plunging into that lot with a truck".

At this point we were hailed from the opposite bank. It was Joseph Kubeka, the catechist. He answered our question immediately.

"Baba, do not try to drive through the river," he yelled.

We were only too ready to accept this advice. If we had reservations about the water, we also had reservations about the ability of the truck, even under normal conditions. A test like that might well provoke it to an attack of temperament.

Joseph indicated a suitable place to attempt a crossing. As we approached the water it became evident that it would not merely be a matter of removing sandals and rolling up trouser legs. The water was deep in the middle and running swiftly. Joseph encouraged us from the opposite bank.

"Baba, it will get worse in the next two hours".

Cos had been hovering before. At Joseph's words he drew back with decision.

"I don't think I can make it through that speed of water". Cos had no cartilage in his knees.

"Well, swim then," I suggested.

"I can't swim, not even in still water and I don't feel that today is the day to learn."

Our options were being narrowed, or rather mine were. I assessed the situation. I had a case of vestments and books to carry across. I took off my habit and trousers and sandals and put them in the case. Unfortunately, I had not acquired the African skill of carrying loads on my head, so with arms aloft holding the case, I began the crossing. Apart from odd alarms as I slipped on smooth stones, I made it. The water was cool, but the day was warm and I was dry again after the twenty minute walk to the church. I paused some quarter mile from the church to dress myself more fittingly.

Some of the grandeur of the service had to be abandoned as Cos was not with us, but Joseph had the hymns and readings well organised and led it all with enthusiasm and gusto. He may not have been commanding in stature, but his voice was powerful, roof-rattling and apparently indestructible. He sang in leadership lustily throughout the hour and a quarter service and ended without the least trace of hoarseness.

He had watched me cross the river before the service with manifest enjoyment, urging me on with repeated advice as where to place my feet. Now after the service he announced that the water level would surely have risen making the return crossing even more problematic. He was right. When we arrived at the river, the waters had risen, and to my eyes anyway, appeared to be running more swiftly. Cos arose from among the grasses on the opposite bank.

"The water has risen", he remarked morosely. It was evident that he had spent a boring, inactive two hours and was prepared to look on the bleak side.

"Baba, you will have to swim," roared Joseph, and laughed heartily.

"Oh, we'll see," I said, trying to be casual about it. I prepared to re-cross in the same way I had crossed previously. However, it was very quickly evident that the flow was much stronger and deeper than before.

"Baba, you cannot swim straight across", Joseph yelled at me, "the water is too strong. Come, you must start up here, and let the water carry you to the slight bend in the river and then you can catch hold on the other bank."

I had never tried this sort of thing before.

"What about the case?" I asked.

"Can you swim on your back?" asked Cos, beginning to enter into the spirit of the thing.

"Yes," I replied.

"Well, then, hold the case above your body as you float on your back."

"But I won't have any hands to help myself across with."

"Yes," Cos said musingly, "but we do need the books. We have got other vestments but we do need the books." Inspiration struck him. "Perhaps Joseph could go the back way through the hills to Besters on his little 'pop-pop'. Do you think you could do that, Joe?"

"Of course, Baba," Joseph called back. And as an afterthought: "And I will stay for the next service and help you.

We were inevitably late back to Besters for the second service of the day, partly, of course, because of the swollen river, but also because the truck limped back for the last three to four miles. We could hear a strange grinding noise from one of the front wheels and detected arbitrary movements of the truck not wholly explained by the bumpy road.

The church was very full as we breathlessly rushed through our preparations and got the service under way. The self-congratulations afterwards were more muted than the evening before. The condition of the truck looked like thwarting the rest of our Easter plans. After uselessly pooling our extremely sparse knowledge of motor vehicles, we asked Graham's opinion. He took the truck up and down the road for a few minutes and returned with a diagnosis.

"I think the bearings in the near-side front wheel are being ground up," he told us.

We looked at each other. Holiday week-end, garages all closed - anyway we were ten miles from the nearest one.

"There might actually be a ball-race about the place that will fit," he suggested. "I could have a go at it for you tomorrow morning, if you like. What time do you have to be out".

"Not until the afternoon," Cos replied. "You think you can fix it?".

"Well, I can at least have a look-see and try. Anyway, I really wouldn't advise you to drive it very far in its present condition."

The next morning Graham found the ball-race, and removed the damaged bearings. Some had been ground to small fragments already and it was only a matter of time before the rest went the same way. He was a little dubious about the ball-race, as it was not specifically for our truck, but he said it should function for a time.

"How long does 'for a time' mean,?" I asked, my suspicions aroused.

"Oh, easily over the weekend; no problem." He sounded confident, and we were reassured.

We dashed about the countryside over the Easter weekend, bringing the joys of the season to as many as possible. But by Sunday evening it was a sense of duty that kept us going rather than our initial enthusiasm. Exhausted, we reflected on the last few days. We decided we should never again perform the services jointly and try to cover both parts of the parish. The solemn grandeur of the monastic church had frankly not been recreated in the African situation nor, with hindsight, did it seem a good idea to try to recreate such an atmosphere in an environment so entirely different.

The truck had behaved well and gave no hint of the trouble we had with it on Good Friday. In view of which we made a further decision. It was the custom among the brethren on Boxing Day and Easter Monday to have local get-togethers at two or three centres throughout the diocese. As the truck had behaved well throughout the weekend we decided to go across to Dundee the next day to join eight or nine of our fellow priests and brothers for a midday meal. I would have to come back in the evening, leaving Cos with one of his friends at another mission for a couple of days. Graham asked if he could take the farm truck and visit a friend over towards the mountains. The farm workers would do the milking morning and evening, but otherwise they would have the day off.

Dundee lay about fifty-six miles to the north-east, but most of that mileage would be done on good tarmac roads. We saw the priests at Ladysmith fairly frequently, when we did much of our shopping there, and we met Marius each week as he came to keep an eye on us. But most of our colleagues, some ex-fellow students, we saw only at Christmas and Easter, or at the occasional clerical conference. So we were in festive mood on the way to Dundee. The gathering was only the second one we had attended since our arrival in the country some six or seven months previously, but it was characterised by two features common to all the gatherings – a great deal of noise and of laughter.

I set off for home about five in the afternoon. When I got to the main Durban to Johannesburg road, it was very evident that the holiday was coming to an end. There was a continuous stream of traffic heading north towards the Transvaal. Luckily I was going south. After a couple of miles a niggling suspicion came to me that the front near-side wheel seemed to have some 'play' in it. I told myself it was my imagination, but I drew on to the verge of the road and stopped the truck. The wheel seemed firm and solid enough, I got back in the truck and drove on.

After a mile or two I got stuck behind a large removal van and such was the flow of traffic in the opposite direction, I was unable to pass. I was reduced to travelling at little over thirty miles per hour, which was both fortunate and unfortunate in a way. Unfortunate, because I no longer had any qualms about the safety of the front wheel – I was travelling too slowly to notice any deterioration in its condition. But fortunate, inasmuch as I was going at no great speed when the wheel came off. The truck lurched giddily to the side of the road and hit a rock about eighteen inches high. The front of the truck became wedged on top of it. The wheel, meanwhile, was seen to be making its own way along a dirt side road, which went off the national road.

I sat in the cab for some minutes. There was hardly a lot of point in getting out and reviewing the damage, I knew what had happened. Nobody on the road had seen the accident; it must have seemed as if I was merely pulling off the road, and as the front of the truck was supported by the rock, the casual observer would simply have seen a truck parked on the verge. After about five minutes of waving at passing motorists, a small car pulled up beside me. I explained briefly what had happened and asked if he could drop me at the garage about six to seven miles along the road. The driver turned out to be a parishioner of the Ladysmith Catholic church and had recognised the habit I was wearing. He was anxious to take me all the way to Ladysmith, but I was even more anxious to move the truck. It was a good bet that the other wheels would also be missing if the truck was left there over-night.

The garage was open – bank holidays were a good time for business. The garage at the Wesselsnek turning was grim evidence and testament to the impatience of holiday drivers, its yard piled high with twisted wrecks, written off or awaiting the decision of insurance companies.

The owner greeted me with friendly recognition.

"Hello, Father. You walking?"

He didn't know me, but he knew the habit, the priest at Wesselsnek was a regular customer.

"Well, I was driving a truck until the wheel fell off, I wondered if you could drag in the remains from the Washbank turn-off."

"No problem," he said, "It's been quieter than usual this weekend, and I was going to call it a day in an hour or so. Most of the Johannesburg traffic will have gone by then."

It was the firm belief of the people in north Natal that the majority of accidents were caused by Johannesburg drivers. Anything with a TJ number plate was to be avoided as dangerous.

"Do you want to come with me?" he asked.

"Well, I rather think that the truck will require a little more attention than just sticking the wheel back on, and there won't be time to do that this evening. If you don't mind I will use your phone to get myself some transport from Besters."

"Fine, man, you do that."

He went off towards the break-down truck, taking an African with him, and leaving another to look after the petrol sales.

I could get no reply at the mission at Besters. I tried the convent. Sister Superior answered, becoming very excited when she realised it was me.

"Oh, Mon Père, Father, there has been a terrible accident, there have been two accidents, and people are hurt; Sister has gone to meet the doctor and the ambulance is coming – we do not know how many, but I saw them go this morning from the mission and there were some, there were many....."

I was having a problem making out what Sister was saying; she was not very coherent.

"Hold on a minute, Sister; who has been injured and what kind of an accident and where?"

"Oh, Father," she showed a little exasperation at my denseness. "You know some of the people went with the tractor and trailer this morning to get thatching grass..."

"No, I didn't know that," I told her.

That at least had slowed her down a little. "And Mr. Crossley, he is not here."

"Yes, I did know that," I said, glad to be in the know about something.

"And he also had an accident with the farm truck." she continued.

40

"Oh, Lord", I ejaculated, or prayed. My own plight paled to insignificance.

I decided to make an attempt at some assessment of the gravity of the situation.

"Let's start again, if you don't mind, Sister. Mr. Crossley, I presume, lent the people on the mission the tractor and trailer to go down to the river to get some thatching grass. Is that right?"

"Yes, and it over-turned, and fell on top of some of the people."

"It didn't hit another car or truck, then?"

"No, Father, it did not." She hesitated. "Father, I think that Miya was driving, and perhaps, Father, he had been drinking..."

A day off from farm work, a day of relaxation, really like a picnic, and they took drink with them – oh, dear. Then one of those idiotically tangential questions came to my mind, in such a moment of crisis.

"Who is milking the cows, Sister?"

"Oooh, Father, I do not know," she replied with some irritation. Then because the image had impinged and unconsciously registered, "But I did see the cows going up to the farm a short time ago. But, Father, the people.... can you not come."

"Ah, well, Sister, you see I too have had an accident."

"Oh, Jesu, ... but this is ... terrible ... mon Pere ... Oh, but where are you now?"

I explained.

"Listen, Sister, I shall ring up Ladysmith and see if the Fathers are back home yet. They were with us at Dundee today and I left them there to have some tea; but they should be home by now. I shall ask for one to pick me up and the other to come out to you, if he can, right away. Alright?"

"Yes, Father. Oh, what a terrible day " I rang off and attempted to get Ladysmith. The priests were home and I enlisted their help – they both said they would set out immediately when they heard of our chapter of accidents. They were both older men and must have thought that the periodic reports they received of the tribulations of Besters Mission had reached their culmination in the multiple accidents of that day.

It occurred to me, as Fr. Alexander and I drove towards Besters, that I had omitted to ask Sister if Graham had been injured in his accident. We were, therefore, very uncertain as to the gravity of disaster awaiting us.

As we neared the mission we saw the Volkswagen of Father Colman, the other priest from Ladysmith, approaching on the road from the river. We followed him into the convent grounds. Sister Superior came running towards us, looking very worried, and followed by several African Sisters.

Father Colman had arrived as the ambulance had been loading those who needed to go to hospital. Old Miya, the driver, had been

41

very carefully removed from under the overturned tractor and it was feared that he had broken bones. He was by far the worst affected and indeed, in the doctor's opinion, the experience could well have killed the old man had he not been at least partly anaesthetised by the African beer which he had been drinking steadily throughout the day. The beer had effectively blunted the sharp edge of shock to his system. Others had cuts and abrasions in plenty, but happily no broken bones. One or two had been taken to hospital in Ladysmith for examination and possible X- rays, but the majority had been allowed to go home after treatment for cuts, bruises and sprains.

"Sister, I forgot in the excitement to ask if Mr Crossley had been injured", I said.

"Oh, no, Father he is alright. His truck slid off the road when it skidded in loose stones and ended up in a dried up river bed. But he is not hurt and will stay the night with his friend and they will get a tractor to pull out the truck in the morning. He thinks the truck will be alright."

Jack Marais had seen the crowd and the arrival of the ambulance and had come up to see what was happening. He and three of his men had righted the tractor and trailer. We heard the tractor approaching and went to meet it. Some of the Africans had hitched a lift to save their bruised limbs. They were silent, no doubt chastened by the day's events. They were cheered when they saw the reception committee and started to brighten visibly when they saw that the priest in charge of the mission was not about to thunder at them for a drunken holiday revel, but was rather concerned about their well-being.

This chapter of accidents was not an isolated period. Accidents continued to happen, but their frequency diminished; or perhaps they just became so much part of the way of life that they ceased to be remarkable. But I jumped ahead several months. I must return to the weeks before Christmas when my first experience of an African summer was causing great perspirations. The planning for the seminary was in full swing and Bishop Harding came to the mission on several occasions for long, sweaty meetings in the fly-filled sitting-room, with its strange smell of old furniture and fly-killer. The fly killer was elegantly scattered about the room in three or four old polish tins. Brother Martin and I, in a moment of wild enthusiasm, had seized some old tins of pale, insipid pink paint, enlivened it with the addition of quantities of powdered ochre and re-decorated. We painted the squared panels of the asbestos ceiling in varying colours, using some gold paint on the dividing laths. This gave more the look of an amusement arcade than a clerical establishment.

"Bit garish, old boy", the Bishop commented, on the second of his visits since we had moved in, "but at least its cleaner than it was when you got here." He stubbed out his cigarette in one of the polish tins containing the fly-killer. The resulting smell was not an improvement.

"Well, now, have you got it all mapped out", he asked. I had been there two and a half weeks and barely even had time to beat the extensive parish bounds.

"Not in the finest detail", I admitted, "but we do have a few thoughts".

"A few thoughts?" He peered over his half-moon glasses, perched on the end of his richly coloured nose. "The rector of my minor seminary had better have more than a few thoughts. I expected you to have it all mapped out in detail by now, what " He finished in a bellowing crescendo, then chuckled away as he sorted through the pieces of paper he had taken out of his brief-case.

"I wrote to tell them in Rome that we were setting up a minor seminary – apparently we are supposed to let them know, so I'm told. I did try to scrounge some money out of the Sacred Congregation while I was at it and there seems to be some hope we might just get some. They also wanted to know who will be running the show; they trust that I have chosen a man of great experience, deep spirituality and holiness of life to be in charge of young aspirants to the priesthood. So I shall have to lie about that, I suppose; I don't see much holiness around this place. I suspect that you drink gin all day, what?"

"Monsignor, I am appalled at such accusations, based on no evidence whatsoever. I am left with no alternative, but to resign as of now"

"Yes, well, I shan't accept it, so you are stuck with the job, old boy. Now, come along, let's get down to business". He lit another cigarette and pushed the tin across to me.

Making lists of requirements was hardly a problem. We should need bunk-beds and bedding, cooking pots, dishes, plates and knives and forks, etc., etc., Brother Martin and myself patiently suffered all this tedious detail, which we could well have managed without his Lordship's assistance.

"And", I ventured, "where and how do we get all this stuff?"

"Well, you'll have to buy it, dear boy", he told me, with the air of a father imparting the basic realities of life to a witless son.

"Indeed, yes, but the money..." I let the sentence hang.

"Ah, yes", some of his bonhomie disappeared. "How well is the farm doing?"

This had to be stamped on. "We are just approaching mid-summer, and have as yet produced nothing apart from the daily milk for the market. That helps towards the monthly wages bill for the farm-workers but we are barely paying our way, and won't be for long if we don't. ..."

"Well, we must have a long talk about the farm later", he interrupted. He not unnaturally believed that an asset in the shape of a farm of five thousand acres must produce some, if not a considerable income. The bit he did not like was the initial capitalisation.

"I am looking to you to do great things", he threw out with an expansive gesture, and returned to his lists.

"Now, Martin, how is the building coming along?"

"Well", he began, settling himself in his easy chair. Martin was roughly of the same rotundity as the Bishop, but slow and deliberate in his movements of mind and body, where the Bishop was impetuous and nervously quick.

"I've gathered a good quantity of sand from the river bed and the first thirty bags of cement arrived at the station yesterday. So we can begin to build by tomorrow. I've also found a local thatcher who can do the roof for us. We can have a look at the site I have cleared, it's outside the side door among the trees between the house and the farm buildings. A block of lavatories can then be built about nine or ten yards towards the farm and just at the back of the house – a kitchen".

"Good, good. But we haven't much time, dear boy, so do push it along, won't you?"

Martin looked slightly aggrieved at the implication that he was hanging about on the job, but there was no way the Bishop could ever be totally satisfied, except by instant execution of his plans.

"You staying for lunch, Monsignor?" I asked him, "because I ought to tell the Sisters."

"Oh, no, I can't be bothered going over there to eat. I brought some special cheese, French bread and cans of beer. Martin, be a good chap and get them out of the car, would you, and ask Doris to tell the Sisters we won't be down for lunch."

Martin made his way to the car in the yard outside, slowly and thoughtfully. I guessed his thoughts. He was keen on his three full meals a day and did not relish a snack of bread and cheese, but the temptation of the beer left him in a quandry. His return was more purposeful; he had made a decision.

"I think I'll step down to the convent and have a spot of lunch – it's a bit late to cancel it now. But", he continued firmly, solving his own dilemma, "I'll just have a can of beer before I go."

"Yes, do, dear boy, but it wouldn't hurt you to miss a meal and lose some weight, you know."

Martin was again a little ruffled.

"So could some other people", he remarked pointedly.

"Well, I have been trying, but I like my food, I'm afraid", replied the Bishop sadly, humbly admitting his distaste for the ascetic life.

"Well, you buzz off and take a can with you for your lunch", he said to Martin, while drawing towards himself the makings of his own lunch.

"Wonderful cheese – Wensleydale – an old aunt of mine sends it over". He set into it with the same sort of impetuous enthusiasm which he had shown in drawing up the morning's plans, eating at twice the speed I could manage. Between mouthfuls we discussed the farm.

"How's this lad Crossley getting on with the farm?"

"Well, alright I suppose. According to his reckoning he is about to break into some very profitable ventures. He has schemes, which only need money to make them work wonders in terms of big profits. He seems disappointed with me for not being able to produce the capital."

"Hm, you'll have to keep an eye on him. We don't know very much about him. We just inherited him with the place. I don't want to be unfair to him of course; if he can make a go of this place I'll be most grateful."

There was a soft footstep outside. Graham came in looking hot and dishevelled.

"Hullo, Monsignor. I saw your car outside and decided you had come to talk about my rise".

"You make a lot of money for me and then we'll talk about a rise. Do you want a beer, old boy?"

"Yes, I do, thanks".

He fell into a chair and pulled the top off a can and drank it straight off.

"Cheese?" invited the Bishop.

"No, thanks, it's too hot to eat".

Graham was very thin and looked as if he needed a couple of good meals, but he appeared to be able to keep going with a minimum of food. His height emphasised his thinness, especially as he invariably went about in shorts and no shoes. While he drank his beer he tried to broach several of his pet schemes with the Bishop. I suspect he thought I had not tried hard enough to get money out of him. He learned quite quickly that though the Bishop was interested in his schemes, especially as money-raising ventures, he had no intention of investing money in them on the dubious promise of good returns.

"No, you must build up from what you have got. Probably have to do it slowly, because we have no capital. But then you let me know after six months how much you have made", he ended somewhat unrealistically.

"Monsignor, usually puts his head back for ten minutes about this time", he said, declaring lunch over and dismissing us.

"Well, I tried", sighed Graham, when we got outside.

"Told you what he is like about money", I replied.

Over Christmas and New Year a lot of activity went into the buildings and the acquisition of the seminary equipment. Several of the priests from different missions had been in touch with me, following a circular letter from the Bishop's announcing our intention to open in January. By mid-January we had sixteen boys ranging from eight years old to fourteen, booked in to attend the mission school.

Jack Marais called one day in early January to see Graham and saw the building that was taking place.

"More farm buildings, Father?" he asked.

"No", I admitted, and told him our plans.

"Oh", he said doubtfully and scratched his head. It was apparent

45

he did not really understand, and probably did not approve judging by his next comment.

"Don't you think it's a bit premature, trying that?" he asked. "You know, I don't think they are really ready for that. The mission school is alright – it's very useful if your workers can read and write a bit – but do you think they really understand Christianity? And anyway – no offence to you, Father, man – but there aren't many bachelors among the Zulus, you know".

I laughed. "I like your delicate way of talking about celibacy, Jack, but the message of Christianity I should have thought was understandable to anyone in its broad simplicity. The Bishop thinks that we are already late in starting to find local priests for local people. Once we do then we imported priests can go back where we came from. We shall have to see whether we are right or wrong by trying. We won't know any other way."

Jack went off to look for Graham, still scratching his head, obviously extremely doubtful about our plans. Back in England I had been very dubious about the advisability of taking young boys into minor seminaries, at an age when, it seemed to me, they could hardly have made up their mind about their future. However, the Bishop had just about convinced me it would be different in Africa. He had been insistent that the boys should not be isolated in a kind of hot-house atmosphere. They would go to the local school, mix with the local community and have a minimum of extra prayer and religious life. At the same time they would be under the eye of priests who would encourage them and foster any incipient vocation to the priesthood. Anyway it was the job I had been given to do. I decided to keep an open mind on the matter. I could at least help to give some Africans the opportunity to attain a decent standard of education, in a country where most were afforded only a superficial introduction to it. In fairness to the Bishop he had agreed in general about the practice of minor seminaries in Europe who accepted boys as candidates for the priesthood at an age when they could hardly understand the implications. The European tradition implicitly involved the dubious notion of vocation as so God-given or inspired that comprehension was of secondary importance and would simply come with time. The important thing was being God-chosen, part of some divine plan. To comply with this plan was virtuous, the more so if acceptance was difficult. Any inability to continue on that road was a sign either that no vocation had been given initially – the aspirant had misread the signs – or the offer to become part of God's plan had been rejected, which presumably left the erstwhile candidate in a very ambiguous position.

I went to inspect the progress on the building which I had not had time to do for several weeks. The Christmas and New Year season had been busy at the mission, with many men home on annual holiday from work in and around Johannesburg. They had been anxious to discuss home matters, their children's schooling and to pay the rent for their two acre plots. The rondavel was now above head height and timbers were being put in place so that the thatcher could start work on the roof the next week. The kitchen had been easy to construct – three walls and a corrugated iron roof. It had seemed a better idea than a totally enclosed room, which would have been unbearably hot in the summer months. Doris had been interviewed about the possibility of her acting as cook for the seminary and had enthusiastically agreed, especially as this would mean additional wages. Her husband was, like so many of the men from the mission, away for eleven months of the year in Johannesburg, so any addition to the pitifully small supply of monthly money through the post was very welcome. Doris had agreed with the design of the kitchen and recommended its siting. The range was not yet installed, but she had found a couple of stools from somewhere and it had become her domain already.

The lavatories were rising unsteadily under Martin's willing but inexperienced hands. Bricklaying looks so wonderfully easy when done at speed by an expert. Martin did not claim this distinction, and even if he had initially spoken with quiet confidence about his ability to mastermind the building programme, he was learning that the actual execution was less simple. The rondavel had been kept in line by anchoring the mechanical builder to a central post. Building the kitchen with large blocks had been relatively simple. But using ordinary bricks for the small cubicle lavatories had quite apparently posed problems. How did one keep the walls from swaying off the vertical? A couple of walls showed correction adjustments of line. I asked innocently the purpose of the resultant small shelves.

"Oh, that", said Martin, "Just a slight correction of line, that's all. Actually", he continued seriously, "it will give added strength to the final construction. And anyway, it will all be covered with a little extra plaster and be quite unnoticeable." The matter was dismissed as a triviality.

I made encouraging noises and wandered away. I could hardly criticise when I had not lifted a single brick and certainly had no illusions about my ability to lay bricks in straight lines.

Jack Marais was returning from the farm-yard with Graham, and if I guessed right, they were bent on drinking tea. I joined them and as we strolled towards the house Doris appeared with the tea tray. Over tea Jack showed some more cautious interest in the seminary. I guessed he had talked about it to Graham after they had done their farming business. I sensed that white South Africans regarded what foreign missionaries did as eccentric, and in the case of the minor seminary, as of doubtful value. It was evident from Jack's remarks that he considered some religion was a good thing for the Africans, but rather as a means of social control, than as bringing good news of salvation and liberation to all men.

"Do you really think you can give natives positions of

responsibility in the church, like being priests, and perhaps even Bishops in time?" he asked. It was apparently a rhetorical question, because he continued, "If I give some of my natives jobs to do and make them responsible for using machinery or equipment about the farm, I have to watch them pretty closely. They break it and don't take any care of it. As I told you before, Father, I think they are like children and it's going to take a long, long time before they grow up."

Graham was smiling quietly at what Jack was saying, and nodding in agreement. He spoke Zulu fluently and appeared to be on good terms with the farm workers. But he was a white South African and no matter how liberal he might appear on most occasions there was a whole culture behind him which considered the black man as inferior. It was a double bind for black Africans. The lowly economic position into which they had been forced, then provided the whites with further justification to regard them as inferior in intelligence, morals and general ability.

"Just supposing, Jack, that what you say is true, and suppose that the child which is growing up is your child. You would take positive steps to rear that child, to educate him and help him to grow up. You wouldn't just sit back and expect that growing up to take place without your help as a parent, surely? So I would think that even the way in which you are looking at the problem ought to tell you to do something positive. And maybe that is what we are, tentatively, trying to do. I don't know how well, or how badly it will go, but I think we must try."

"Father, we live with these people, we know them through and through." Jack did not regard imported priests as a threat to his way of life; we were acting in ignorance, we had not the knowledge that he had. "And one thing you have to learn pretty quick is that you can't trust them. They'll steal from you, they'll lie to you, and all the time they'll be all smiles and touching their forelock to you". Jack was now speaking very earnestly, trying to prevent me from making terrible mistakes.

"Part of your trouble is that you priests and brothers think well of everybody and trust too much. You don't think there is a hell of a lot of wickedness in this world" – he must have felt that his language had overstepped the bounds of propriety to be observed in the clerical presence "if you'll forgive the expression, Father."

I laughed at Jack apologizing about his language, but I also laughed to relieve what was becoming a slightly tense situation. Jack was getting into full stride, obviously saying what he had ached to say to a cleric for a long time.

"Jack, I haven't been here long enough and haven't seen enough to know about the Africans' morals. But just in general terms, any priest who has been hearing confessions anywhere, for even a few weeks, soon loses any idealistic notions about the inherent goodness of human nature. Apart from that it isn't very surprising that people who are living on very low wages, and have no power to change their situation sometimes give way to the temptation to get a little extra for themselves and their families. What surprises me is that in spite of my carelessness in leaving things about and never locking my door, I have not found anything missing. But that says nothing really; it's merely my personal experience of a few weeks. I am loth to believe that one people, Zulu or British or Afrikaner, have a monopoly on either wickedness or goodness. I rather suspect there are people of all nationalities or ethnic groups who will give way to the temptation to get something for nothing, if the opportunity arises. Not that I approve of it", I hastened to add, – "just in case you think to quote the recent clerical arrival as advocating self- help through theft..."

"Well", said Jack, finishing his tea, "we could argue all day, I suppose, and probably still have different opinions." He got up. "I must get some work done before the rain-cloud descends on us." He stuck his battered old hat on his head. "Thanks for the tea, Father". He waved and went.

"Do you think we are in for rain?" I asked Graham.

"Well, it looks likely, man. If you can see the beginnings of clouds over the hill there at this time of the morning, there is a good chance of a storm by mid-afternoon. I hope so; we need some rain for the mealies."

It did rain very hard by four o'clock. It threw down four inches of rain in an hour and a quarter. The old iron-stone house had been built on strong foundations, the stoep and the rooms off it being raised up some two and a half feet from ground level. From the end of the stoep facing the road you could see the tops of the convent buildings some fifty to sixty yards away on the other side of the road, but below eye level. From the stoep at four-fifteen on that summer afternoon, we stood marooned, watching a river of water rush down the driveway, across the road and, as we learned later, straight through some of the rondavels in the convent complex. It swept away several of their outbuildings, flimsy hen houses and many of the hens, caught unawares and unable to find perches in the nearby trees. Graham regaled us with stories of floods he had known and seen; of cattle and cars swept away in flood waters; of crops destroyed and top-soil washed away. It was this sort of storm which caused so much of the widespread erosion seen everywhere.

An hour and a half later as the worst of the flooding flowed away to the stream – now a raging river – behind and below the convent, we went to assess any damage. Apart from the room at the farm end of the house, which had faced the onrushing water, the house and the church appeared to be unscathed. We all tore off shoes and socks and gingerly felt our way through the muddy river to the convent. Sisters were busy sweeping water from their rondavel bedrooms and carting furniture to higher ground. The rain had practically stopped, but the clouds were still threatening and it seemed unlikely that the things being placed outside would be dry before nightfall. Sister Superior was ruefully bewailing the loss of her hens.

"Father," she said, "this is a violent country you have come to." The twinkle in her eye suggested that her comments were as much about political forces as the forces of nature. "At least there was no hail to destroy the mealies," she noted philosophically.

Chapter Four

The boys arrived on January the eighteenth to begin their long haul to the priesthood. There were two nine year olds among them. They seemed to be very young and I feared that they would be feeling immense homesickness. The boys arrived in twos and threes, brought by the priests of their respective missions. A couple of the priests were honest enough to wonder whether their boys would make the grade, but they all said what wonderful boys their boys were – faithful altar servers, sons of the woman who does the house, or of the catechist – they all had magnificent references. Happily some spoke at least some English. My priestly colleagues eagerly dropped their charges and left me to cope with the coming eighteen months and all those young bodies to feed and bed down each night.

We had got the bunk beds and disposed them round the walls of the big rondavel. It looked clean and cheeful, with its new thatch and the coat of white paint Martin and his assistants had given it. Temporarily, the boys would be living out of suitcases, until we had lockers for each of them. Martin also set up two enormous corrugated galvanised tin tanks to catch every drop of water, from every available roof in order to provide washing water for both bodies and clothes.

The kitchen was functioning. The range had been installed the previous week and had a couple of trial runs, mainly making tea for Doris and her friends who called after mass in the mornings. I had somewhat foolishly canvassed opinions about what Zulus eat from Gareth and Jack Marais. They had both replied without hesitation, and doubtless very truthfully, that they ate mealie meal. All I had to do was to make sure that the cook had a constant supply of the meal, with which she would make porridge in the morning, or a drier mix in the evening to eat with gravy and a few vegetables. I discovered about two weeks later, that Jack and Gareth were not exactly accurate. I was watching Doris stirring a huge pot of mealie meal cooked almost dry of water. I commented that it appeared very dry and I wondered that the boys actually liked it like that. Doris was always very gentle when explaining to the ignorant foreigner.

"It is not so dry, Baba, when they eat it with milk from the farm in the morning."

"But what about now?" I asked. It was time for the evening meal.

"Perhaps Baba can afford to get meat sometimes so that we can make a gravy," she said very shyly, hardly daring to look at me.

"Would they like that?" I asked in my naivety.

"I think that they would," she ventured; which being interpreted meant that she was absolutely sure that they would. I was to learn that Doris's thoughts about the boys were usually prompted by what the boys had told her they would like, with the added suggestion that she should make this known to me.

51

I fled suffering internal shame, whilst I gravely promised to look into the food question. While not intending to set up an establishment of gourmet delight to every school boy within a hundred mile radius, I did want to give a basic good, and if possible attractive, menu to the boys. And I had committed the sin of not asking them what they liked to eat. I had not even asked Doris or local parishioners – I had asked the white men.

The first two weeks consisted of ad hoc solutions to problems. I had started the whole thing off with a short talk in English, translated by a thirteen year old, Jeremiah. I had appointed him as my first lieutenant, not because he was one of the oldest, but more particularly because he spoke the best English. I was very conscious of my lack of more than very basic Zulu, though after two months I was improving. My ear was beginning to be attuned to it to the extent of starting to understand oft-repeated phrases. But regardless of the lack of first-hand communication with some of the boys, I felt we must have a general meeting about mutual problems. I called Jeremiah and asked him to gather the boys after the evening meal. I let drop that food and meals would be prominent on the agenda and a gleam of interest fought its way through his quietly deferential manner. I could tell he had told the other boys about the topic for discussion by the heightened buzz of conversation in the rondavel where the boys waited for their evening meal.

As things turned out my ghastly lapse about the matter of food worked to the advantage of all. Boys who had satisfied themselves up to now with greeting me in a respectful manner, became quite animated over the question of food. It became very apparent that mealie meal prepared in different ways was favourite. It was familiar and it filled the tummy, though it hardly fired the appetite or the imagination. It crossed my mind that the cheapness of mealie meal might have had some bearing on the suspiciously unscientific theory of many whites that blacks' taste buds were differently constructed from those of their white superiors. Years later I came in contact with an enterprising black man who was making a lot of money by selling fish and chips in the Soweto African townships.

The results of this meeting were apparent within months. The seminary boys were obviously better fed, fitter and more able in both academic matters and sport than the local children. On the mission farm itself there was no severe and obvious malnutrition – though we did see some most appalling cases in the district – but when the comparison was made with the seminary boys, enjoying a more balanced diet, it was not hard to see why underfed workers were characterised as 'lazy kaffirs' by white farmers or why hungry children were 'slow' at school.

Another result of the meal meeting was to teach me a lesson. The necessity for consultation is a commonplace and I had failed to do it. I wondered why. Of course, I was a quasi-infallible catholic priest – that may well have been part of the trouble. A priest's role is said to be that of servant and minister, but in fact the opposite tends to be the case. We possess the power, the status and, even more important in the South African situation, the white skin. Add to that the fact of my being landlord to my immediate parishioners at Besters and my supremacy was assured. In such circumstances barriers were inevitably there. But another reason was that I had also unthinkingly fallen into the South African way of life. I had consulted white men about the African.

I remember, some months after this, being present at a clergy conference of mainly white priests, with just two African priests present, where the discussion centred on the problems of adaptation for the African clergy into the clerical life imported from Europe. After an hour of different opinions being voiced, Father Marius stood up in some exasperation and pointed to our African colleagues, who had remained silent throughout the discussion, and enquired why nobody bothered to ask them. There had been a quite total insensitivity to their presence until it was pointed out to us. Generally there was little embarrassment in talking about the adaptation of African clergy into 'our' system without consulting them. We, the whites, set the standards, we set the pace – because we knew.

About this time Cos crossed swords with an elderly German priest through the letter columns of the South African Catholic weekly. He had been in the country for nearly forty years. With the usual European arrogance, the old man dismissed African customs. He saw no possibility of any sort of marriage between the trivial beliefs of the Africans and the imported Catholic creed. His logic was simple: Rome was so totally right about everything that anything not conforming to such infallible recititude was, by implication, and necessarily wrong. Therefore, there could be no adaptation of anything to do with, say, ancestor worship, because this smacked of idolatry. Such opinions were given with only a superficial appraisal of the African beliefs. It was necessary to show only minimal non-conformity in order to invalidate any suggested incorporation into an African style Christianity. The recommended method – which coincidentally was more congenial to the missionaries - was to sweep the existing African beliefs and practices away altogether and give them a whole new and better way of Christian life. Unfortunately, one result was to drive the old customs underground, as far as the priest was concerned. In some places there was an odd mixture of old and new which had the backlash effect of bewildering the clergy. They were left confused as to what the Africans really did believe. Then they sighed sadly and opined that it was going to take some time before these people were able to latch on to the real truth. There were only a few I met who thought that Dr Voerword might not be right after all. The answer of many Africans was to combine Christianity with their local beliefs and to form their own churches.

Before Easter we had fallen into a pattern of daily life centred around the presence of the boys. From half past eight in the morning until three in the afternoon, the boys were out at the mission school, apart from a brisk run down the hill at midday for dinner. In the late afternoon and evening there was homework to be done and various household chores, rotated among the boys. And football. They were keen on football and, under the pretence of supervising, Martin and myself also turned out twice a week to play. We rationalised this activity to ourselves on the grounds that we could do with the exercise. Anyway if the game was supposed to teach the boys the desired disciplines of sportmanship and team co-operation, it was fitting that their mentors in matters spiritual should also be actively involved in this fine example of community activity. Having said all that, it just so happened that I enjoyed playing, although as the years went by, it became apparent that a man of thirty was no match for very fast-moving youngsters of fifteen and sixteen. Another happy spin-off was the vicarious admiration and respect I received for the abilities of 'Ace' and 'Speeds' and other stars of the team, who were often referred to as 'your boys'. I took it all with proprietary modesty, like a first division manager who does not, of course, claim credit for natural ability, but has blended the various natural talents of his players into a well-run team. In retrospect, about all I can really claim is dissuading them from chasing round after the ball like an untidy loose-scrum on a rugby field and endeavouring to introduce some rudimentary form of positional play.

The Bishop thought they ought to start learning some Latin. I had learned to read it fluently – as students we got plenty of practice, both in church and refectory – though I have to admit I was not always entirely clear what I was reading. So, like any good teacher, I kept one lesson ahead of my pupils. More interestingly, my preparation had to include some three-way translation: ringing the changes from English through Zulu to Latin. Fortunately at these basic stages, this could all be done with the aid of a dictionary and half an hour's intensive research before the class. This was fine while we stuck to the acquisition of basic vocabulary but the comparative complexities of accidence and syntax in the three languages often left my class with bemused or glazed expressions of bewilderment. I wondered how much, if anything, any of them retained from my trilingual attempts to pass on a language I had only grudgingly and half-heartedly learned myself.

After about six months the Bishop felt the experiment of the seminary was going quite well.

"Bit cramped, aren't you though, dear boy?" His remarks often sounded like criticism, though he was only expressing the regret that reality failed to live up to his private fantasy. He would have liked an impressive building with ready-made customs and traditions, but he was reasonably content that at least there had been no palpable disasters. Nonetheless, I guessed plans for the future were already beginning to be framed in his mind.

"Need to be separate, really, to do the job properly.... and you shouldn't have to run the parish as well.... couple of teachers and yourself and you could have your own school...."

Such remarks, half muttered to himself, gave me the clues about the direction his mind was taking. For myself, the longer the project went on the more I became drawn to it, the less critical, the less sceptical. I suppose I wanted to defend the work I was doing and justify it in the face of the criticisms of my brethren who felt the whole idea was a waste of money. However, with the project having started up and running, we no longer heard such rumblings. It was now a fact; we pursued it energetically and even sought to give it an aspect of respectability.

Not having the funds to build the imposing fantasy establishment, he decided to start on the boys.

"I think they should have a uniform, dear boy; what do you feel?"

If I ever expressed a contrary opinion, he would usually fret about it unhappily for a time and then ignore it. So I made a half-hearted attempt to caution him about injudicious spending at a time when we could hardly afford unnecessary extras. It was a novel reversal of roles and I had given him the opening he needed.

"But, dear boy, these things are necessary. They define our aims and the boys' aims and aspirations, give them a feeling of belonging to something, d'you see? If we use the money this way, other things will just have to wait a little longer. We must get our priorities right. You and Cos will have to swig less gin, what?" He tried to wrap the whole thing up in jocular vein.

"Actually, we prefer whisky", I told him austerely, as if he was accusing us of a more pernicious decadence.

"I'm looking at the colour of your nose", he said, laughing with the good humour of one who has won the argument. His mood then quickly changed to one of busy organisation.

"When do the boys finish for the holidays?"

"In a fortnight's time".

"Good. On the Monday after they go home we shall go and get uniforms from Johannesburg".

"Johannesburg? That's about two hundred and fifty miles away", I said. "Surely, we can find something a little nearer than that".

"Well," he explained, "I have a couple of letters of introduction to wholesalers up there. And anyway I have to visit a film distributors there. I'm at Ermelo that weekend then I'll come and stay the night here on the Sunday and we can make an early start. We might have to stay the night somewhere on Monday; but that's no problem." He was brisk and business-like. He had quite evidently thought it all out beforehand, and short of a direct refusal coupled with my resignation,

I don't think I could have stopped him.

"Meanwhile, dear boy, you get busy with the tape-measure and write down all the vital statistics of the boys."

The boys treated the whole thing, when I explained it to them and measured them, with excited interest and a good deal of laughter. As African boys they had never been measured for clothing before. In many cases they had to make do with what clothing they could get from elder members of the family and parish jumble sales. Eventually out of all the noise and clowning, I managed to get a fairly coherent list of the sizes needed to provide all eighteen of them with 'Sunday' best and everyday uniforms. They wanted to know if they would have the new clothes the next day and were a little dampened when I told them the uniforms would not be ready for them until the start of next term.

In his initial enthusiasm over the uniforms it appeared the Bishop had entirely forgotten about some confirmations at Ermelo which were scheduled for Sunday evening. On Saturday evening while his lordship and Cormac were chatting before going to bed, the Bishop casually said:

"I shall be going down to Besters tomorrow afternoon, old boy, so perhaps you can tell the Sisters I shan't want any supper."

Cormac put his head back and guffawed.

"Shall I do the confirmations then?" he asked.

"What confirmations?"

"The twenty youngsters you promised to confirm here tomorrow evening?"

"I did?" he asked, anxiously. "I didn't," he stated with no great conviction. And then after a pause, now biting his fingers: "Did I?"

"Oh, yes, indeed, Monsignor," affirmed Cormac, thoroughly enjoying the situation.

"Oh, crumbs," the Bishop commented typically and sadly. He relapsed into thought, while Cormac laughed heartily.

"Can Sam come up here and stay the night on Sunday, do you think, Cormac?"

"Of course," said Cormac expansively. "So you'll do the confirmations then?"

"Well, yes, if I promised; but I haven't prepared a sermon and there's no time now."

"Good heavens," shouted Cormac, "you've got time tomorrow. Confirmation isn't until the evening."

"Yes, yes. Well, I'd better ring Sam."

So I went up to Ermelo arriving shortly after the Bishop had started his oration to the candidates. He was a good preacher, but he did like to prepare his sermons thoroughly. That day it showed he had not given the matter his usual attention. He rambled on, touching on most aspects of Christian teaching, to the growing restlessness of his congregation. It became painfully clear to Cormac and myself as he attempted to draw together the strands of thought after thirty-five minutes that he was having problems in finding a conclusion. He furtively glanced at his watch – a move as well-disguised as a stage-whisper – and concluded by promising all present a remembrance in his prayers.

"Well, not too bad; didn't go off too badly did it, Cormac?" he asked afterwards in the sacristy.

"Wonderful, Monsignor," boomed Cormac, "You knocked 'em for six."

"Yes, well, I don't really think that I did that." He was pretty sure that Cormac didn't think so either.

We made our way to the priests' house.

"I could do with a drink," the Bishop announced.

"A cup of tea, perhaps," enquired Cormac, knowing very well tea was not what the Bishop had in mind.

"Well, no," replied the Bishop, somewhat diffidently. He always felt he had to justify having alcohol as a reviver or reward.

"I did think perhaps something a little stronger.."

Cormac threw open a cupboard door and produced beer, gin and whisky.

"What will you have, Monsignor?"

"Well, I think I would like a gin and tonic, if you have it"

"With ice?"

"Oh, please, dear boy," said the Bishop, lighting a cigarette and beginning to relax.

"Sam, you can help yourself" called Cormac.

"Thank goodness that is over," admitted the Bishop frankly, "I get so sticky in all those vestments. Did you think I went on a bit too long with the sermon?"

I was about to reassure him, when Cormac burst out in reply.

"Yes," he said, baldly, chuckling while preparing his own drink.

"Mm, I thought maybe I had," said the Bishop, sounding a little disappointed at not receiving some reassurance. We finished our 'revivers' and went across the road to the convent for supper.

After prayers the next morning the Bishop was all haste to embark on the day's plans. He didn't actually hustle me through my breakfast but he did finish his remarkably quickly and then gave every indication of impatience. He tapped his feet, bounced his left knee about beneath the table – unseen, but the vibrations could be felt – and drummed the table with his fingers. I finally put my cup down and he sprang up.

"Shall we go, dear boy?" It was a rhetorical question.

"Have a wonderful time", Cormac bellowed after us.

At the house I changed from my habit and put on a dog-collar, and a light-weight jacket.

"Not too formal are we?" I called to the Bishop.

57

"What do you mean, old boy?" He appeared from his room.

"Thought I'd leave my sandals on."

He looked down at my feet with faint disapproval, and mused a moment.

"Well," he started, "we don't want to make a show of ourselves in the big city. Do you have shoes with you?"

"Oh, yes," I admitted. He gazed at me sadly while continuing to fight with his back collar-stud.

"I'll put shoes on if you think that better."

"Oh, would you?" He brightened, as if the whole idea had come from me. "Probably better, don't you think?"

He went whistling back to his room.

Ermelo was only about one hundred and fifty miles from Johannesburg over tarmac roads and we arrived by midday. After some circling of our target, we found a parking place. The Bishop got out, stuck his hand in his pockets and went off at a fair speed, whistling down the busy city street. This was the man who had not wanted me to make a show of myself in the big city by wearing sandals. I hastened after him. I nearly caught up with him by the first corner, but by the time I turned the corner he had disappeared. He could only have gone into the first shop around the corner in the short seconds he had been out of sight. The shop was a music store. I found him at the record counter, trying to make himself understood by an assistant. There must have been a dozen or so youngsters around, listening to the latest 'pop' hits being played. The Bishop was gesticulating at the record-player.

"Can't you turn it off for a minute?" he requested.

"What?" asked the assistant blankly.

"Turn the bally thing off " the Bishop bellowed.

"Oh," said the assistant flatly and the teenagers nearby looked aggrieved, though curious to see what the Bishop wanted. So for that matter was I. I had been treated on the way up to his lordship's whistling parts of Vivaldi's Four Seasons, which seemed to be his current favourite. In a small Volkswagen, however beautiful the original music might be, I found the episcopal whistle a little piercing. In view of his obvious liking for the classics I wondered whether he might not be about to denounce all this noisy pop music as beneath human dignity, or something like that.

"Can't hear yourself talk, can you, dear boy?" he remarked to the assistant.

"Now, I want a copy of that."

"Of what?" enquired the assistant.

"Of that, the one you were just playing;" said the Bishop, a little testily, unable to understand the young man's obtuseness.

"Oh, that," said the assistant enlightened at last.

"Yes, yes, dear boy," agreed the Bishop, beaming affectionately at the young salesman. "Wrap one up, will you?"

58

He leaned against the counter and surveyed the scene. He caught sight of me.

"Do you like it?" he asked.

"Like what?" I asked in reply.

"The latest record, dear boy."

He turned to the assistant. "You can start the machine again if you will, young man."

"Oh, thanks," said the young man, with no trace of sarcasm in his voice.

"I didn't know you followed all these pop groups," I said as we left the shop.

"Not all of them, dear boy, not all of them. But some of them are good and we must keep up with the times, what? Now I think we should have a bite to eat. We shall get nobody worth having to serve us in the wholesalers at lunchtime. Better to eat now and try to get to the wholesale place about two, don't you think?".

We ate huge bread rolls stuffed with salad and great mugs of coffee at a sort of lunch bar. Then we proceeded to the clothiers. The Bishop was in good humour. He appeared to be at home in the city and to know his way about. I did not and his public relations were poor. He seemed to assume that I would know where we were heading. He forged ahead as one with a pressing purpose in life, with me desperately trying to keep up and follow his sudden changes of direction. After ten minutes of this disjointed travelling, the Bishop turned into a multi-storied building, paused at a floor sign-board, asked me if I had my list at the ready and bounded into a lift just as it was closing its doors. We went up several floors. When the doors of the lift opened, we entered the calm of a heavily-carpeted, spacious sales area, scattered with counters, and ceiling-high sets of shelves filled with clothing of all sorts. Business appeared to be carried on with quiet dignity, unruffled by indecent haste. It all made a sharp contrast to the noisy activity of the streets outside.

His lordship was obviously satisfied at having reached our goal. He paused, looked around and then signalled his satisfaction by emitting an ear-splitting whistle. Conversations had been subdued as we entered. Under the impact of the whistle they ceased altogether and everyone looked round to see who had perpetrated the unseemly noise. It was both embarrassing and amusing. Embarrassing to think we were the object of the disapproving attention; but amusing as it became obvious that the sight of our clerical collars and the episcopal purple led on-lookers to believe we could never have been the culprits. Puzzled momentarily they all went back to their various tasks and we began to view the display of clothes for boys and young men.

I had not been shopping with the Bishop before, but had been warned that he had eccentric methods. He began by disparaging the quality of the articles in a fairly loud voice, peering at things over his half-moon spectacles in a faintly disapproving manner.

"Yes," he began doubtfully, fingering a blazer of evident quality "the nap will be worn off that in three weeks. Not really what we want, dear boy. No I'm sorry, old boy".

The impression to an eavesdropper would have been that I was sold on the said blazer and he was talking me out of it. A tall young assistant approached, looking some-what affronted at having heard the company's stock dismissed as of inferior quality.

"Can I help you?" He articulated it slowly and austerely, without any ingratiating smile. He obviously assumed we had wandered into the place by accident, and could not possibly be bona fide retailers.

"Ah," the Bishop said, swinging round on the young man with a pleased smile, "I'm sure you can, Mr -" he leaned forward to read the small plaque pinned to his white coat, displaying his name – "er – Brits, isn't it?" He thrust a letter of introduction into Mr Brit's hand, but then hurried on before the poor man could read it.

"We are looking to rig out the boys at my minor seminary with uniforms – everything from socks to ties – and I'm sure you will be able to help us admirably. We shall of course require good quality materials - as I was just explaining to Father Sam here, quality is all important in getting clothing for boys. But of course for the poor missions we shall want it cheap, as cheap as possible. You do understand, Mr Brits, I'm sure."

Mr Brits unbent somewhat after reading the letter and receiving this assurance of the Bishop's faith in his ability to help us. The Bishop continued to pour oil all over Mr Brits. He forgot me for the moment. I had fulfilled my purpose as straight man in his double act; all his attention was on Mr Brits. He asked his advice; he sometimes wondered delicately if Mr Brits' judgement was exactly right; asked if he had something just a shade more or less of this or that and if so perhaps Mr Brits could be so kind as to show it to us. The comments, the discussion went on almost without interruption, mainly directed at Mr Brits. I was occasionally included when he wanted to make slightly adverse comments about certain garments. Within twenty minutes the counters were covered with all the things he wanted to see – it seemed he was keen to view the entire stock of the warehouse – most of which he rejected as unsuitable. Mr Brit's calm was being sorely tried in his attempts to please this whirlwind customer. By this time the Bishop was keeping him going with encouraging pats on the shoulder and he had started to refer to him as 'dear boy'.

After he had made the choice of the colour and quality of blazers, trousers and shirts, socks and ties, he turned to me and stage-whispered:

"Lists, lists, lists, dear boy, where are the lists; don't tell me you've lost them, what?" He knew jolly well I had not lost them and I passed them to him.

"Ah, good," He turned to Mr. Brits. "Now, dear boy, here are the different sizes, very clearly made out by Father Sam here. I want to leave it all to you, as I know you can take care of everything for me."

"Er," interrupted Mr Brits, "The socks and ties are from downstairs..." But there was no escape for him.

"Never mind, dear boy, I am sure that you can manage. If you can have it all parcelled up, we shall call back in" he looked at his watch "shall we say one hour? Many, many thanks, Mr Brits, you have been most helpful and kind."

There was not a lot that Mr Brits could say or do, especially as the Bishop was already moving towards the lift. Mr Brits stood gazing at the turmoil created in his department in so short a time. He looked a little lost and forlorn. The Bishop turned as he was about to enter the lift and called back.

"Don't forget the five per cent off for the poor missions, dear boy."

The lift bore us downward, the Bishop whistling happily as we went. I viewed him with a new respect and awe after watching his performance. He affected not to notice my expression.

"Helpful young man, Mr – er Brits, what?"

He beamed ingeniously.

"How do we spend the time while your Mr Brits prepares the parcels?"

"Well, I have to see the film people, remember. It's only round the corner."

We went through the same performance as before. He never bothered to mention which corner it was round, consequently we kept disengaging and having oddly fragmented conversation. I had been trying to find out what film he was trying to hire. I certainly didn't manage it on that short walk through the Johannesburg streets. The film place was the local office of Twentieth Century Fox. We located the manager's office, but there was someone with him. The Bishop had ascertained this by popping his head round the door, but he courteously withdrew when he saw that the man was engaged. We stood for a while; we sat for a while; we read the notices about different films; then we paced for a while in desultory conversation. We ran out of waiting room chat and again we paced, now in different directions, passing each other from time to time, the Bishop whistling, but this time gently and unobtrusively. In the meantime, different employees kept buzzing in and out of the great man's office, bearing sheafs of paper, or sometimes huge round tins of film. Apparently they supplied many cinemas in the Transvaal. His lordship's patience was getting frayed and he was tutting quite audibly - he had been waiting a full twelve minutes. Suddenly he popped his head round the manager's door and called out in a vexed voice:

"Come along, come along, come along."

A couple of secretaries came out and looked at him anxiously as they hurried away. I laughed.

61

"Do you know him well?" I asked.

"Know who?"

"The manager."

"No, never met the man. They do mess about endlessly, don't they?"

He was getting quite cross.

He gave the remaining member of staff another minute to get out and then seeing the exhortation had failed to shift him, he beckoned to me and we walked into the manager's office. The employee was talking earnestly to the manager and looked nervously over his shoulder at us as we entered. He gathered up his bits of paper from the desk and began to retreat, obviously under the impression that a personage of some importance had entered. The Bishop sank wearily into a huge leather armchair and tossed his hat onto the manager's desk. He put his head back and closed his eyes a moment while the underling uttered his final words before disappearing out of the door.

The manager was undecided. He half stood, vaguely wondering if he or his secretary had forgotten this appointment.

"Can I .... do I ...." he began apologetically.

"Bishop Ulyatt", the Bishop announced, "and Father Sam, one of my priests. You seem awfully busy". It sounded like a complaint.

"Well, I am rather ... Did you ...?"

"I want a film," stated the Bishop; which seemed to put the manager more at ease. "It's a little film of Zulu dancing. I'm afraid that I don't know the title, or who produced it, but I understand that you do have such a film".

"Yes, I'm sure we do, but...." he reached for one of the three phones on his desk.

"I...... I shan't be a moment." He went out to organise the matter.

"A full-length film on Zulu dancing, is it?" I enquired.

"Oh, no," the Bishop corrected me, 'It's only a ten minute thing."

Again I was impressed. The manager of a large concern who had previously been king in his own office receiving and sending forth minions, had been totally usurped, and all for a 'short', a mere ten minute fill-in.

The manager came back within about three minutes, bearing a small film and bits of paper requiring the signature of the hirer of the film. The whole deal had been completed within about six minutes of our entering the manager's office. Such was the presence of his lordship that the manager rose at the end of the transaction and told us how glad he was to have been of service to us. I followed the Bishop out, fixing my face so as not to reveal my amusement. The Bishop was an impressive operator. He managed to get superb service and leave those who served him feeling the privilege had been all theirs.

We walked back to the car, drove round to the clothing

warehouse, and found the parcels waiting for us at the service door. Mr. Brits must have called in at least 2 assistants to help in order to have had it ready so quickly.

There was a great deal of merriment and mutual ragging when the boys returned from holidays and were issued with their new uniforms. But the next Sunday there was no merriment as they walked across to the church for mass under the eyes of the local parishioners. They walked with a slightly self-conscious pride. One or two lifted their chins an extra inch and affected an almost indicernible swagger. The more vociferous parishioners showed no reticence at all in expressing their views: the boys looked marvellous. Old Dora, who spoke quite good English, delivered a short speech about the wonderful delight it was to see 'their' boys, looking so smart, thanks to the good Bishop – and Father Sam, she added in a hasty afterthought. Having finished the more formal speech, she then grabbed two of the boys and had them parading like models before the parishioners outside the church, as she gave a commentary – in Zulu, this time – interspersed with delighted laughter. The boys picked out to be the male models were a little embarrassed but also quite pleased to be the centre of interest. Dora rounded off the occasion by pronouncing the general approval of the minor seminary and especially, its siting in their parish. When the parishioners had gone away, the boys walked about the house, preening themselves and enjoying their new-found elegance.

I had occasion to speak to the Bishop the next day on the phone and reported all this to him.

"Well, of course, dear boy. You leave it to your uncle; he knows all these things, what?" He chuckled happily at the success of his plans.

Chapter Five

The final term of the year passed very quickly. We now had a routine which ran itself. We seemed to have passed through our initiation period of disasters and crises, accidents and acts of God. We had come out of it more wary, and perhaps wiser. Martin had gone through the year gradually making the place more habitable and providing more room. Cos had become steadily busier as he got to know his area and we saw less and less of him at Besters except in the evenings. He was even playing with the idea of having a pied à terre in his own area. As it was an officially designated African area he was, as a white man, forbidden to live there. This was one of the reasons why he had been living at Besters. The other was the adherence, on the part of his ecclesiastical and religious superiors, to the principle of community living and mutual support. Initially we had ourselves seen the sense of this, especially as we were extremely raw recruits. With the passing of time and gaining of experience Cos now felt confident enough to go out on his own. He had also had time to weigh up the likelihood of getting away with breaking a law. We considered such laws immoral anyway. Cos established that a local police commandant was not totally hostile to our point of view and, while having his job to do, was likely to direct his forces towards more important matters than chasing Catholic priests out of African areas. There was a school of thought that saw churches and the instilling of a bit of religion into the 'natives' as a good, and more importantly, a useful thing. The reasoning was simple: the Church generally taught people that if they behaved in an approved manner in this life they would be rewarded in the hereafter. Of course, set against this were the cases of clerics who interferred in politics and dared to promote such ideas as the equality of men before God. Such priests preached about freedoms that were manifestly denied to the Africans - freedom of movement; of speech; the right to vote and to make decisions about how they were governed. There was the real threat of being thrown out of the country if the government put you in this category. There were regular examples to prove it. However, Cos started to make preparations to move his base to the area he worked in by the New Year.

About a week before Christmas Sister Colette, the district nurse, came across one evening and asked if one of us could provide her with transport. Her little motor-bike was out of action and she wanted to check on a couple of families she had seen during the day. We were sitting on the stoep after supper and relaxing after what had been a particularly hot day.

"We'll both come, if you don't mind, Sister?" Cos said.

"Of course not", she said, and laughed, "I shall feel very honoured."

Colette was French Canadian, full of amazingly ceaseless energy and laughter which was always very near the surface and ready to bubble over. It was already starting to get dark as we set out on the road towards Ladysmith. On either side of the road there were white-owned farms, and dotted here and there, the homes of the African farm workers. Happily the home we were to visit was close to the main road. Visiting the parishioners on the farms meant coping with the attitude of the white farmer. In general they implicitly regarded the Africans, as part of the property, their property, and thus any approach to them needed the farmer's permission. Of course, the farm did belong to the farmer and as a matter of courtesy, if not also of legality, a case could be made for obtaining permission before entering. In our view the visiting of one person in his own home by another could not justifiably be under the control of a third party. So we tended not to ask permission. Another reason was that it might be refused, and we preferred not to push matters to a confrontation.

This home consisted of two thatched huts set in an area of baked earth which, under the hot summer sun, was almost as hard as concrete. We called out as we approached. A female voice called out to us to come in. We entered a small round hut and found a young woman and three small children, sitting on grass mats, in the light of a single candle. The mother was rocking her baby on her knee, and the other two children were sat, almost motionless. They did not glance up as we entered, but continued to gaze at the floor. The woman greeted us with a slight nervous smile as if she were a little ashamed of something.

Sister Colette had explained to us on the way over the reason for her concern about this family. The children, she said, were all suffering from very bad malnutrition and needed urgent medical attention. She had advised the mother to take the children into Ladysmith to the hospital, but though the mother had given a half-promise, Sister Colette feared she would not go. If she did not go, the result would almost certainly be the death of the three children. We had listened with polite interest to Sister Colette but it was only when we saw the children that we became involved in what might so soon become a tragedy. I think Sister Colette sensed that we had not met cases like this before. So she began very gently to take the mother through the problem of the children's well-being as she saw it. She knew it had to be done slowly if we were to understand, for our Zulu was still barely adequate.

"Has your husband returned?" the Sister asked.

"No. I have sent someone to call him from Ladysmith, but he has not returned yet."

"Is he working?"

"I do not think he is working." The woman spoke in a tired monotone.

"Then what is he doing?"

"He is trying to find work. He is staying with my brother in the location."

"But I think we need to take the children to hospital tonight, because they are very, very sick."

"I will tell the father when he returns," she said, with her eyes cast down, not looking at us.

"But", Sister said very slowly and gently, "you do not know when he will return and then it might be too late."

"Yes," she said. "But we must ask him".

There was silence in the hut for four or five minutes. The only sound was the laboured breathing of the children, who seemed preoccupied with trying to breathe and had no eyes or ears for the conversation.

Cos and myself had come as chauffeurs to Sister Colette – a little drive in the cool evening air – but we were, without having uttered a word being drawn into this dreadful situation of watching needless death. We began to feel anger, and frustration, but were not sure at whom to direct these feelings. After five long, silent minutes Sister Colette looked at us and saw our tense faces.

"Have you met the farm workers' situation before, their conditions of employment?"

"I don't think so", I said, "unless you mean the sort of situation we have on the mission farm, where I am ashamed of the amount we pay the men each month."

A little chuckle escaped the Sister, in spite of the tense atmosphere.

"Father, your workers are poorly paid, of course, but relatively they are living in luxury. I will explain it later. Now I think we must try to get the children to hospital."

"But she wants her husband here," said Cos, "Should we pressurise her?"

"Mon Père, yours is the ethical problem. For me it is more simple. I see that at least one will die by the morning, if we go away and do nothing."

Cos and I looked at each other and mentally put away the text-book of moral theology. Our Zulu was poor but our anger and worry chased away any inhibitions about sounding foolish, as we tried to persuade the mother that she was left with no choice about the children. To us the situation required no consideration. Once the brutal fact had been plainly put to the mother, that in twenty-four hours at least one of the children would be dead and the others would surely follow if nothing was done, she was in anguish. Her quiet monotone of resignation broke and she sobbed. We looked at each other in perplexity. She calmed a little, then blurted out, without looking at us:

"Children die in hospital, they die, they all die in that hospital. My husband will blame me when it happens; he will hate me. Perhaps he will leave me."

She sobbed again. Then after a while, "Perhaps he will agree for them to go, when he returns."

"But when will he return?" asked Cos.

She was silent for a minute, then she whispered, realising what her answer meant for the children, "I do not know."

"Look," said Cos, getting practical, "where does he stay in the location. We'll go and see him."

"I do not know. I have never been there," she replied, despairingly.

"Well, we know his name and we know your brother's name; we can ask around."

But even as we thought about that we realised we were grasping at straws. The amount of time all this might take could be fatal to the children. We might ask officials at the town location, only to find they were not known there and we would have revealed them as illegal residents. Or they might be staying in the African areas which began a couple of miles outside the town.

We tried again. Children died in hospital, often enough because they were taken there too late. If we went now there was just a chance that we could get help in time. And meantime the longer we discussed the matter the worse the children's condition was becoming. Her eyes flickered recognition of the soundness of the argument.

"Could we not dash back and get some soup, or something from the mission?" I whispered to Sister Colette.

She shook her head "it is too late for that. They need intravenous feeding slowly for some days, if they are to survive."

We sighed and thought again.

The breathing of the eldest child of four and a half years – he looked about one and a half – could be heard worsening in the silence. This turned the tide. The mother looked very frightened and put out a hand to the child whose situation was deteriorating.

"Asihambeni", she said, "Let us go."

Cos and I scrambled to our feet and staggered with limbs numb from sitting on the floor so long. Sister Colette grabbed the four and a half year old child, I the middle child and mother carried the baby. The woman blew out the candle and closed the hut door. Cos had the doors of the car open and the engine running as we emerged from their home. He drove the few miles to the hospital like a lunatic and we rushed the children into the casualty department.

Some hour and a half later when the preliminary work had been done and drips set up for the children, we met a young doctor who had been examining the children. She took it all very matter-of-factly. This sort of condition was a commonplace to her. There were of course many different diseases in the hospital wards, but most of them, she admitted could be traced back to malnutrition.

"Will the children survive?" we dared to ask.

"Oh, I think so," she answered quite cheerfully, "but you were right to get them here when you did. They would not have survived

67

much longer at home."

"Well, that's wonderful," we said, full of relief.

"Is it?" the doctor shocked us by saying, "What will happen after we discharge them? We get children coming back again and again, until they are so weakened they die anyway."

We gaped at her in horror.

"Don't think I'm cynical, Fathers, I'm reporting what happens. You ask Sister Colette, if it's not true. But I must go. Good-bye, I promise we shall look after the children."

The mother had gone with her children into the ward and we went to find her to tell her what the doctor had said. She was sitting, very calm now, with her children who were asleep. A hint of a smile shyly crept into her eyes as she saw us approaching. She was first to speak.

"The Sister says they will live, but we have been lucky. We thank you, Sister Colette. My husband will not be angry now." She looked at Cos and myself, hesitated, then said softly to Colette: "The white men, the reverends, they have been kind too."

Sister Colette offered the mother a lift home. She looked at her children, who were sound asleep.

"Thank you, yes; I shall come back early in the morning."

Cos said he would be passing through Ladysmith the next day en route to his mission and would give her a lift. She was delighted at the suggestion.

She was quietly happy as she waved us goodbye at the roadside near her home.

"And the other patient you had to see, Sister?" asked Cos. Sister Collette laughed heartily, and remarked mischievously:

"Father Cos you are afraid I will insist on my chauffeur taking me on another call. But no, it is too late now to visit the old man. They will all be asleep at the house and there is nothing really I can do for him. He is dying, but of old age and no hospital can cure that. I wanted to make sure he was comfortable for the night, but we were a long time with the children." She looked at her watch. "Gracious, it is past midnight. The sisters will wonder what has happened to us all. But no matter, they will not worry; I am quite often out on late calls. However, my chauffeurs – you must be tired." She laughed, giving no evidence of remorse at keeping us out so long.

"You haven't finished yet, Sister. You said you would tell us about the woman's husband and his work on the farm," I reminded her.

"Ah, yes. You do not know the farm labour system which operates on most white farms. The farmer allows the workers onto his farmland and for the privilege they get a place to build and a little land to cultivate rent free, providing they agree to work for him for six months of the year at a wage of ten shillings a month."

"What? No one can live and bring a family up on ten shillings a month," said Cos. "No wonder the kids were dying of malnutrition, of just plain lack of any real nutrition. No one can really believe that a family can live on that amount of pay. It isn't even enough to buy a sack of mealie meal – or even a quarter of a sack."

"Oh, Father, you are telling me this, when I see it every day", said Sister Colette. "The theory is that the man has a plot of land, he pays no rent, he can grow some vegetables and mealies, and has a bonus of ten shillings a month. All that for six months while he works for the farmer. For the other six months of the year he is free to find other work in town, or wherever. This will earn money to help out in the six months he is working for the farmer."

"But who is going to employ him for six months? And what sort of work will he get that only lasts six months? Nothing that pays a decent wage."

"Of course, Father, of course. The theory sounds better if you do not ask those questions. So there is widespread malnutrition and under nutrition, and many, many children die. How many babies and young children have you buried this year, Fathers?"

"Yes, it's true," I said, "and I was putting a lot of the blame on problems like enteritis which dehydrate the children so quickly in this hot climate."

"Well, that is true," said Sister Colette. "But it is also true that the people simply have not enough money to buy the food their children need. The father must be kept strong because if he cannot work there will be no money to feed the family. Fathers, there are miracles all round us in how these people continue to live on so little."

"Doesn't it make you angry, Sister, the system that allows this to happen, the appalling poverty, trying to cure diseases that should never have happened in the first place?" asked Cos, getting angry.

Colette laughed at him.

"Oh, Father, of course. But getting angry will not cure a wicked system; somebody helping the victims of that system is a good thing perhaps, don't you think?"

We had arrived back at the mission. Sister made her way to the convent, where someone had stayed up to let her in. We went thoughtfully to bed.

On the Sunday before Christmas – Christmas Day was on a Tuesday that year, as I remember – the men working in Johannesburg were all home for the holiday. The church assembly looked like a society wedding. The men from the big city all in suits and the women dressed in their best clothes so as not to be outdone by their returned husbands. The previous Christmas I had, on advice, chosen this Sunday to have my annual word about money. I don't suppose there are many priests who actively enjoy this chore. Many different approaches are adopted, dictated by the personality of the priest or his theological presuppositions. Some clergy imbued with ideas about the elevated quasi-sacred status to which they have risen use an

69

authoritarian approach. Others try to spiritualise and appeal in terms of giving not to them personally, or to the visible church, but to God, who will undoubtedly reward the generosity of the faithful. I, and a growing number of clergy, much preferred the simple presentation of the facts. I explained what the parish needed to keep going and looked at the whole matter in a purely economic way.

The Bishop constantly made impassioned pleas about parishes being self-sufficient. In the case of Besters, his dream was of a successful farm to keep the parish and seminary going, and even, in moments of wild fantasy, giving him some surplus to assist the poorer missions. He knew very well he was asking the impossible. As far as Besters was concerned, the parishioners wanted the school for their children and were prepared to pay for it. We couldn't say that out loud because it was illegal. Since the late fifties the state had taken over Bantu education, claiming to provide for the Africans at state expense. What was provided was a system about one-tenth of the quality of white education for only some of the African population and almost entirely at primary level. The pyramid rose very, very sharply after primary education so that only a tiny minority of Africans were afforded the privilege of secondary schooling. Private schools for Africans were allowed to continue to operate, but only if they demanded no fees. As a denominational mission school we were private and therefore could not legally ask for money from parents to support the school. So at Christmas I talked about rent to be paid for the privilege of living on mission ground and we all knew what I was talking about. Even then I found the task difficult, as I knew very well that in some cases the payment of ten pounds a year per family was well nigh impossible. From memory I can't say how we made up the short-fall, though I can remember putting in my budget for the seminary an item 'Education for the boys' and charged the Bishop for it. He tried to wriggle out of it by saying the school was there anyway and it cost no more if his boys attended. I threatened to resign over the matter. He promptly refused to accept my resignation, but he paid up.

After mass that Sunday while I was renewing acquaintance with the men on holiday, I was approached by a tall elegant man in his mid-thirties. He spoke very good English and introduced himself as Emmanuel Hlongwane. He lived just over the boundary fence of the mission on the north side in a small African enclave, delicately termed by the authorities a 'Black Spot'. He told me that he was a teacher and had previously been a teacher at the mission school. He was now out of a job and asked if there was any possibility of being re-employed at the mission. I was delighted at the idea. I had seen his name in the school books, had heard excellent reports of him and indeed knew his family well. He had been away teaching during the year, but I had visited his wife and children on several occasions and used his house as a mass centre for some local elderly people. There was in fact a vacancy at the

70

school because one of the African Sisters from the convent was going to do a further course of training. I was also under pressure from the Bishop to improve the quality of the school, now that 'his boys' were being educated there. He was, in his male chauvinist way, urging me to find a male teacher to make sure the boys got the required discipline, the firmer hand of the man.

"All these women about the place," he had said disparagingly, wrinkling his nose in distaste at the female monopoly. "We are dealing with young Zulu men and they need a man, d' you see, dear boy?" Whether I necessarily "saw" or not, Emmanuel Hlongwane seemed heaven-sent. I did not commit myself immediately, but said there was a possibility. I would let him know in the near future. I'm sure he already knew about the vacancy before he talked to me but he seemed happy with my reply.

I was glad to have an opportunity to improve the quality of teaching at the school. The government ban on payment by parents, meant the stand made by the Catholic church to keep its schools was not a total victory. At first a huge campaign had brought in a million pounds to support the schools but this sum soon disappeared over a few years. Then standards began to fall as less qualified and less able teachers were employed at lower wages. The continuance of Catholic schools was then only justified because it was doubtful whether many African children would have received any education at all in their absence. Happily there were notable exceptions to this general decline. Some of the schools run by the German Benedictines and the Mariannhill Missionaries were excellent and well-funded with money which the German Catholics seemed to donate in a never-ending flow.

Emmanuel Hlongwane came into the mission later in the same week, on the Friday after Christmas, by which time I had spoken to Sister Superior at the convent and asked her not to replace the Sister who was going on the training course, as I wanted Emmanuel Hlongwane to take over as head teacher. Apart from the Bishop's quite explicit preference for a man, I preferred a layman to a cleric as head teacher. I was vaguely aware that the domination by clerics and the religious professionals made lay people look like second class citizens. I am sure I was selective in my consciousness on this point, but at times a sensitive nerve was touched by the injustice meted out by arrogant clerics, who liked to think of themselves almost as the holders of the power of God. Apart from all that, Emmanuel was well respected and acceptable to the local people.

But I have jumped across Christmas. I must say I can see a certain sense in having midnight mass in the southern hemisphere where Christmas falls in the hottest part of the summer. At least it is cooler than mid-morning. Against that, at Besters there was always the unpredictability of the old engine and generator I had inherited. The house and the church were wired up together (even to my untutored eye the wiring seemed to be in a mighty dangerous condition), and if we put off all lights in the house, only then did we have enough light in the church. Even so the engine appeared to have a faulty heart beat. It stuttered about once a minute – that was on average; there was nothing regular about it. We all held our breath hoping it would not die on us. Graham, who 'knew' about the engine, and frequently swore about it, had gone on leave for the Christmas holiday. Martin was anxiously in charge. He pretended quiet aplomb, but this was belied by the nervous bobbing up and down he performed during midnight mass each time the lights appeared to be failing. In fact, our fears were misplaced. The thing was sick, but it fought on bravely. Two days later it finally, did die, but we were ready in the house with Aladdin's lanterns and candles. Martin used some of Graham's words on it but it still refused to respond until its own doctor came back from leave a week later.

I felt a lot more confident about the big occasion, than I had my first Christmas. The church was packed to capacity; the Sisters had prepared some special carols, and the singing of the congregation in four part harmony was thrilling, helped by the addition of the powerful voices of the men home on leave. I was intensely nervous about my sermon – I suspect I wanted to show the men who had been away for a year that I had made great strides with my Zulu. I probably had no need for such worries, as few would be listening anyway. A fair number had already started the Christmas celebrations and even I concentrating on the paper before me in the periodically dimming lights, caught two of the worshippers with their eyes closed. They were not in attitudes of ecstatic prayer.

After mass there was general hand-shaking and exchanging of Christmas greetings. Frank Zikalala, who seemed to be the accepted parish spokesman, approached me with grave courtesy. He asked if the parishioners could use the parish hall that afternoon as a small concert was being organised. He also cordially invited me to be present. I explained that in the morning and early afternoon I should be travelling to different places for the Christmas masses, but I should be delighted to come along in the late afternoon. I knew I should feel about dead by then, but I had no intention of missing a concert given by the parishioners and their children.

Cos came back from one of his stations about half-past two in the morning. We had a quick celebratory drink and fell into bed, knowing we had to be up for three more masses each the next morning.

I said another mass at Besters on Christmas Day morning for the children and older parishioners who had not attended the midnight mass. After mass I appeared at the front of the church with a fifty-six pound box of cheap sweets which I had obtained from a friendly wholesaler in Ladysmith. Polite interest gave way to a mad scramble as the children clamoured, calling: "Me, Baba, me Baba" until all the sweets had gone. Some of the older members arrived on the periphery of the circle and with a twinkle in the eye and the raising of a brow, indicated that they might not refuse a few sweets for themselves.

Before going on holiday, Graham told me that the previous incumbent had a practice of having a drink with the farm workers at Christmas. I had not known about this for my first Christmas at the mission but I promised to reinstate the custom this year. What kind of drink, I had asked. Graham looked at me as if I was simple.

"Well, I didn't mean tea," he said.

"But isn't it illegal to give Africans alcohol?" I asked.

"Oh, yes", he answered, "but then you don't have to announce it in church, you know. Man, just tell the induna that you want to see all the men at the house after milking on Christmas morning, and then give them a drink. They will really appreciate it, I tell you."

So I did and they came. I had set a bottle of brandy and glasses on the table plus a plateful of biscuits. They all filed in, clutching their cloth caps or battered trilbies and I attempted small talk about farming matters, telling them of my efforts at milking. I poured out the drinks and wished them all a happy Christmas. I was still raising my glass to my lips, as most of them were replacing theirs on the tray. One by one they thanked me smilingly and began to shuffle out again. I was impressed by the speed at which they had disposed of neat brandy, a half tumbler per man. At least no more small talk was needed. The induna paused at the door, the last one to leave, thanked me again and invited me to join them for milking the next morning. I thanked him, but did not commit myself.

I arrived back on Christmas afternoon only shortly before Cos, and we decided to have a look at the concert. We would have our Christmas dinner later, hopefully in the cool of the evening. We prepared ourselves for the concert by pouring a quick can of beer down our throats, in my case to replace some of the sweat, I had lost during the day. Cos did not seem to sweat, nor did the sun seem to affect the colour of his skin -he became known as the 'whitest man in Africa' among the brethren. But he had a beer, chiefly because he liked the taste, he said.

The parish hall was a delapidated affair behind the church. I do not know what its original purpose had been but I doubt if it had been built as a parish hall. Whenever the parishioners wanted to have a meeting about anything, they held it under the trees next to the said hall, which was very sensible. It was considerably cooler under the trees. Cos and I sat, cheered, and sweated and felt clammy for an hour, among the parishioners who did just the same. It was evident that a good time was being had by all, including ourselves. One group of youngsters followed another, all singing and dancing. Occasionally a group of the mothers would advance onto the stage, embarrassed and trying to hide their faces and, at first, hardly able to perform because they were giggling too much. The older ones always got the best applause and provoked the greatest mirth. It was apparent that both audience and entertainers, enjoyed themselves immensely.

At about half past five we all came out into the open air, the parishioners to continue their revels at home and Cos and I to have our belated Christmas dinner. Of course, the Sisters had excelled themselves with the traditional English Christmas dinner. We sat back at the end slightly regretting our gluttony.

I awoke the next morning to the whistle of the men calling and driving the cattle in for milking. I suddenly remembered the invitation to join them milking the cows. It was very pleasant in bed and I had not actually promised to go. I lay there wrestling with myself and the wrestling woke me up. Anyway, my honour was at stake; I had half-promised. Oh, hang it, I thought. I dragged myself out of bed, dressed in haste and then strolled down to the cow-shed as if I had been up for hours.

Most of the cows were in and already tied up. One man was washing the udders, while another was following behind him and appeared to be massaging the already washed teats. I went to see what he was doing and found he was smearing grease on the teats of the cows. A third man was binding the back legs of the first cows to be milked. Two or three men started the milking and I saw why they found it necessary to tie the cows legs. They used a long stroke, pulling on the teats to extract the milk. It must have become irritating to the cows after a short time. Probably the grease lessened the irritation but the whole process made for a much slower style of milking than I had been used to in England.

I was offered an opportunity to try my hand. I told them how we milked in England, quietly thinking I was passing on a good tip for their future use. It was obvious that in spite of their show of polite interest they considered my method as quaint. I tried to show them how I had been accustomed to milk, but even after wiping the teats some grease remained, making it difficult to get up any rhythm or speed with the thumb, two fingers and wristy action method. The cow became restive under an unfamiliar hand and I was glad its legs were tied. Apart from anything else I had forgotten how painful my method had been on the forearm muscles until the muscles had become accustomed to it. I laughed and explained how long it had been since I had milked cows, and gracefully withdrew, leaving them to get on with their work in the time- honoured way.

Cos was rising reluctantly when I got back to the house. He was going across to the convent, so that the sisters could indulge in the luxury of a mass in their own chapel, while I said mass in the parish church. We went to the traditional Boxing Day gathering of the Brethren in Dundee and vied with each other in claiming vast congregations of faithful for the Christmas services. The implication being that the people were drawn by the charisma of our preaching or just our saintly personalities. We all belied the latter by eating and drinking far too much.

Graham came back after the New Year expressing fresh determination to achieve huge successes on the farm. His statement caused me some fears, for it sounded as if he was trying to convince himself. It reminded me of my responsibilities, wished on me, by the Bishop, I was supposed to be looking after the interests of the farm and supervising the farm-manager. The seminary had so dominated my previous months that I had just left Graham to his own devices.

"Ah, yes," I said, "perhaps we can get together in the next day or two and have a conference about how the farm is getting on." I saw a flicker of anxiety in Graham's eyes.

As we went through the accounts the next day, my first impression was that, although the farm was not exactly booming, the income had not dropped off from milk sales or sales of cattle, but had increased slightly compared with my predecessor. Latterly up to November of the previous year, a new venture by Graham had been quite profitable. He was buying day-old chicks and breeding them for the table over a period of several weeks. Unfortunately, that was the bright side of the picture and the reason for Graham's apprehension was revealed as he told me that the latest batch of day-olds had caught some disease and the lot had been wiped out, thus also wiping out the profit of the previous six months. On the further debit side, the bills from the garages for new spare parts for the tractors added up to a formidable amount and frightened me to death. Of course, that wasn't Graham's fault. We had inherited the old stock and were trying to make do with it. We mulled it over for an hour and a half, trying to think of ways around the problem. Of course this sort of thing is repeated the world over day after day as people try to seek methods of managing on less than the ideal. The net result must always be that there is really no way of making progress without investment of money. I think we could both see that things were not going to get better by themselves or even with the most strenuous efforts by Graham. Neither of us said as much to each other, though Graham did tentatively wonder if another approach to the Bishop might not be .... perhaps..... I said I would tell him how things were and see what he said. Inwardly I had little hope of getting cash from him.

While we were talking I kept noticing a pungent aroma surrounded Graham. Eventually I asked him what sort of after-shave he was using. The question lightened the tension and he told me that it was a Christmas present. He thought it probably repelled all known insects and could prove useful at a place like Besters.

I mentioned the after-shave to Martin in a joking way at lunch and mused on its qualities as an insect-repellant; or, I said as an afterthought, as a disguise against bad breath. Martin gave me an old-fashioned look and said that should be useful to Graham. I gathered he was making a serious remark and asked him what he meant.

"You haven't noticed," he asked. "Graham has been having a couple of sharp swigs from the bottle by ten in the morning."

"Good lord, has he?" I asked, "I'd never noticed. Oh, dear, when did this start?"

"He was drinking before you came to Besters. Not first thing in the morning, but by midday certainly. How long is it since you saw him here at lunch with us?"

"Yes, you are right, now I come to think of it." I mused on that for a minute or two. "I don't suppose that the worry of trying to make a go of the farm is helping him enormously. Has he talked to you? Does he see it as a problem?"

"No idea, Sam. He knows I know, and even occasionally offers me a tot of brandy, but not with any sense of shame or concern that I might have caught him at it. I think you're right about his finding the farm a bigger problem than he anticipated. He was full of optimism to start with and spent time out and about with the men. If you just keep an eye open you'll see he is about the house a lot more than he used to be. I see a lot of what goes on when I'm working out at the back of the building".

"Very difficult to tackle him on the subject, isn't it? He can drink if he wants to, but it doesn't seem a very good idea to be starting before ten in the morning."

The more I thought about this in the next few days, the more worried I became and I decided to see the Bishop as soon as possible. I rang and found that he would be visiting a nearby mission on the following Monday. I arranged to see him there.

"All very mysterious, dear boy, what's your problem now?" he asked, when we met the following Monday.

"Yes, I'm sorry I couldn't say more, but you know where the phone is at Besters; it's a bit public and everyone can hear what you are saying. And anyway its a party line with ten subscribers using it, so we don't indulge in confidences over the phone. It's about farm matters."

"Oh, crumbs" he said, "what's happened now? Crossley run off with the cook, or something?"

I told him about the meeting between Graham and myself and then the conversation with Martin over lunch the same day.

He sighed resignedly.

"You don't seem able to control your household, do you?" His voice rose in a crescendo to the end of the sentence. He was merely letting off steam, as he met yet another example of the inadequacy and inefficiency of human kind. I think that he felt some slight injustice that he should be saddled with such an undue portion of human failure.

"I suppose I shall have to come and sort it all out for you. I don't know, you all rely on your big uncle", he said, his spirits reviving a little, because he liked being the shepherd of his wayward and, at times, idiot flock.

"I suppose that you introduced Crossley to the demon drink, you and Cos and Martin. The lot of you pickled most nights, I expect, what?" he said giving his imagination free rein.

"But seriously, dear boy, don't go splashing the stuff about when Graham is there, d'you see?"

"Actually, I don't. We only have a drink on a Sunday evening."

"Mm, oh, dear, Well," he said getting practical, "I'll come down on Thursday and we can have a big discussion on the farm's future. And don't bring the bottle out, d'you hear?"

"It's a bit late in the day to be hiding bottles. Anyway he's quite capable of buying his own."

"Yes, yes, I know, but we must do what we can," he said virtuously, not to be gainsaid.

Graham was pleased at the prospect of the Bishop's visit, though a little worried at first that the great man might be holding him responsible for the poor fortunes of the farm. I tried to reassure him on this count, telling him that I had been at pains to point out to the Bishop that we were trying to manage with clapped-out tools.

The Bishop bounded in on Thursday morning looked over his half- moon spectacles at Graham and roared accusingly at him.

"I understand you are pouring all the farm profits down the drain, young man, what?"

Graham half took him seriously and started to explain.

"I don't think it's really as simple as that, Monsignor..."

"Yes, yes, yes," Bishop Ulyatt brushed his explanation aside "I know, dear boy. Anyway, let's get down to the facts and figures, shall we? Did you say tea, Sam?"

I hadn't, but I knew he would want some and was about to arrange it anyway.

We went over the same ground as Graham and I had covered the previous week and arrived at the same deadlocked position. Eventually the Bishop told Graham to get both tractors overhauled and to send him the bills.

"Of course, it may well be the garage will tell us that it is hardly worth bothering because of their poor condition," Graham told the Bishop.

"Well, we'll discuss it if that proves to be so," the Bishop said briskly.

"Sam, you can buzz off," he told me, "I want to have a word with Graham about a salary review I promised him."

I supposed he was also going to try to bring up the drink matter delicately. Since Martin had told me about Graham's drinking it had been possible to penetrate the after-shave and smell the brandy on his breath, even by mid-morning. He had been drinking that morning, doubtless worried about the meeting with the Bishop.

Half an hour later the Bishop came out of the sitting room, followed by Graham.

"Are you giving me lunch?" he called out.

"I have warned – that is to say, told the Sisters of your presence and they are expecting you."

"Oh, dear, do we have to go all the way down there? I was hoping for cheese and biscuits here, or something. I'm trying to lose some weight and I don't go in for lunches in a big way."

"Well, they do rather expect to see you?"

"Oh, crumbs, I suppose I shall have to go down there, then."

The Bishop took me aside for a second after lunch and told me he had advised Graham against too much drink on the job. Graham had replied that things were actually getting better, he relapsed a bit over Christmas but was in control of any slight tendency to over-indulge. We were both relieved.

The tractors were mended and able to carry on with far fewer break-downs than during the previous year. Graham tried rearing half-a-dozen pigs at a time for the market, and this venture, though small, had some success. For that year and into the next, the farm ticked over much as before.

Chapter Six

The seminary was running well according to the pattern we had set. The boys were no problem, for the most part they were under the eye of Emmanuel Hlongwane, who was taking a personal interest in the seminary. The only slight worry I had was on Sundays when the majority of the boys were left very much to themselves, while I went out to the out-stations to say mass. Cos had now moved to his own area and Martin had gone to help building at another mission some miles away. The custom was for the boys from the seminary and the boys from the mission to play football on Sunday afternoons. This seemed to be a good way of keeping them occupied in my absence. However, about half way through the year an incident made me worry about leaving the seminary untended. I arrived back one Sunday evening to a subdued greeting from the boys who were just getting ready for their evening meal. I was taking my books and papers to my room when Sister Colette arrived looking very serious. I was out on the verandah about to ask the boys how the football had gone, but paused as I saw the grimness of her face; the boys began to drift away in an over-casual manner.

"Father, I must speak with you," Colette said, sharply.

"Of course, Sister," I said, feeling apprehensive, "Come in".

We went in and I closed the door, taking a quick look to see if any of the boys were lurking near enough to overhear us. I suspected from their behaviour it must be something to do with them.

I turned to face Sister Colette, whose grim seriousness I had not seen before, to find she was actually trying hard to suppress her laughter. I felt bewildered.

"Oh, Father, excuse me," she said taking out a handkerchief to wipe her eyes.

"I had to be very serious before the boys."

"I am now thoroughly intrigued," I told her.

"I will explain. You have not seen Alfred, no?" She asked.

"Well, no, unless he was with the rest of the crowd out there."

"Ah, no, I think not, Father. But I will tell you. I was coming back about an hour ago from some calls. As I passed the clinic up the road, I saw several of the seminary boys coming down the road. They were helping one of their number to walk. I thought he had been injured playing football, so I stopped and called to them. Jeremiah came over to the car – I was using the convent car today – and I asked what the matter was. He said that Alfred was not able to walk properly because his legs were weak. Oh, Father, Jeremiah had a sad face and he looked so concerned. I asked if Alfred had hurt himself playing football, and he said no. They could not understand why his legs were so weak. I got out of the car and went over to the group. I was looking at Alfred's legs, but when I got near, Father, I understood about his legs." She paused to suppress the laughter once more bubbling to the surface. "He was drunk, that was why he could not walk."

"Oh, Lord," I said, "That's a nuisance, isn't it?"

"Of course, they all think I am scandalised and very angry this should happen when you are out at the out-stations and they are supposed to be on trust. I told them all this and they were very quiet. But, Father, it was so funny. The big boys must have known what had been happening, but they think Sisters do not understand all that."

"Well, yes, I can see the funny side of it, but unfortunately I can't let it go like that, can I? Presumably, the parishioners have seen him in this legless condition anyway, and who had given him the beer to drink?"

"Oh, Father, it will do him no harm, except for a headache. I am sure you have been drunk yourself sometimes.

"Good heavens, Sister, what a monstrous accusation. I never do things like that. I am nearly all pure spirit. But I'm not really worried about Alfred's headache. It's the breach of discipline that I have to think about. How many times has it happened before? Will you hang on a minute, Sister, while I have words with Jeremiah?"

"Of course."

I went outside the door and bellowed "Jeremiah". Jerry came in from behind the house with a look of deep concern on his face.

"Come in, will you, please. Jerry?"

"Yes, Father," he replied, looking puzzled, as if mystified as to the reason for this summons.

He saw Sister.

"Good afternoon, Sister," he said with grave courtesy. Sister Colette had a little trouble with her face as she returned his greeting.

"Jerry, Sister has just been telling me about what happened this afternoon. Now you know that Alfred had been drinking, don't you?"

"Maybe he did have a drink," said Jeremiah slowly, as if giving the matter great thought. "We were playing football, Alfred too for a time, but then he was talking to some of the people. Perhaps he did have a drink."

"I think perhaps he did," I agreed heavily. "Where is he now?"

"He is in his bed asleep."

"O.K. Jerry, I'll see him when he wakes up. Now what about the rest of you; did anyone else drink?"

"Oh, no, Father," said Jerry, much taken aback by the suggestion.

"That was a silly question," I muttered to myself. "Alright, Jerry, will you see that everyone gets his things in order for tomorrow and make sure all homework is done. I shall be in later."

"Thank you, Father".

He went out.

"Father," said Sister Colette, "they are boys and some of them like

80

Alfred are really young men. You must not be hard on them."

"Oh, heavens, Sister, I know that. But it takes a fair amount of beer to knock you over, so it wasn't a casual sip of the stuff. As a matter of fact Betty used to leave a large container of it for Martin and myself every Sunday. No, I am really only looking ahead. If I do nothing about it and regard it as a boyish prank, it might be taken as licence for regular Sunday drink-ins, when Father is away."

"What about Alfred?" she asked.

"Oh, I'll go through the charade of a severe reprimand, I suppose".

I think Sister had enjoyed the whole episode. She had another hearty laugh, before straightening her face and going outside in view of the boys. Alfred declined to wake up that evening. I might have been a little worried except for his loud snoring.

The next day was a public holiday – I forget which now – so the boys would not be at school. There would be a later mass time, breakfast and then free time. I had forgotten about the public holiday and had arranged nothing for Monday, though I knew that a football match was always welcome to the majority. After mass I told Jeremiah that I should like to see Alfred after they had finished breakfast. I had been sitting at my desk for about half an hour when a tap came at the door.

"Come in," I called.

It was Alfred, looking timid and concerned. He was a heavy, well-built boy of sixteen, one of the oldest there, and a fast, bustling centre-forward on the football field. I asked him what had happened the day before.

"Yesterday, Father?" he asked, as if searching his memory for some forgotten incident. "Oh, I was very tired after the football and the others helped me home."

"And the drink, Alf? You had a lot to drink, did you not?"

"Hawu, Baba, it was very hot after playing and maybe I did drink some beer."

"You were drunk, Alf, and slept the rest of the day. You all know I expect you to behave yourselves on Sundays when I'm away at the outstations. The people here see you as young men preparing to be priests of the church in Natal and therefore expect you to behave respectably. I don't think that getting drunk fits in with that. No doubt you are not used to beer and got drunk very easily, but I want an assurance from you that it will not happen again. I really don't know what people will think."

I really didn't know what people thought about it. I doubted they would all be wildly scandalised but I suspected that some of the older ones might be. Anyway, I felt I should make the point before the boys all thought it a free-for-all when I went off on a Sunday. I added a footnote:

"I shall, of course, have to mention this to your parish priest.

Alright, Alf, you can go and behave yourself, do you hear? Because if anything like this happens again, I shall ask you to leave."

It so happened that the Bishop had moved into Alfred's parish about a month earlier. The priest there had been sick and gone on extended leave and Bishop Ulyat had decided a little pastoral work at grass-roots level would be a good thing for him. He had already paid us a visit -his mission was only about thirty five miles away – and taken great delight in telling the three boys from his parish he was now their parish priest. In consequence he was going to take a very special interest in their progress at the seminary, especially with regard to behaviour and discipline. He had looked at all three severely over his half-moon spectacles and they dutifully looked awed. I barely managed to keep my face straight during this lecture. The Bishop was the most gentle and kindly man, and a most unlikely disciplinarian.

Whether it was concern about what I had said or apprehension at what the Bishop might say, I don't to this day know, but it appears that Alfred was very worried about his misdemeanour of the previous day. About two o'clock in the afternoon, shortly before we were to have a game of football, one of the boys came running to my room, calling for me as he ran.

"Father, please come, Alfred has hanged himself."

"What?" I yelled, incredulously.

"Alfred has hanged himself from the tree by the school."

I rushed out with him, and came upon a group of boys bearing a body down the hill. It was Alfred. He was not dead, but lay in the arms of his friends with his eyes closed. From his throat came strange gurgling noises, as if he was trying to get his breath. The nearest room was the farm office. I told the boys to bring Alfred into the room and lay him on the couch. I sent another boy to fetch Sister Colette.

As they laid him down a hank of rope about his neck became visible. Alfred kept jerking his neck about and continued to make the strange gurgling noises. I was totally at a loss. He was certainly still breathing, and there appeared to be no cuts on his neck, nor for that matter was it badly marked by the rope. I was somewhat reassured, but still very concerned about the boy's well-being.

Sister Colette came running up the drive-way, gasping out questions to my messenger. She came in and went straight to Alfred, without a question or a glance to anyone present. She took his pulse, lifted an eye-lid, felt his heart and then started on an examination of his neck. I drew Jeremiah aside and asked about the sequence of events. He told me in a whisper that someone had happened to see Alfred with the rope around his neck, first in the tree, then jumping from the tree. There was a shocked air among the boys some of whom were in the room and the rest looking on through the door. Sister looked up after about five minutes examination and said that it would probaby be better if Alfred was not so crowded by us all. I shooed the boys out, and started to follow Sister out. As an afterthought I called

Jeremiah and asked him and another of the boys to stay with Alfred, while I had a word with Sister. We walked along the verandah towards my room.

"There is nothing seriously the matter with him," Sister told me.

"Probably the worst thing is shock. Were you very hard on him Father?" she asked, looking at me a little reproachfully.

"No, I don't think so," I protested. "As far as I was concerned the matter was over. I did, as an afterthought, tell him I should have to report the matter to the Bishop, who is now his parish priest. But can you see anyone being terrified out of his mind about being reported to the Bishop?"

"Not you, of course, but maybe Alfred," she said. "Anyway, I think he will be alright. The doctor will be at the clinic tomorrow, and I shall be in the rest of today – after all it is a holiday, Father," she added ironically, reminding me a district nurse is always on call.

Of course, I was feeling some guilt about Alfred. Could my words have induced feelings of such rejection as to drive a boy to try to take his own life? I went to see how he was. His condition was unchanged. He appeared to be sleeping, still periodically stretching his neck as if in some discomfort. I asked Jeremiah who had seen him about to jump from the tree and Jerry told me it had been Philip. I called Philip and we went to my room. Philip told me he had been in the farm-yard at the time and looked up to the school to see Alfred in the tree with the rope round his neck. He had called to some of the other boys and they all ran up the hill towards Alfred.

"Was he hanging from the tree when you got there?" I asked.

"Oh, no, Father," Philip replied, "he was lying on the ground".

"Oh," I replied lamely. I had supposed the boys had rushed up the hill and saved Alfred from a ghastly death. "And then you carried him down?" I asked.

"The big boys did," said Philip, who was only a small boy and still quite frightened by all the events. I thought I had better end his inquisition and get Jeremiah to fill in some of the details.

"Philip, ask Jeremiah to get someone else to stay with Alfred, and then he can come and see me."

Jeremiah arrived looking dutifully concerned. He gave me much the same story as Philip had done. I decided to go with him to the scene of the suicide attempt. As we stood by the tree and looked down the hill, it crossed my mind that if one wanted to make a dramatic act, this was the place. There were many other trees, bigger and better suited to Alfred's purpose. But this one by the school stood out starkly against the skyline. Under the tree we found the remnants of an old rope. I picked it up. It did not look very serviceable, and I gave it a sudden tug. It came to shreds in my hands. A nasty suspicion was beginning to form in my mind.

"Yes, well," I said to Jeremiah, "let's go down again".

I went into the farm office, where Alfred seemed to be sleeping peacefully, and looked for the piece of rope that had been attached to his neck. It was the same quality as the rope under the tree. I beckoned to Jerry. We sat down again in my office. I decided as tactfully as possible to test my suspicion.

"Jerry," I began slowly, "did Alf seem very upset after seeing me this morning."

"Father? he enquired, as if not understanding.

"Oh, come on, Jerry, you know what I mean. Did he seem upset because I had told him off yesterday?"

"I think so, Father, a little. He was afraid that you might send him away."

"But I only said.... No matter. Now, did you or any of the others get any idea he would try to take his life?"

"He was quiet all morning, Father, but he is always quiet really. Then after dinner he went round, shook everybody by the hand and said 'goodbye' and started to walk slowly up the hill."

"Oh, he did, did he?" I ejaculated. Then more calmly: "Did he say what he was going to do? Did anyone ask him?"

"Well, we asked where he was going, he just smiled and said 'You will see' and walked away. So we all watched him."

"You all watched him: Not just Philip? Why didn't you tell me this at the beginning, when you brought him down the hill."

"You didn't ask, Father."

After a pause, Jerry asked:

"Do you think he will be alright, Father?"

"Oh, yes, Jerry, I think so and hope so. I don't really think he had any intention of killing himself. He was just trying to tell us, and perhaps especially me, that he was very upset. I am sure he will get over it."

I knew that Jerry would pass on what I had said to the others. I was particularly worried about the younger boys who had been goggling wide-eyed and perhaps a little frightened by it all.

In fact, Alfred did not come out of it all afternoon. Sister came up in the evening and I told her what I had learnt. She said that fitted in with her own observations. She had wondered, though not out loud, just how serious a suicide attempt it had been. Alfred meanwhile was still behaving in the same way. We carried him to his own bed and then, out of sight of the boys who might have misinterpretted our actions, we tried to wake him, with a few sharp slaps and some cold water. He refused to respond. I asked the older boys to organise themselves so that someone was with him during the evening. At night three others shared the room, so there would be no problem then.

The next morning Alfred was awake in a dazed sort of way, still making noises in his throat and declining to speak. Sister came and saw him after breakfast. She thought he was in some sort of hysterical condition. She told me to bring him along to the clinic at two that afternoon, to see the doctor. Alfred drank a little milk, but would not eat. He declined to speak, or made out that he could not do so.

I rang the Bishop.

"Hello, old boy, everything alright with you?" he asked.

"Well, yes, apart from Alfred trying to hang himself yesterday."

"Alfred who?"

"Your Alfred at the seminary, Alfred Mazibuko."

"Oh, crumbs, what did he want to do that for?"

I told him the whole story. At the end of it he said "Oh, crumbs" again and lapsed into silence. Then after a thoughtful pause:

"What are we going to do?" he asked in a thin voice.

"Well, I don't really know yet," I replied. "We shall see the doctor this afternoon and then I'll let you know what he says later today."

"You really need an assistant there, don't you, dear boy? I'll have to think about all this." He sounded worried.

"Don't worry about it. We were worried at first yesterday, but everybody seems alright this morning – except Alfred, of course, – but I am sure all will be well."

"Well, I hope so," he said doubtfully. "Do let me know, old boy." And the line went dead.

At two o'clock I took Alfred along to the clinic, assisted by Jeremiah whom I had kept off school for the purpose. Sister had told the doctor some of the story and he was prepared to have a look at Alfred as soon as we arrived. He tried to get Alf to answer his questions, but he continued to make guttural noises in his throat. The doctor called me aside into his litte dispensary and closed the door. He was a pleasant man of about my own age, and gently amused by the talk of what had happened over the weekend. For a white man he was kindly disposed towards the African, and Sister told me he really took pains to help his patients. He was untypical of most white doctors who were more interested in their fee than in the well-being of the blacks whom they considered over-numerous anyway.

"I think we have a case of quite deep hysteria here," he told me, "as a reaction to shock. I'm afraid we shall have to get him out of it by shock also. Now if you will allow me I shall inject a small amount of ether into his veins. It will have the effect of making him appear a little drunk for a very short time. Thereafter, he will also have what drink gives – a hang-over. But it should shift the hysteria. O.K.?" he asked.

"I suppose so, Doctor, you are the expert. We did try to shake him up a bit yesterday evening, but with no result."

"No, I'm afraid it's a bit deep-seated by now. Alright, I'll just get a syringe ready."

Alfred was still sitting in a dazed condition as we re-entered the surgery. The doctor pushed up the sleeve of Alf's shirt and gently inserted the needle. Alf looked at him and then at his arm in a slow bewildered way. Then suddenly he gave his head a shake and

85

brightened. A smile of recognition came over his face as he looked round at us all.

"Alright, Doctor," he said, "Alright, Father, Sister, Jerry," he greeted each of us in turn. He was speaking in English, though normally he was shy of speaking it and preferred to speak Zulu.

"I am fine, doctor, absolutely fine; I am fit and well, ready for anything," he prattled on uncharacteristically.

"O.K.," said the doctor, smiling, "Now let's see you run up the road about a hundred yards or so, eh?"

"Of course," said Alf expansively, "anything you say, doc."

He walked out of the front door of the clinic, followed by the four of us. He started to run on the spot, picking his knees up high.

"Now watch this," he admonished us seriously, and he sprinted up the road, turned some hundred and fifty yards away and sprinted back again.

"What do you think of that?" he asked breathlessly as he drew up beside us.

"First class," the doctor told him. "Now you will feel a little tired later and have a bit of a headache, but you will be fine in the morning. So back to the mission and take it easy, alright?"

"I'm fine, doc, fine, don't you worry about me."

Jeremiah and myself walked back to the mission with Alfred, who did not walk, but kept running in short bursts ahead of us and then returning to tell us how well he felt. When we got back, Jeremiah went up to school and I saw that Alfred got some food from Doris in the kitchen. She foolishly asked Alf how he was, and he told her he was fine and then demonstrated how well he was by the sort of athletic display he had treated us all to at the clinic. Doris was both amused and a little concerned and kept looking at Alf as she warmed up his dinner. Alfred proved his fitness further by disposing of food very rapidly. He must have been extremely hungry.

In the evening I rang the Bishop and brought him up to date. However, he had spent the day reading implications into the affair and wanted to discuss the matter with me, and with Alfred. He guessed it had probably all been very traumatic for the boy, and indeed for the others, especially the younger ones. Perhaps it might be better if Alfred were to come home for the rest of the term – only a couple of weeks anyway. He would come over in the morning, he said, and I should tell Alfred that he could have leave for a couple of weeks at home. I rather suspect he thought that Alf might have some deep psychological problem and would be better under his eagle eye for some weeks.

I spoke to Alfred after supper and outlined what the Bishop had suggested. Alf, was now rather low. He did not remember much detail of the last few days, but he cheered up slightly at the prospect of going home early. I peeped out about five minutes later to see him telling the rest of the boys what had been arranged. He was wearing a smile on his face and the attitudes of a couple of the others suggested the whole business was most unfair. Of course, I could not hear the exact words being spoken, so cannot tell what version of our conversation Alfred was relating.

The next day it was evident that the Bishop had been giving matters a lot of thought. Once he had a scheme in his mind it was very difficult to shift. The idea of a separate, self-contained minor seminary for the diocese had been mooted before. I would be rector with teachers to direct the studies of the boys, so that they could get individual tuition. The Bishop had recently bought a property in a small village on the edge of the reserve, a doctor's surgery with about an acre of ground attached to it. The village was the home of Jack, an Indian builder-handyman who had been doing various jobs for the Bishop. Jack seemed to be an integral part of these new plans.

"So there we are, dear boy, what do you think of that?" He continued without giving me time to answer – another rhetorical question "If we are going to do this thing, we had better do it properly. We have experimented now for nearly two years and we ought to be consolidating, what? And you need to be full time on the job. Your time is far too divided between all those other matters, farm and parish, as well as the seminary". As usual he spoke as if this was my fault and of my choosing.

"Well, you have spent a sleepless night working all this out," I said admiringly.

"Not really, dear boy, I have been giving it a lot of thought in the last few months. I have even asked Paschal to get some plans drawn up. You know how Paschal loves making plans for houses and buildings – schools and churches – well, we must use what gifts we have, mustn't we? So, you see, things are on the move."

"It will cost an enormous amount of money, you know."

"Yes, it will; I know that, dear boy," he said tersely. "But I am pretty sure I can get some from Rome. They are keen on diocesan seminaries currently. They want young men to study in their own areas, and hopefully keep in touch with their own people."

"Like Alfred was doing, you mean"

"No, I don't mean like Alfred was doing", he replied, grimacing at me over his half-moons. "Anyway, we shall have to get together over this pretty soon. But as you mentioned Alfred, I think perhaps I ought to have a word with him. He will be fretting over the pending interview with his spiritual father, what?"

I went out and found Alfred, not noticeably fretting, though he might have been in turmoil within of course.

The Bishop greeted him with meticulously enunciated Zulu, but after the usual pleasantries he had more or less shot his bolt and lapsed into English. A week ago I would have been worried about Alfred's ability to understand what the Bishop was saying, but having seen him under the effects of ether, with all inhibitions removed, I knew he would understand. Anyway the Bishop was at pains to take it slowly.

Indeed, he was very gentle and considerate.

"And so," he finally summed it all up, "Alfred, dear boy, I want you to have a couple of weeks at home to get over all this trouble. We shall see a lot of each other. You can come up to the mission each day and I shall have some little jobs for you to do, and we can have chats about your future and about all sorts of things, d'you see; and then we'll make decisions about when and if you come back here next term. Alright young man?"

"Yes, thank you, Monsignor," Alfred responded.

"Good. Well, we'll be off then, Father Sam. And remember, I shall want to see you very soon – say as soon as the term has finished -and we can make plans about the future of the seminary. Bye bye, old boy." And they went.

Cos came in one day later in the week and I told him the whole story. It amused him greatly, though he chided me about the final solution of the problem.

"And you consigned the boy to the care of the great Ulyat? Are you mad? The poor lad will be totally confused. But seriously," he continued, "don't you think he ought to have stayed here? His removal from the scene will look like banishment for a heinous crime and God knows we are hardly the advocates of total abstinence. It's likely to look like one law for the boys and one law for the fully fledged priests."

I protested, "I think that in this instance, it was better for Alf to have a break away from what was doubtless a rather embarrassing scene for him."

"I don't want to harp on this," said Cos, "but think about Jeremiah's elaborate pretence that Alf was not drunk, but rather suddenly afflicted with a strange disease of the legs. Aren't we, as the priests, teachers and leaders, to blame for that as well? Haven't we brought in the old eleventh commandment 'Thou shalt not be found out'.

"Well, thank you professor. Having said all that, would you like a drink? I feel the need for one."

"Well, I hardly know what to say," Cos said, pretending surprise and reluctance, "Well, – alright then, if it will please you."

"I have six or eight cans of beer."

"What no whisky?" he complained, "I did intend to stay the night."

"Oh, Lord, that's the end of my beer then," I remarked gloomily, peeling back the metal openers from a couple of cans.

"I give you a toast," said Cos, "Alf, and may you learn from your mistakes," he added mischievously.

"Now look you," I started defensively.

"Alright, don't start again. I withdraw any offensive remarks. I must merely say that you did your best in a difficult situation, which is definitely not covered in the manuals of how to be a good and successful parish priest."

"Actually", I confided, "I do hope that Alf comes back, he is a fine centre-forward and the team needs him."

"Good grief, you sound like the coach at an American University giving out places to promising athletes."

"And what better reason for taking boys on? Oh, I didn't tell you. One of our local farmers was passing while we were out playing football. He must have seen me among the boys, all playing together. He leaned out of his truck and yelled Kaffir Boetie, which I took as a compliment, but Graham tells me it isn't meant as one apparently. He says it means something equivalent to 'nigger lover'."

"I suppose you will now justify your wild behaviour on the football field as a model for racial integration and present it as a prime feature of your mission and Christian witness," remarked the cynical Cos. I regretted giving him my beer to drink.

On the first Wednesday of the school holiday the Bishop got together Cormac, as his second-in-command, Pascal with his plans, Jack the builder and myself. We met at his little mission, crowded into the office to discuss the grand project of the independent minor seminary. It was apparent that Cormac was quietly sceptical, and had been telling the Bishop so before the rest of us arrived. It was all good humoured enough. Cormac like the rest of us, knew that once the Bishop had got his teeth into something it was very hard to make him let go. Like many of the Bishop's meetings virtually everything had been decided beforehand. He would gather all the interested parties together to pool ideas, but it was really a PR exercise. Only details still had to be decided, such as timing. From my point of view I wanted to start the new venture at the beginning of a school year, if at all possible. Pascal said that making plans was no problem and he had in fact a few ideas sketched out already, but he needed to know what sort of room I wanted; for how many boys; how many classrooms etc., etc., Anyway how long would it take Jack to build it all; what was the site like, what depth of foundation would be needed...?

The Bishop cut into these discussions after about half an hour.

"Why don't we all go there now and look at the place?" he asked with typical impetuosity.

"Why didn't we meet there in the first place, Monsignor," asked Cormac and laughed heartily at the Bishop's slight discomfort.

"Yes, well, never mind, we can go there now, can't we," he answered tartly, looking over his glasses at us all and challenging us to disagree.

So we all squeezed into the Bishop's car, throwing our papers and his case into the boot. We travelled for about an hour on very dusty, sandy roads, through some places I knew. Finally we came out of a wooded, shady section into hot sunshine and saw stretching out below us a valley, the far end of which was lost in the heat of the haze. Directly below was a village, into which we gingerly dropped by means of a winding mountain road. It was rather like landing in an aeroplane: the houses, trees and people slowly taking on clearer outlines and increasing in size. It took six miles of twisting, stony mountain road to drop the thousand feet until we rushed through the village in a vast cloud of dust, making it difficult to see very much. Just as I thought we were passing through, the Bishop turned abruptly into the last built-up part of the village and drew up in front of a single-storey house made of the same stone as the mission house at Besters. We gratefully prised ourselves out of the car, and stood stretching and loosening limbs made half numb by the cramped journey. It was appreciably hotter than the Bishop's mission or Besters; we were at a lower altitude than many of the local missions and the temperature was increased correspondingly. There was a sound of movement within the house, then a rangey mongrel came out, looked at us with disinterest and moved off. It was followed quite quickly by a rangey human being, wearing a gentle smile and shaking his head in disbelief at the sudden invasion. It was Father Jo Banks.

"Hello, Jo, dear boy," said the Bishop, "Sorry to butt in like this, unannounced, but we wanted to look over the site while we were all together."

"Well, here I am," said Jo, "what do you think of the sight?"

"Very funny, I'm sure," said the Bishop impatiently, "the site for the seminary, I mean".

The Bishop and Jo had both been in the Air Force during the war though in rather different capacities – the Bishop as a chaplain and Jo as a navigator on a bomber – and they had different perspectives on life in consequence, causing little sparks of occasional friction between them.

Jo knew what the Bishop thought and quietly teased him by playing up to the image the Bishop had decided on for him.

"Jo's a dear boy in many ways," said the Bishop to me once, "but he still thinks like one of the boys in blue during the war, the same spirit is still upon him."

"Well, shall we get on?" the Bishop asked in a business-like voice.

We had parked at the back of the house where there was a considerable plot of land, at present covered with weeds. The Bishop led us into the house. We entered through the kitchen at the back and into a passage which went down the centre of the building. The end of the passage led into a large room which ran across the whole front of the house. At both outside corners of this room were two big rondavels, which projected beyond the front of the house. In the middle of the front wall there was a door which opened onto a large roofed porch which connected the two rondavels. Off the through-passage there were another three rooms and a bathroom. I was intrigued by the design of the house and privately determined that if this move did take place and if I came to live at Pomeroy – the name of the village – I should have one of those rondavels as my room. The other three sides of the house were surrounded by a verandah which was from roof to floor protected by a wire-mesh screen.

The Bishop passed through the house pointing out its features in a perfunctory manner, then went out on to the front porch and with a sweeping gesture, drew our attention to the view.

"What do you think of that?" he asked, his eyes glowing with pride as if he owned the view along with the house.

"I don't think much of the garden," said Cormac, "It just looks like a piece of veldt".

"No, no, no, not the garden, dear boy," said the Bishop with irritated disappointment, "the mountain; that's Msinga," he pronounced, proudly effecting an introduction. And it was magnificent. The ground fell away from the front door of the house for about a mile or so, and then the road in the distance, having disappeared in the valley, re- emerged rising up towards the mountain which completely dominated the background. In the hazy, early spring sunshine it appeared grey-blue in colour. The foreground did indeed look much like the Transvaal veldt, but it quickly gave way to bush land, interspersed with huge aloes which gave the landscape a distinctive aspect, quite different from the parts of the country I had seen up until then. Even at this first encounter I was captivated by this country. No wonder the house had been built with its back to the road and its face towards the stunning view.

"Well, now," the Bishop broke in on my thoughts, "shall we get on? We'll go round to the back again, I think, and look at the proposed site for the seminary building." For the next three-quarters of an hour we measured and argued about where and how big, and could we avoid cutting down any trees – this from the Bishop, who had a phobia about cutting down trees.

"I think that we should leave this one," he pointed to a gnarled and stunted specimen in the middle of the open ground, "it will form a focal point in the middle of the campus." He looked round, aware that the word 'campus' betrayed his fantasies about his new pet project. He blinked at us amiably over his spectacles and chuckled his odd hiccoughing laugh. "What?" he said to underline it all.

"The University of Pomeroy, mm?" said Jo Banks, experimenting with the sound of it. He put his hand on my shoulder. "And Professor Sam Torkington, I suppose."

"Yes" agreed Bishop Ulyatt, chuckling again, "Well, I think that about covers it for the moment. Now it's over to Paschal and then Jack. You say that we are aiming at fourteen months hence, Sam, as your ideal? I think that that will suit Jack as well, because he has enough work about the diocese to take him into the New Year and then he can start here."

Jack was obviously delighted with the prospect, as he lived in the village.

"I hate to introduce a jarring note," said Jo Banks, "but are you expecting food?"

"Ah, no, dear boy," answered the Bishop, "I am aware of your frugal habits, not to say, hand-to-mouth existence. So I took the precaution of bringing a little something." He moved towards the car and opened the boot. The reason for the case became apparent. I had vaguely wondered why he needed to take a case with him for a few hours visit. But as always he had thought of everything.

"Shall we lunch on the porch, do you think?" the Bishop asked and then made off through the house with the case, not waiting for a reply. We followed. He was already opening the case when we arrived to reveal bread, butter and cheeses, some cold meat and cans of beer. There was an old settee and two or three chairs on the porch.

"Sam, be a good chap and bring that small table through from the living room, will you?" asked his lordship as we arrived.

I drank in the view again as we had the picnic lunch, and regretted the year I had to wait before I could move into this beautiful place.

Chapter Seven

Towards the end of the year I began to get really worried about Graham, I had hoped things were improving on the farm and that it would at least break even. But Graham's frustration seemed to be increasing, judging by the number of times he took occasion to tell me of this machine breaking down or that piece of equipment no longer being serviceable. The tales of woe had been growing during the past winter months. It was also frustrating for me, knowing there was no chance of finding any capital to renew worn out tools and machinery. I had, as usual, passed on Graham's complaints to the Bishop. As usual too, the subject of money turned him stone deaf. Interviews invariably ended up with:

"I'll have to leave that to you for the time being, dear boy; I just cannot spare the cash on what might well be a case of throwing good money after bad, or something like," he waved it aside with a gesture of dismissal.

"Yes, but what about Graham," I had asked, with some little heat, "We can't just leave him to rot away with the farm and then say, 'Oh, what a shame, but then perhaps he was never the right man for the job in the first place.' He has had to make do with clapped-out equipment. It's hardly right to judge him in such circumstances."

In fairness to his lordship he had taken the point. After frequently suggesting we might seek someone else's opinion about the viability of the farm and Graham's competence, he finally admitted that none of this would change the basic situation. So the problem was left with me.

The Christmas school holidays gave me my first opportunity to get to grips with the situation and to make some preliminary assessments. The Bishop had told me to make it clear to Graham that we were in no way holding him responsible, nor expecting him to go down with the ship, if it really was sinking. He had added that if Graham saw a good job, we would entirely understand if he took it. I had kept this to myself. I felt certain that saying this to Graham at this juncture would almost certainly have sounded like giving him the push. However, as we discussed the future, I reconsidered my decision.

I had screwed up my courage for a painful interview, as I was very unsure of the best way to approach it. I really need not have worried as is so often the case with such dreaded interviews – Graham was only too glad to talk about the problems of the farm and his own problems as well. He was extremely honest, even embarassingly so. His excuse for his dangerously heavy drinking was the frustration of trying to make two go into one in the management of the farm. He had never really been given the tools to do the job. Not that he threw all the blame onto the impossible task of trying to make the farm viable. He admitted he had already been a heavy drinker when he came to

Besters. Now the problem was out of control. He needed a drink by ten in the morning or he had the shakes and he was only able to get through the day with regular doses of the same mixture, or frankly of any mixture, as long as it was alcoholic.

The farm problems became of secondary importance very soon after we had started talking. It was so clear cut. Either we invested large amounts of money in it, in the hope of future profit, or we got rid of it altogether. For Graham there was no such clear cut decision in view for his future. But as he talked one thing became very obvious.

"Father, I've had it as far as carrying on here is concerned, I know that. Actually, I have never said it to myself, but I know it all the same and I'm glad we are talking now. Man, there is no way I can get sorted out and carry on trying to make this job work. I promise myself every morning I'll stop drinking, but by midday it gets to me so badly that I break the promise and I'll go on and on like that until I drop, or something."

He told me about the various jobs he had held. He had usually worked for someone who had given him explicit instructions. In those circumstances he had been happiest. But he had wanted to be in charge of something; to achieve; to be creative. He had achieved more autonomy when he worked at the chicken farm and that had given him the confidence to think he could make a go of the mission farm. Unfortunately that confidence had all but disappeared and his courage to continue was now all coming out of a bottle.

I felt, and indeed was, helpless. I had no experience of dealing with alcoholism. Happily by some fluke I managed to avoid saying anything as crass as 'Pull yourself together, man', but apart from that I floundered. I offered sympathy. I apologised for my ineptitude. It was clear Graham could not stay at Besters in his present state. He needed a holiday; he needed help. Even if I could possibly have helped him, staying at the mission would have meant staying in the midst of the problems which were at least partly the cause of his present condition. I told him I would see the Bishop the next day at the latest and that he should make plans for getting away immediately.

The Bishop was in that very afternoon, so I went straight over to see him. He gave me a cheque for Graham, with instructions that his leave was indefinite. His return would depend entirely upon himself or his doctor's assessment of his health. With regard to the farm, the discussion went on for some time – to sell, to invest afresh – this alternative did not really appeal to either of us – or to let off portions of it. Of course, the Bishop said, the whole matter would have to be decided by his council, but my opinion was important. I was 'the man on the spot' – he set great store by the view of men on the spot – and the person who was going to have to carry out any plan that was chosen. I knew very well that our neighbours would be pleased to get their hands on more land for running their cattle. It was important not

94

to appear too desperate to keep the price up. We wanted to be able to run the mission off the proceeds of such leases.

I got back to Besters in the evening to find Graham 'mellow' but more relaxed than I had seen him for many a month. He admitted to feeling better now that the inevitable had become a reality. He had told the men on the farm that he should have to be away for some time. I imagine he had told them it was for medical reasons but I never did find out. I recounted my conversation with the Bishop about the future of the farm. Graham warned about selling the whole thing, as he knew very well that any security of tenure for the African tenants would immediately disappear. He was quite right. That was why we preferred to sell leases on terms laid down by the Bishop and his council.

Graham assured me that, at this time of the year, the farm would run itself. It was only early spring and until the rains came the ground was too hard to plough. The men were engaged in milking twice a day and in going round the whole area mending fences. There was enough silage to feed the cattle for the rest of the dry season, unless the first rains were late; but we should worry about that when the need arose. There were some pigs being fattened up and enough food for them for several weeks.

I drove Graham to the station the next morning to get the train to Pietermaritzburg, where his mother lived. He planned to go there first and just rest and see how he coped without all the worries of the farm. He left me that address as his base. We parted as if he were going on an extended holiday. In fact I never saw or heard from him again. The Bishop sent him monthly salary cheques for the next three months and then, not having heard from him either, sent him a final cheque and notice that as we had disposed of the farm, his job no longer existed. About a year later we heard that Graham had happily found a job as a long-distance lorry driver. We presumed that he must have mastered his drinking problem in order to hold down such a job.

I thought over Graham's advice about safeguarding the interests of the Africans living on the farm. When I first arrived at Besters I had received letters from the Bantu Affairs Department concerning the number of 'natives' resident on the farm. The usual justification for Africans living on white farms was that they were labourers, living with their families. Any others were deemed to be squatters and legally could be evicted. The mission was stuffed with files of letters from the department which my predecessor had received, all enquiring how the process of getting rid of surplus natives was coming along. I chose to ignore all these. The Department could and did on occasions enforce the law and removed "surplus natives" off designated white area farms. However, they much preferred the farmer to do it for them. If they forcibly removed Africans they had some obligation to make sure they had alternative places to live. If they were evicted by the farmers, they could turn a blind eye to their plight. They would be left to go begging for a place to live from some other farmer who was entitled to employ more labourers, or from a chief who might accept them into an area designated for Africans. With missions the department appeared to be more conciliatory in its approach. Not because they had any great respect for missions, especially Catholic ones which they regarded as the 'Roman danger'. But because missionaries had international contacts and what was done to missions, often staffed by foreign personnel, was news in South African and, more embarrassingly, in overseas papers.

When the first letters arrived after my arrival at Besters, I had left them for a few weeks and then, asked for clarification, telling the Department that I had just arrived, could not make head nor tail of the whole matter and was therefore unable to comply with a law I did not understand. After two months I received a letter patiently explaining to me the law and policy of the South African government with regard to Africans inhabiting white area farms. Finally it asked for my co-operation in bringing the mission at Besters into line with the aforementioned law and policy. I allowed several weeks to elapse again before explaining that many of the people on the farm had been there all their lives. Indeed their fathers and grandfathers had been there before them. In such circumstances, how could they be described as 'squatters'? Some ten weeks later a letter arrived explaining that the word 'squatters' was a technical term describing someone illegally living in a white area, and not registered as a farm worker. Length of tenure had nothing to do with the matter. What might have been acceptable twenty five years ago was not so now.

In this vein the correspondence was protracted for three years, and the department eventually became convinced they had got the message across to me. The last letter I received asked me to give the numbers of natives I had evicted from the mission and the number remaining. I wrote back with relish, telling them I had evicted no-one and had no intention of evicting anyone. I think I must have been a disappointment to them. I acquainted my successor with the procedure to follow in order to avoid the moves as long as possible. The moves had been threatened, I understood, for at least ten years, before my arrival. At that time, there were fifty five families resident on the mission farm; the usual allowance was six or seven for that size of farm.

I passed on these thoughts to the Bishop. He and his council decided that we should offer leases on selected parts of the farm and that the leases should contain clauses protecting the Africans' land and their grazing rights.

For the next three months there was a game of 'catch the lessee'. To start with I did nothing at all. But within ten days of Graham leaving on his extended holiday for medical care, as the official report described it, Jack Marais had come to see me. He offered sympathy about Graham's 'illness', fishing for further details, and gave assurances that if he could help in his absence, I had only to call him. I thanked him commenting that Graham was badly run down with all the worries of having to make do, patch up and run on a very tight budget. I hinted that we might have to re-think the future of the farm, especially if Graham was away for a long time or felt unable to continue. I left it at that.

He was back a week later – just dropped in to see if all was well and to ask if I had heard from Graham. As he got up to go he added, as if it had almost slipped his mind:

"Oh, Father, by the way, if you should think at any time of letting the farm or any part of it I should be interested in more grazing for my cattle. And I happen to know that Tim Muir, over the hill, would be too. Just thought I'd mention it, you know, Father," he added with a knowing grin, "I should hate to think you would let our friend Van der Merwe in before having a word with us, eh?" We laughed and he went, but negotiations had been started. I rang up the Bishop and in guarded terms, remembering the party line, I appraised him of developments.

"Ah, Monsignor; Sam here. About the special service of prayers for a fruitful year on the land, I think we ought to arrange it fairly soon, if you can manage it."

It took a few seconds for him to catch on.

"The special service?" he queried, "Oh," as comprehension came, "Well, indeed, yes, good. But mm, not too soon I think, dear boy. Round about the time of the first rains, don't you think?"

His idea was that the fields would look so much more inviting and desirable once the grass had begun to grow. He might have had a point, but I felt that Jack Marais was a thorough professional and knew the value of the grazing even in its dry, brown state before the rains.

"Well, just as you say," I agreed.

"O.K., old boy. I'll wait to hear from you."

Before final decisions were made, I was determined to get a bit of expert advice. I had met a veterinary doctor about a year earlier. He had recently become a Catholic and lived in another part of the diocese. His name was Lionel Steel. His practice covered a wide area, but he did not operate as far south as Besters. However, I rang him. It took three days to get the busy man who was out most of the day on the farms. I told him about the plans for selling up Besters. He said he had visited the place once, but could not comment on whether it would be a good idea or not. He agreed to come and have a look at the cattle and pigs when he was next in our area.

Lionel called two days later to say he would be coming the following Monday afternoon. I told the men to have the cattle in for milking rather earlier than usual, as the vet was coming to examine them. When Lionel arrived he was able to go to work immediately. He asked for a bucket of soap and water and put it beside the first cow to be examined. I speculated on the use of soap and water in the determining of pregnancy in cows. Unfortunately I did it out loud and Lionel gave me a withering look.

"The soap and water, Father, is for me, you will soon understand why."

I did. He thrust his bared arm into the backside of the cow and groped around inside the cow. He explained that he was looking for a calf.

"But surely," I said, "it might still be too small to be recognisable to your hand".

"Yes, it might, but very soon after conception you can feel something like a tennis ball inside the cow, if you know just where to look."

He washed his arm after examining each cow. When he had looked at eight or nine, his face was showing disappointment. He shook his head in my direction, then stood back from the line of cows.

"Father, this is really a waste of time. If you are selling cows that are in calf people will buy them because they will soon be giving milk. But I have tried half of them and found no calves. There is little chance of finding any in calf amongst the rest."

He tried a couple more without success.

"I'm afraid there has been a bit of neglect here about seeing that they get to the bull; unless there is something wrong with the bull of course. Sorry, Father if you want to sell them, you can't advertise them as with calf, or even as having run with the bull."

"Well, I'm sorry, Lionel. I've dragged you out here on a wild goose chase – rather a mixed farmyard metaphor. Have you time for a cup of tea?"

"I'd love one," said Lionel, "I've finished for the day, there are only a few pets at surgery this evening."

He was interested in the seminary and we had a long conversation about it. Then he told me he had decided to go away and train for the priesthood. The Bishop had obtained a place for him in the major seminary for whites in Pretoria. He was to begin the following January. I invited him to come and have a look at us, when we got settled in Pomeroy in about fourteen months time. He promised he would. He ventured the opinion that the church submitted too easily to the demands of the South African government that such establishments should be racially segregated, couldn't they all be more closely linked he wondered. I was pleasantly surprised to hear a South African white speak in this way. I had met very few white Catholics as Besters was an entirely African parish, apart from the handful of white sisters at the convent. I had heard from my colleagues that there were many white Catholics who approved of the racial discrimination, quietly in most cases, but in a few quite outspokenly.

Lionel left, promising that we should meet again soon.

For the next five weeks, the Bishop played hard to get in order to impress aspirant lessees. He left them with the impression that we were highly spiritual and therefore scornful of the financial

98

arrangements and also that the matter was so weighty that long deliberation with endless committees was necessary before a satisfactory formula could be devised. While this charade was being played out I was stuck in the middle. The first thing I did after speaking to the Bishop was to ring Jack Marais and tell him that I had passed on his ideas to the Bishop, who was considering the possibility but whose first reaction was of favourable interest. Jack and his friend Tim pressed me in the ensuing weeks for further progress reports on the state of the Bishop's mind. I kept them going with the news that the matter was now in the hands of the Bishop's council; or the religious superiors in England, the Apostolic delegate was being sounded out for his opinion; or Rome was being consulted. Some of this was on my own initiative and some on the advice of the Bishop, whom I kept informed. Latterly I had to warn him that my excuses were beginning to sound a bit thin and were, I fancied, beginning to exasperate the prospective lessees.

Eventually, at the end of this five week period, Jack and his friend Tim Muir came to see me to ask to meet the Bishop. Their request carried with it just the faintest suggestion that they were beginning to suspect that the Bishop was just a myth, and that there were other, more Machiavellian reasons for my delaying tactics. I agreed that seemed to be a good idea; certainly better than passing messages through me, the middle man. I pretended I had been on the point of suggesting such a course myself, as most of the preliminary discussions had taken place and the necessary permissions obtained.

It was arranged that we should all go across to the Bishop's place.

"No, dear boy, I do not come over to Besters. You all come here. Don't want them to think they're doing us a favour, what? It is us doing them the favour, d'you see?"

And so it was arranged. We should all be there at the Bishop's mission the following Tuesday at two-thirty in the afternoon. I arrived just after the prospective lessees. Bishop Ulyat was greeting them in front of his massive rondavel, which served for everything – office, bedroom and little kitchen, with thin partitions for dividing walls. I was suspicious when I saw him. He had got himself all rigged out in full pontificals, as if about to enter a plenary session of the Bishop's conference. As I approached he was oozing charm:

"So good of you to come across here. I was telling Father Sam how much better it would have been to conduct all this in situ, as it were, but one is so busy; so I am most enormously grateful to you for coming here." He spread his arms and beamed on us over his spectacles, as if about to impart a blessing. He ushered us all into the small office.

Jack and Tim Muir were all dressed up in suits and ties. I had never seen them like this before. They appeared somewhat awed and nervous at meeting the great man. They sat together in front of the Bishop's desk. I took a chair and placed it to one side and slightly behind my farmer neighbours – the middle man retires to the shadows when the principals get together.

"I think we should go through the contracts I have had drawn up", The Bishop stated abruptly.

He passed us each a copy, which we started to read, when to our surprise Bishop Ulyat began to intone the document as if reading the gospel of the day. He must have seen, and been prepared for our surprise, because he looked at us benignly as if somewhat surprised at our reaction.

"I thought it would be easier if I read it aloud and then I could comment on anything I think might need amplifying. I imagine that's the best way," he beamed again over his glasses, challenging anyone to disagree. I was glad I had pulled my chair back, as I felt laughter begin to rise up from my stomach.

"Good. Well, I'll carry on then." And he did, pausing from time to time to look at us over his spectacles, to make sure we were getting every word. Some passages he would emphasise by reading extra slowly, and pause a while for the whole import to hit us. This he did portentously when insisting on the rights of and the non-harrassment of the resident Africans and the continued employment of those working on the farm. When it came to passages about the rights of the lessees, he sped along, or dismissed the rest of the paragraph with a "yes, yes, well, we know all about that."

"Now," he said, having finished the reading, "if you have any questions, we can discuss matters and if not, we can sign it. Alright?"

There were a few practical matters about how payment was to be made. His lordship had first thought that they could pay me directly. Later he decided this would lower the tone and they should pay him, the Bishop, with whom after all, he said, they would be completing the contract.

"Mr. Marais, you sign here.... good, thank you; and now Mr. Muir, you sign here. The 'T' is for Theodore, is it not, Mr. Muir?" He knew damn well it was not.

"Timothy, actually," corrected Tim Muir.

"Oh, very biblical," cooed the Bishop, nauseatingly. I got up and looked out of the window, turning my back on them. I had begun to sweat in my effort not to laugh out loud by this time.

Jack Marais, after signing all the relevant pieces of paper, said he thought that they should all bear equal cost of the production of the documents of the lease. The Bishop waved away the offer with a saintly expression on his face.

"I shall see to all that," he said. "I am conscious of all the help you have given to Sam here and feel I should like to make some little gesture of gratitude." He gazed at us demurely.

They murmured their gratitude, disclaiming having done anything special – any neighbour would have done the same. I was not

100

as impressed as my neighbours, I happened to know that a legal friend of the Bishop had done the whole job for nothing.

The formalities completed they all shook hands and the Bishop invited the gentlemen to have a drink, tea, coffee – or a beer perhaps? The last sounded like a concession to their rough, bucolic tastes. But I think that they had done the business they wanted to do and declined his offers of hospitality with excuses of commitments at their respective farms.

We all left together, so I had no opportunity to make any remarks to the Bishop about his staging of the whole signing ceremony.

When I got back to Besters I found Cos there. I told him of the Bishop's performance. He said he was seeing him the next day and would pass on my comments about the torture I had been through trying to keep my face straight.

Cos reported later that the Bishop was quite unrepentant. He claimed he deserved an Oscar for it. He told Cos that the whole staging had nearly been ruined by the kindness of the children at the school. He had been away for several days in another part of the diocese and on his return had been confronted by crowds of smiling children, waiting for him to see their new handiwork. They had cleaned up the whole mission compound, weeded and swept the area in the front of his rondavel and the church. They had to his embarrassment marked out a path between his house and the church with old beer cans which they had discovered in sacks at the back of the house. They had half-buried these at an angle of forty-five degrees along both edges of the path to form a neat border.

The Bishop told the children that he was delighted by the magnificent work they had done, and the pathway ... well, what could he say. On reflection, he told them, he feared the tins would go rusty and spoil the effect of the beautiful job they had all done. But he had an idea ....

With typical impetuosity he jumped into his car and drove some fifteen miles to the nearest little rail-stop, where he knew there was a builders yard. He purchased enough stout red flooring tiles to replace the tins, plus a large quantity of sweets from the general store and raced back to the mission.

The children agreed that the tiles would make a much better and more attractive edging and offered to replace the tins the next day. Any disappointment they might have felt at the slight implication of adverse criticism of their work was very quickly banished at the sight of the sweets the Bishop had brought for them.

Jack and Tim Muir now became business-like. They had agreed, for a percentage to arrange a sale of all that was still serviceable about the farm. I had explained the new arrangements to all the workers on the farm, before the contracts had been drawn up, and most of them had been willing to carry on working under the new management, though one or two felt that they were now too old to carry on working.

101

The new situation had been explained to the other parishioners at church on a Sunday some weeks before. Their one fear had been for their security of tenure. Once I had explained that no land they lived on was to form any part of the contracts and that in any case they were not to be harrassed in any way, under pain of breaking the contract, their fears were allayed. They understood, they said, that Father was too busy with many other matters to be able to run the farm as well; kindly they did not add that they knew very well that Father was quite incapable of so doing.

A fortnight after the leases had been signed, all that was saleable had been sold. Stout fences had appeared between the farm yard and the mission house, church and seminary buildings, which I, at first, regarded as a blunt hint to keep out, but soon realised was sound common-sense. The two things were now separate – farm and mission – and it was better for all concerned that it be physically emphasised by a solid barrier.

In the months that followed I came to appreciate the lifting of the worry of the farm, and the steady income from the leases. The money went to the Bishop, but was added to the money he sent to me for the upkeep of the boys each quarter.

Christmas and New Year came and went. Alfred did not come back when the others did after the summer holidays. The Bishop reported that Alf had faithfully come in every day for about three weeks. He had done a lot of work at the mission; had lunched with the Bishop and they had had several chats about Alf's future. Then one day he came in and asked the Bishop for a reference for a job he thought he might get at a builder's yard at the rail-stop fifteen miles distant. The Bishop had gladly given him a reference and he had got the job.

Soon after the boys had returned I had a visit from Paschal to consult me about the plans for the new seminary to be built at Pomeroy. Jack Ramana, the Indian builder, was ready to start. He had begun to dig foundations in the evenings, while finishing off another job at nearby mission. Jack was work mad. His complaint was never about being worked too hard, but about not having enough to do. Paschal and myself managed to agree about the outside walls at least, so work could begin. I had reservations about his plans for the rooms inside, mainly because I found it difficult to visualise what our needs would be.

Now that the farm was no longer a constant headache. I felt freer and more able to get about. I managed to visit belatedly forgotten corners of the widespread parish. I even suggested going to a couple of the out-stations once a fortnight instead of once a month. I was surprised and probably a little hurt when this suggestion was not met with universal enthusiasm. But with one or two hints from the local catechist I arrived at the answer. The people treated me to a chicken dinner every time I visited them. Pleased as they might be to see the priest, the cost of killing two chickens per month instead of one was considerable. I tried to put myself in their position and after some thought I ended up laughing at myself. I had foresworn the idea of the priest as the sacrament machine, yet here I was unconsciously falling into the trap. I was behaving as if I had something to offer over and above what the local catechist offered. I made a comparison in my own mind. I was a white man, speaking the language poorly and spouting out far too much theological jargon often unrelated to my parishioners' lives. I came in a car, stayed two hours, and then went back whence I had come. The local catechist or church leader spoke the language, was able to relate the gospel to a life he understood, because he was living it with the people. I was virtually superfluous, except for births, marriages and deaths. But if that was so, I had better find myself a more relevant role. I fell asleep before I had worked one out.

The rest of the year passed quietly enough with many planning meetings for the new seminary. My new role there would at least avoid my dilemmas over my value as a priest. One day at the beginning of December the Bishop arrived out of the blue with a Volkswagen Kombi. He had decided that the new beginning at Pomeroy demanded better transport for the boys. With his usual business-like alacrity he explained the idea, said he would take my Volkswagen beetle to get him home and went within ten minutes leaving me astonished. The Kombi was a great help. I had been planning the loan of a truck to cart all the seminary beds and bedding. Now I thought that with the help of Cos and his Landrover the pair of us could manage the lot.

By Sunday, I had everything ready for the move on Monday morning. I said the three masses – at the mission and at two out-stations, and was back by mid-afternoon for my farewells. I was presented with the money which had been collected much to my embarrassment. I knew the parishioners could not afford it and strictly should not be giving it to me. I made a formal little speech with knots in my tummy and wished for Monday morning. After a short time I slipped away and went to see the Sisters.

I was alone at the mission that night. I wrote out all the last minute things I could think of for my successor, Father Godfrey. He had made a couple of visits already and we had gone through the duties and the places he had to visit to say mass. There was no problem with guides because the Sisters had been going with me to out-stations for the past two years and knew them well. They had been catechising and also taking simple medicines, chosen as safe to let people dispense for themselves and their children.

I drank two stiff brandies and slept.

First thing next day I loaded the Kombi with the last few things to be packed. Then I said mass for the last time at Besters. There were a few more people than usual at church that morning and they stayed around afterwards to wish me goodbye; Dora laughed and shook like a jelly; Doris looked sad. I had a quick breakfast and as I walked back from the convent I took a last look at the place.

Everyone had lined up to see me off. I felt sad and awkward. I shook hands so solemnly that we all ended up laughing and while the mood lasted I jumped into the car and, with a wave of the hand, I went off up the dirt road in a cloud of dust.

Chapter Eight

As the crow flies from Besters to Pomeroy it is probably about thirty miles; by road it is almost fifty miles. For the first ten miles my eyes were a little moist and my heart heavy at parting from a place in which I had been happy. After the next ten miles I started to look forward. I knew that there would be a lot to do before the boys joined me in January. I had intended, after the first visit to Pomeroy, to make it my business to go and watch over the progress of the buildings so that I could make suggestions and even ask for additions and alterations. This remained like so many fine resolutions, unfulfilled. I had received reports about progress; I had been consulted from time to time about different aspects of the building, but I had not been back to Pomeroy myself. My only visit had been so sudden and unplanned and of such short duration that my memory was hazy and patchy. Were there three or four rooms off the main corridor? Was there a water tank behind the kitchen and anyway was it going to be big enough to cater for all the boys' needs?

My memory of the route was vague but I was sure that I was on the right road when I passed a small convent which Joe Banks had set up with English and Irish Sisters, who in turn were teaching African postulants and novices. I knew the convent was only seven or eight miles from Pomeroy. Within two or three minutes I came out of the trees and before me was the view of the valley with Pomeroy nestling beneath the steep hillside and shimmering in the heat a thousand feet below. The Bishop had been driving last time we had made this impressive drop down the hillside. I was able to appreciate why he had gone so slowly. The road had been cut out of the side of a very rocky hill and was strewn with stones which caused the car to slide about, inspite of anything I might be doing with the steering wheel.

As I struggled to the foot of the hillside I remembered the character of the landscape, quite different from what I had been used to, with giant aloes and cacti everywhere. I gazed at the little village stores on either side of the road, with their verandahs in front; a small stone building just at the entrance to the village, which looked official – it turned out to be the police-station – the dusty and dilapidated trucks; the occasional horses; the huge blue-grey mountain which filled the background. I felt as if I was entering a wild west frontier town. The villages and small towns I had seen in north Natal and southern Transvaal were dull, sedate and prosaic by comparison. I felt I had fallen down the hill into a different dimension, not a sinister one, full of threats and menace, rather a dimension evocative of romance and adventure. Almost reluctantly I turned off the road into the driveway I remembered from the first visit. I was expecting to see Father Neil who had beaten me there by about a week. He had been appointed as parish priest – I was to have no responsibilities for the parish, apart from occasionally helping him out at weekends during holiday times. We had been students together and knew each other well. Like everyone else I always called him Fred. Fred had been blessed by God and his Irish parents with an almost perpetual smile, set on a round shining face, which was itself set above a round short body. He had a beautiful singing voice which we, as students, maintained was better than that of his great hero, John McCormack. He regarded this opinion almost as sacrilege.

However, it was not Fred who greeted me; it was Jack. He was on top of the roof of the new seminary building, which faced me as I got out of the car.

"Welcome, Father; hey, what you think?" he demanded cheerfully. Jack laughed a great deal, and only became serious when he was in need of materials to keep the work going.

"Well, Jack, this is wonderful," I said, though I was a little disappointed that the job was not finished. Jack was perched on a roof as yet comprised only of rafters. Jack must have read my mind.

"No worry, Father, we finish very soon. Work very had," he assured me.

After the initial slight disappointment, I was impressed by the facade. It spread across the whole of one side of the open area behind the old doctor's house and yet did not seem to diminish the size of the open space. I had, of course, seen the area covered with weeds and some old tree stumps on my previous visit; all that had been cleared to expose the Bishop's 'campus' or even professorial lawn, if your imagination was vivid enough.

I was hailed by an Irish tenor voice.

"Hey, I didn't hear you come", called Fred, "It's coming on, isn't it?" he said, nodding towards the building. "Only trouble is that Jack needs a whip across his back to keep him at it."

Jack laughed at him. "No, the days are very short, Father, very short. We need more time."

"Well, at least come in, will you?" said Fred; and to Jack: "I'm just going to make tea, come on in about five minutes, will you, Jack:"

"I'll be there, Father".

In the week that he had been resident Fred had been working hard on the house. Joe Banks had only used the place as a pied-à-terre, when working in that part of his parish and had lived virtually in one room. The furniture which the doctor, the previous occupant, had left behind in the house had been piled up in one of the two rondavels. Fred had spread it through the house, and the place looked inhabited, even inviting. He said it was all superficial show for my arrival, there was still an enormous amount to be done. As he put a kettle on and got cups out, we talked.

"Before Jack comes in, Sam." He looked through the window to make sure Jack was not yet coming. "Jack is a supreme optimist. He is blithely convinced that the building will be ready for habitation by the time the boys come in January. It won't. Jack makes estimates assuming that there will be no hitches, snags or unforeseen delays. He does not take into account the amount of time taken in going back and forth to Dundee for supplies, that might not be available anyway. If it wasn't that he works all the hours God sends, the building would not be as far on as it is. So I'll show you later what sort of provisional arrangements I think we could make for the boys for a few weeks until there is more accommodation ready, O.K.? But not a word to Jack, or he will think you are criticising, and heaven knows that's the last thing he deserves.

Fred finished talking as Jack arrived, not quietly.

"That tea ready, Father? Come on, I'm a very busy man," he called out loudly as he approached, laughing.

We sat in the large living room and drank tea and ate biscuits. For most of the time Jack allowed himself a break, he rattled on to me about his problems – the difficulties of getting materials from a long distance over dirt roads that did no good to the springs and shock absorbers of his laden truck; the quality of the sand from the dried out river bed about a mile and a half away also over very rough ground; the scarcity of cement and a hundred and one other things that were holding Jack up. Being held up in his work was the supreme irritation to Jack. Happily there were so many different jobs to be done, that Jack could always get on with something else, if blocked in one direction. He finished his tea and jumped up.   "Right, Fathers, must get on," He went out laughing. If it were not for the fact that Jack was usually laughing, he would have looked like a bandit. It was mainly the moustache that gave that impression, that and the way he swung his shoulders almost arrogantly as he walked. He was far from being arrogant or for that matter anything like a bandit. He was, I think, a Hindu but during his time at Pomeroy he used to come to mass on Sundays and spoke vaguely at times of becoming a Catholic. Neither Fred nor myself ever pushed this point. There was a strong suspicion in our minds that Jack did not really know what to do with himself on Sundays, and really came up for a look at his handiwork and to assess the jobs for the ensuing week. We guessed he wanted company too, he would spend time sitting in the living-room drinking tea – and, as the day wore on, to have a little drink before dinner.

When Jack had left, Fred and myself settled down to a planning discussion. I asked tentatively if he had chosen himself a room.

"Yes, the one down the corridor opposite the bathroom," he said. "That was the first job I did," he added with a smile. Then a thought struck him: "If that's alright with you Sam?" he asked anxiously, "after all I'm the paying guest; you're in charge of the seminary."

"Good grief, I hope you don't feel like that. No, I asked because I have been harbouring for a year a secret yearning to inhabit one of those rondavels and I didn't want to tip my hand until you had expressed an opinion. Not that it would have mattered, because there are two rondavels anyway."

"No, they seem a bit big for my liking," Fred confessed.

"Well, I had in mind that I could keep all the school books and various bits and pieces of equipment for sport etc., in my room."

"Good idea, certainly for the time being," Fred agreed, "because you will be short on space until Jack has got the new building ready. I have suggested that once he has the roof on, which should be by Christmas with a bit of luck, but anyway by early New Year, he should then concentrate on completing one room at a time, so that you can start to use part of the building, while the rest is being completed."

"Good idea". All the doors of the one-storey building would open onto a verandah running along the front, so it would be possible to use a completed room without getting in the way of continuing building operations.

We arranged that the boys would use the other rondavel and a further room in the house for temporary sleeping quarters. This was possible using the bunk beds. The present living room would have to be used as a dining room for all of us and the easy chairs would go into my rondavel once term started; and my room would then double as a staff sitting room, hopefully only for a few weeks.

We unpacked the Kombi, transferring the bedding into the rondavel designated as the boys' dormitory. The bunk beds were already there, delivered by Cos the previous Saturday. I gathered Cos had arrived swearing very creative oaths. The metal parts of the beds had been moving about over the rough roads, periodically hitting him across the back of the head as he tried to drive as steady a course as possible.

"Oh, by the way", remembered Fred, as we finished a hasty lunch amid the chaos. "You have an appointment tomorrow. We may have a teacher for you. Joe Banks knows him very well and I have had a chat with him. He finished teaching on Friday when the schools broke up, but he agreed to stick around to talk to you about the possibilities of a job here next year. You probably know more about this than I do; Joe told me that he had spoken to you about this man a few weeks ago. Joe tells me he is quiet and competent, but a little fed up working under Sisters at a mission school. He wants a change.

"Perhaps I can appreciate his feelings," I said, "but how will he take to working for the clergy, I wonder? Perhaps better men than women as bosses, I suspect, for a Zulu man. Anyway, that's fine. I will need at least one teacher, and he must be Zulu. I might make some pretence of teaching other subjects, but there is no way I could attempt Zulu," I clutched my head, as my imagination caught hold of the idea, "What a totally ludicrous notion", I grimaced at the ridiculous proposition.

"Incidentally", a thought struck me," I suppose I ought to ring the boss and let him know I have arrived. You do have a phone?"

"Oh, yes," he laughed, "It was a doctor's house, if you remember. I know the whole setting looks ultra-primitive but there are minimal amenities. There is even a bus passing once a day."

I rang the Bishop that evening and announced my safe arrival at my new appointment.

"Good. Now, dear boy, how about teaching staff for my bush university? Have you got anyone?"

I told him about the interview the next morning.

"Yes, you can't manage without a Zulu teacher. But now a word in your ear," his voice dropped to a whisper, "Lionel Steel has left the seminary, for all sorts of reasons we needn't go into. I thought that you might ask him if he is interested. I haven't said anything to him. He's a bit raw about it all at the moment and undecided about his future. So you might jump in, but" he added hastily, "with tact and delicacy, dear boy, with tact and delicacy."

I mused for a second. "Where is he at the moment?" I asked.

"He's staying with a friend at Volksrust for a few days, probably over Christmas, so you could ring him there."

"Well, thank you," I said thoughtfully. The Bishop gave me the phone number, leaving me to wonder about the possibility. Lionel had seemed really interested in the seminary when he visited me at Besters, but what now? Had the experience of being inside a seminary changed his attitude? I could but try, anyway.

Daniel Makhaya arrived to see me at about ten the next morning. He was older than I, probably approaching forty. He was quite a small man, but dapper and well-dressed. He spoke softly and a quiet smile appeared from time to time as we spoke and he began to appreciate the situation. He was not the sort of person given to outbursts of excited enthusiasm, but I sensed that his interest grew as we talked. To the recommendations of Joe Banks who had known and indeed employed him for several years and the reactions of Fred, I needed to add my own assessment. Could I work with him? I made up my mind quickly. I was impressed that he grasped the issues so easily. I could see his mind weighing up myself as a prospective employer, and as an untrained teaching colleague.

"Mr. Makhaya, you do understand the situation? You will be the professional in the set-up and myself and, I hope, another man I shall be seeing later will be relying heavily on your experience."

He smiled modestly, "I hope I shall be able to help".

"I hope by that remark I can assume you are prepared to take the job, because I am more than glad to offer it to you. You know the area well, and you certainly know teaching well after so many years in the profession. By the way, where is your home?"

"Oh, many miles from here, Father, near to Durban".

"Oh, dear, I'm sorry you have had to wait to see me when you might have gone home at the weekend."

"No, Father," he reassured me, "that is no matter. I had decided that it was time for a change of a job and otherwise I would have been busy looking for a position during the holidays."

I felt a twinge of conscience. "Had you in mind finding a job nearer to your home? I don't want you to feel that I am preventing you from finding a job that will allow you to be with your family more."

"Oh, no, Father," he smiled again, "My wife had already looked around near our home, there are no vacancies. So the next best alternative is the area I am used to. I shall be glad to work here, as long as," he appeared a little worried by a thought, "I am not expected to be on duty every weekend as well as teaching."

"Good heavens, no, Mr. Makhaya," I protested, "I shall be grateful if you can help with homework in the evenings, but the weekends you must have free; any involvement with activities at that time is up to yourself."

He nodded and got up to go.

"Thank you, Father," he said, as we shook hands, "and my name is Daniel – please?"

"Fine; then we shall meet on the twentieth of January."

That evening I phoned Lionel. I didn't know how he might feel about my proposition, so I dissembled. After offering my sympathies, about his decision to leave the seminary, I said that I should be passing through Volksrust the next day or the day after and thought I might call in and see him. He obviously thought it was a kindly act of charity to cheer him up, probably motivated by a suggestion from the Bishop. He told me he was bound to be in. He was trying to sort out his future in his head and did not feel much like going out and visiting people.

Lionel looked a little tired and worn when I eventually found the house in Volksrust. His friend, John, was out at work and would not be in until the evening. John was also a bachelor and so Lionel and myself had the house to ourselves until evening. By the time I arrived the morning was already well advanced and before lunch we talked of his experience at the major seminary. I let him, in his own time without any questions from me, tell me about his reasons for leaving. It was, he said, a combination of things, mainly, his inability to accept the seminary regime and way of life. He was far older than the majority of the students, and hence more set in his ways; the teachers and lecturers were from overseas and he thought that they were paying no attention to local conditions. They were trotting out the same text-book teaching as was used in Europe as if it was equally valid in South Africa. Latterly he had been ill and spent a few weeks in hospital and when he had been able to lie back and review the situation, he made the decision to leave. I had got bits and pieces of his feelings, still probably somewhat mixed up, but what came through fairly clearly was that he had had enough of clerics for the time being. He had experienced what he considered to be their over-authoritarian attitude; the arrogant assumption that they had all the answers and their consequent patronising manner in dealing with students as if they were little boys.

110

I kept my mouth judiciously closed through all this.

Over lunch I prompted him about his plans for the future. He did not really fancy starting from scratch again and building up another veterinary practice. When he sold his old practice he had signed an undertaking not to set up practice again in the immediate area for at least five years. Thus he would have to restart in an unfamiliar area. So he was mulling it all over and after Christmas he would make a decision. John had said he could stay as long as he liked and he would stay certainly until the New Year.

As gently and tactfully as I could I brought up the subject of the seminary at Pomeroy. He apologetically asked how the move was going, feeling guilty for talking only about his own affairs. I told him about the building, about the enchanting place and how I had been interviewing a teacher, taking him on and was now looking for another. He listened with detached interest, politely.

"Lionel, I have a confession to make," I said.

"You to me, Father? That's the wrong way round," said Lionel.

"Not sacramental confession," I said laughing. "No," more seriously, "I mean about coming to see you. I had in mind that you might like to consider the idea of teaching at Pomeroy."

He gaped at me. "You're joking," he said.

"Well, no, as a matter of fact, I am not joking. You have been telling me about the way the major seminary is run and the way you think it ought to be run. Well, how about getting involved and putting your ideas into practice? I hope I am open to suggestions. I want to learn the best way to do the job I have been given. Here you are with ideas; I'm in need of them and a teacher."

"Good God, you do mean it, don't you," he said slowly, as the truth dawned on him.

"Oh, yes, I do, Lionel."

He snapped out of his first surprise.

"No, Father, sorry, I couldn't do it. I have had a belly full of clergy and their establishments. You know, I felt walled in eventually. They were so rigid and rule-bound. No, I am sorry, Father, I couldn't face it."

"I think Pomeroy might be just a bit different from Pretoria, you know, Lionel," I suggested quietly.

"Father, with all respect, you are a priest, and you will have the same sort of mentality that they had in Pretoria. No, I couldn't do it."

John came in at about six in the evening and found us still at the table from lunch and still arguing back and forth. We had got to the stage, where Lionel was calling me Torkington and I was referring to him as Steel, but without any animosity.

"Look, Steel, you said..." I would say and he would reply with,

"You are contradicting yourself again, Torkington...." This seemed quite promising to me – he had not told me to go away and

111

leave him alone.

John was quite surprised at the change in Lionel, who had been rather withdrawn and uncommunicative. I had at least aroused him, though not to the extent of taking my job.

"Torkington, stay the night," he commanded, "John won't mind a bit, even if you are a Catholic priest."

"But haven't you to get up to Standerton tonight?" John asked, puzzled.

"Of course, he hasn't," shouted Lionel, "he was lying about that. But what can you expect – he's a Catholic priest. You can't trust them, John, not for a minute, man".

John, not himself a Catholic, was slightly embarrassed, until I joined in Lionel's laughter.

"I merely dissembled, John. I didn't lie, I partially withheld the truth." I told him virtuously. "But I would like to stay if I may, John. It is late and I still want to try to convince this man that he ought – as some sort of duty, or something – to take on the prestigious post I am offering to him."

Lionel had regained his spirits through the afternoon and some of his frustration and anger were dying down. Hopefully he was beginning to look ahead instead of backwards, but inspite of my brave words about trying to influence him, I did not really believe I would succeed.

John prepared an excellent dinner, with the aid of one or two tins. We ate it to the accompaniment of a bottle of red wine and a record of an African penny-whistle player called Spokes Mashiane, playing traditional tunes in a modern style. It was the sound of the locations and African townships, polished and captured on record. Both wine and music helped maintain the friendly mood.

After dinner the subject of the job was declared taboo, mainly because neither Lionel nor myself wanted to inflict it on John. We talked instead of the South African race situation and its eventual outcome. It was an education listening to two white South Africans, who were by normal white standards, very liberal-minded. I discovered with what difficulty and heart-searching they had arrived at their current positions, so different from the unthinking acceptance of discrimination and apartheid of their backgrounds. Tongues were loosened by the bottle of brandy that followed the wine. When it was empty, we went to bed.

After breakfast Lionel and I started again. I found Lionel much better organised in his defences. The best I could get by lunch time was an admission that perhaps it would be a great idea, but.... The 'but' turned out to be a new idea that had not been mentioned the day before. I fancy the idea had been at the back of his mind when he had been in practice, namely, the offering of his training and professional services to his African countrymen – to help them to improve their stock, keep them free of disease, to make sure they had the best possible care. He must have seen the state of African animals which never got enough grazing or the ensured services of a vet. He would have seen all this as he travelled round the white farms and I suspect that the injustice of the system had been slowly pricking his conscience for years. Anyway, by lunch time he was beginning to describe what had been lurking in his mind.

I was delighted and cast down. It was a marvellous idea. I could hardly fight against it and press him to come and teach at the seminary when he had such a laudable plan – extension work, he called it.

"Fine", I said, "that sounds great. But on a practical level how and where do you start."

"I really haven't worked out details. Basically the plan is this. We both know what the chances are of a white man walking into an area inhabited by Africans and trying to tell them how to run their farms or small plots. Nil. There are government advisers but they are ignored because they are government men and because they act like government men, trying to impose a new system on the African. What I plan is literally to sit by the road and let people get to know you and what you do and wait to be asked to help. Once your help is seen to be good, you are in and others will come along. But the essence of the thing is to be of service, when asked and not before. The Africans must be in charge, as it were, not like another white boss-man giving orders."

"Just a point", I hated to be so mundane, "but how do you live? Money, you know?"

"I know that. It will take time, time when nothing is happening. So it needs some sponsorship, at least for a short while. I did speak to the Bishop, but you know what he's like. He wants to see results the day after tomorrow, and sooner, if possible."

"And where do you start this?"

"Well, anywhere; the problems are everywhere and the need is so vast."

"Like Pomeroy, for instance?" I queried gently. "I mean, while the people are getting to know you, you could be putting in a few hours teaching, becoming a known figure about the village, walking about the countryside, taking the boys on nature rambles, examining at close quarters the flora and the fauna .... get the picture?" I asked.

"My God, Torkington," he roared, "you don't give up, do you? And I thought you were genuinely interested in the plan."

"Oh, I am, I am," I told him earnestly, "and I was about to give up all ideas of trying to get you to the seminary, when you first outlined your plan, but I don't see why the two things can't go together. Not only that, but I could speak to the Bishop maybe get him to look more favourably on the project. You could do some teaching at the seminary, on the understanding that when your extension project started to take off, you would be released to that full time and we should have had time to get hold of a replacement teacher. How's that

113

for salesmanship?" I finished triumphantly.

"Torkington, it is all wonderfully logically worked out, but can I trust a priest ever?"

"Such cynicism; I am shocked and disappointed."

"No, I am really not ready to make decisions like that yet. Perhaps, next year, when I have sorted myself out. I don't think I would be a good influence on the boys at the moment, anyway. I can't pass on to them my wretched cynicism and turmoil of mind, now can I? No, Father," he said with finality, "I appreciate your kindness in thinking of me and trying to help me at a difficult time, but no. We'll see next year."

It was lunch time and we fried bacon and eggs. Over lunch I cleared up the last point Lionel had made.

"Look, Lionel, thank you for listening to me and not throwing me out. But I want to make one thing very clear. I might indeed be glad of your services next year, but that is a long time away. I came to you to try to capture your services now because I need someone now, and off hand I can't think of anyone I would rather have at the seminary than you. I did not in all honesty come to offer you a job to help you out at a difficult time. If that was the happy result of your coming to Pomeroy, I should be delighted, of course. But my need is now, come the twentieth of January."

"Oh, I see," said Lionel thoughtfully, "I suppose that should make it easier for me to say 'no'. But actually I don't think it makes any difference to my decision. I really feel it must still be 'no', though I do appreciate your need."

"Well, O.K.," I conceded, "I see your point of view as well. It's ultimately a matter of how you feel and what you feel able to do. Do you know Pomeroy, by the way?"

"I've passed through a couple of times, that's all."

"Forgetting what we have been talking about, you are most welcome to come and stay with us. I've only been there a few days, but I am entranced by the place and the whole surroundings. A shimmering, little back-water of tranquility. It seems untroubled by the ghastly problems of this country. You should come and see. The view from the front porch is spectacularly beautiful.

"Father, I might well take you up on that."

I wound my way back round Majuba, tired because I was a bit dejected. I thought that I might as well go and report to the Bishop on the way back, as it was only a short distance out of my way. Bishop Ulyat had only just got in himself when I arrived about five in the afternoon and he looked tired. I reported the discussions of the last two days and asked that if perchance Lionel did change his mind, I might have permission to link work at the seminary with the ideas about extension work.

"It's all a bit airy-fairy, don't you think," said the weary Bishop, who quite evidently did not want to be bothered with such intangible matters.

"Mm, I think the idea is excellent. Whether it will work or not would seem to depend very much on the individual. Anyway with Lionel at the seminary we would get the best of both jobs, as it were. If his extension thing doesn't take off, we have him there teaching. And if it does start to happen, we can then decide about making him a full-time worker and you have lost nothing."

"Yes," he said doubtfully, "well, alright, you can have the permission to negotiate on those terms, but I rather think that you won't get Lionel. He is still very mixed up."

I shared a pound of sausages with the Bishop and did not get home until about half past seven, when it was already dark.

"Oh, you've come home then," said Fred, when I entered. "You look as if you need a pick-me-up."

"Well, after all the last two days I feel a bit shredded."

"You've only just missed Lionel on the phone. He wants to come down after New Year."

"Oh, I see. Yes, I invited him for a few days any time he wanted to come. He's been through it a bit – I'll tell you later – needs to sort himself out."

"No", said Fred, impatiently, "not a holiday. He said you had talked him into teaching here."

"What" I yelled, and then I laughed so loudly that Fred's face showed concern, as if I were hysterical.

I calmed down a little and went to the phone.

"That you, Steel?" I asked when a reply came.

"Ah, Torkington, I thought you might ring," Lionel paused and I could hear his distinctive chortling laugh at the other end of the line. "I take it Fred has given you my message."

"Indeed, yes. I must confess to finding it an amazing about-face, though of course extremely heartening. Nothing I said, I presume?"

"Well, of course it had a lot to do with what you said, Father. I was going over it all by myself, after you left, and then with John when he got in. His ideas of bringing undue influence to bear are not as upstandingly British as yours, you know."

"How do you mean?"

"Well, after hearing what you had said and my reply, he threw his hands in the air and said 'You bloody fool, Steel, you want your head looking at. It's damn-well gift-wrapped for you.' Anyway, he came across with some pretty strong stuff and said the least I should do in my own best interests was to go and have a look-see. So I thought that I could come down and give it a go for six months anyway; and then we can review the situation. So what do you think?"

"You have swung right over to the opposite viewpoint haven't you? There is a middle road, like coming and having a look before the thing starts on January the twentieth."

"My dear Torkington, you appear to have no grasp of the

115

situation. Schedules, rotas, timetables, division of subjects have to be sorted out; books and equipment have to be bought or checked over; desks obtained; to say nothing of the central matter of the kitchen with menus worked out on a weekly basis, a system for buying in bulk and discounts to be obtained for that. We need all the time we can get. Perhaps I should come down immediately after Christmas."

I was hardly able to believe my ears. I was dumbfounded, and speechless, as I strove to take in this change. A voice came down the phone.

"Are you there, Father, are you there?"

"Yes, Steel, still here. A bit dazed, you know, but still here. Funnily enough we had thought of one or two of the things you mentioned, but you are right about the need to push on with the job. Listen, you come down whenever you like, but for the rest of this week, which means virtually up to Christmas, we shall be engaged in throwing furniture about and it seems a bit of a waste of time for you to be here during that. My suggestion would be that you come down certainly on January the second, or between Christmas and New Year, if you want. O.K.?"

"O.K., Sam, that's fine. I'll give you a ring about the date I'm coming, but see you soon, eh?" He sounded positively happy.

Fred was sitting in the living room with a broad grin on his face. The telephone was situated on a wall-stand in the corridor and Fred had listened to the conversation with interest and no small amusement.

"I gather you have had a bewildering two days."

"You could say that," and I sank into a chair. "Fred, you spoke earlier of a pick-me-up; do you have the makings of one?"

"I do, I do," he replied with the air of one about to reveal hidden treasure.

"I opened a cupboard in the kitchen and found right at the back two or three bottles. One was cheap sherry, which I sampled just to be sure it was not poison."

"Quite right too."

"I remain uncertain about that one, because it tastes nasty. But there was also an unopened bottle of Martell brandy."

"Fred, I have need of it, or some of it, that is."

"I thought you might," he said rising.

"It has been a hard day, and the mind is still reeling a bit. However, as well as treating the brandy as a medicine, I see no reason why we should not also allow it to fulfill the function of a celebration. All's-well-that-ends-well sort of thing."

"Exactly," agreed Fred, and poured two medicinal tots. The second tots would be celebratory.

Just as we had begun to recover after a healthy sip each, the phone rang.

I was nearest the door and went to answer it.

"Hello," said a familiar voice by this time.

"Steel," I said sharply, "Are you drunk?" I asked, as he chortled at the end of the line.

"Not yet Torkington," he spluttered.

"Tcha," I said, "I shall be pretty firm on this sort of behaviour among the staff on the seminary, Steel, I ought to warn you."

"Now, listen, Father, I do feel I owe you an apology – well, about all sorts of things probably, but I seem to remember being rather anti-clerical."

"Well, yes, you were, but that hardly calls for an apology. Some of my best friends among the clergy are quite anti-clerical. Good Lord, I agreed with the bulk of what you said. If I appeared to wince on occasions, it was because your shafts were hitting home and I was being forced to admit to myself my own short-comings. No, no, no, say on in such matters, you will act as my constant conscience."

"It wouldn't be that you are having a drink too would it? You sound very jolly, as well as magnanimous."

"Well, to be truthful, Fred is just plying me with medicinal brandy, required in part to soothe me after some of the barbed remarks you made about the clergy. But I am now recuperating, you have no cause to worry. Well, if that's all this time, I had better be getting back to Fred who will be lonely. See you soon, Lionel."

The house itself was fairly well sorted out by Christmas. Happily, the Sisters at the top of the hill heard we had only just moved in and offered us Christmas dinner. I strongly suspected that Fred had deliberately dropped hints about our disorganisation and the Sisters offered a meal after we had been out and about saying masses. After eating their Christmas dinner, we asked the Sisters if they happened to know anyone locally who could cook for us. We really wanted to find someone we could try out in the holidays before the boys arrived. They said that they would ask around and so they did.

We were rather nervous about the candidate the sisters produced. Prisca was only about twenty. We wondered what experience she could have had and, more important, could she cope with the numbers, feeding up to thirty mouths each day? She was also of an age to have the eyes of the older boys on her. We discussed the matter – to no purpose, all we could do was to wait and see. She had only been with us a few days and we were very satisfied with her cooking so far.

117

Chapter Nine

Lionel arrived on January the second, or rather I went to fetch him, as he had no transport. By the time he came the place was looking lived in and the roof was almost finished on the new building. We were very anxious to get a roof on as soon as possible, complete with gutters, and tanks to catch the water. The summer was half over and there was a desperate need to increase our supply of water. At the convent at the top of the hill they appeared, judging by the vegetation, to get a good supply of rain. But at the bottom of the hill in the much hotter climate of the valley, you could almost see a line where the lusher vegetation ceased and the more arid scrub began. So Jack was hell-bent on getting the roofing iron on, and the tanks in place.

Lionel seemed unimpressed by my worries that Prisca, our young cook, might become the focus of attention of the older boys.

"They are human beings, aren't they? One or two of them are bound to feel attracted to a young woman about the place. I know that they are seminarians, but you can't cut them off from all contact with the rest of the human race. It seems to me that the price to be paid for keeping celibacy going in the Catholic clergy is too high."

Fred and myself looked at each other and laughed.

"Well, you could be right, Lionel," I said, "I suppose the theory is that in the period of decision during training and what is known as 'formation', which I presume can be translated to 'indoctrination', the distraction of female contact should be eschewed as far as possible", I spouted the official line.

"Let's be practical, Torkington", retorted Lionel, "how many of these boys will arrive at the priesthood do you think?"

"Yes, well, you would have thought of that, wouldn't you?" I had rather expected this question from Lionel. "Well, I should think from twenty boys, we might get one, if we are really very lucky, two".

"We might, you say. Or none at all, perhaps. In that case, we should be weeding out as soon as possible those who are manifestly unfit, according to whatever criteria you use, and sending the unsuitable away. Isn't that the policy? It obviously was at the major seminary in Pretoria".

I smiled quietly. "Alright then," I said, "I know very well that very very few, if any, will ever attain to the priesthood. As far as I am concerned, I shall never send one of the boys away from here, merely because I feel he will never become a priest. One boy did go and it forced me to take a hard look at the principles guiding me in keeping or dismissing boys. Frankly, I have now reached the position where I don't care if none of them ever become priests. As long as we are able to give some education, and as good as possible an education, to a few boys in this country that's fine. They need every possible aid to combat the enormous disadvantages they have to suffer. It isn't much, is it – twenty boys? But at least I feel we might actually be doing something worthwhile, in a small way."

"Well spoken, Torkington," said Lionel smiling his slow, slightly crooked smile, "those are my sentiments exactly. Mind you, I didn't expect to find yours so similar. I was going to be diplomatic and keep quiet for a bit. Does the Bishop know of your thoughts on the matter?"

"No, not exactly, though he does know of my reservations about minor seminaries. I find it difficult to accept the belief that vocation to the priesthood means God sends down some massive illumination into the mind of a boy of eight or nine and at that tender age he knows indubitably he is destined for the priesthood. In reality I tend to believe that the idea is to get hold of a favourable subject at an early age and indoctrinate him. Personally, I prefer the boy to be somewhat older and thus more able and likely to make a rational decision and choice. I am sure Fred would agree as he was already an adult before he decided to be a priest, as I was myself; not forgetting you Lionel."

"Right; I am glad we agree, Torkington, but enough of policy, what we need is action, man."

And so it was. The next week we worked on schedules, timetables, menus, the lot. One afternoon, as we were seeing light at the end of the tunnel, Lionel's thoughts strayed further afield.

"Sam, what do you think of this place? What do you know about it?"

"Well, you know I love it. Every morning I go out the front door and look over the reserve up to the mountain in the distance. It's a wonderful sight – with the mist sometimes filling the valley and the rising sun shining through it. The whole aspect is so totally un-European – even in South African terms, it is different from what I have been used to – the cacti, the twisted and gnarled and stunted bush, the outcrops of rock. Why, how does it strike you?"

"Oh, yes, all that, I can be lyrical about it too. But what about the neighbours, for instance?"

"Well, our immediate neighbours are an Indian couple. They're Muslim and he's a doctor, I'm told."

"Have you met him?"

"No, only to wave to in passing."

"I think we must introduce ourselves more formally. We are going to need medical attention for the boys from time to time, apart from anything else."

I took Lionel's point. It was time we introduced ourselves to all of our neighbours.

We started to walk about the place, introduced ourselves at one or two of the stores, receiving enthusiastic bids for our custom. The doctor's house and surgery were set back from the road some twenty-five yards. Near the gate was a small, rather old two-storey building, which could only have consisted of two rooms, one up and one down, connected by an outside wooden staircase. The doctor's wife opened the door, smiled as she recognised us and asked us in. The doctor must have heard our arrival, he came out of the living room to greet us.

"Malardi, Dr. Malardi is my name and this is my wife."

"Father Sam Torkington, and this is Dr. Lionel Steel."

"Actually, Father and Doctor, everyone calls me 'Mally', and" he gestured to his wife, "Lindy".

"And Sam and Lionel, as far as we are concerned, Mally."

"Sit down, sit down," Mally insisted. "Now listen, I know Father Joe, and he used to pop in here whenever he wanted, and you must do the same."

Mally was about thirty-five, so we were all about the same age. He had an open manner, suggesting a generous personality, tolerant, friendly and warm. Lindy seemed more watchful, summing us up, but judging from her gentle smile willing to follow her husband's lead for the moment, giving us the benefit of any doubts she might have.

"Well, what do you think of Pomeroy?" asked Mally.

"I think that we both love the place already," said Lionel. "Though we have only just started to look around properly, and to get to know the village and the surrounding country."

"Are you kept busy, Mally? It seems such a delightful backwater here, peaceful and away from the rush of life," I said.

Mally and Lindy exchanged quick glances, Mally chuckled and Lindy forsook for a moment her watchful attitude and in a broad smile revealed a perfect set of white teeth, which gleamed against the background of her smooth brown skin. She was a beautiful woman. She relaxed a little more after that and seemed less guarded towards us. She got up.

"Would you like a drink of tea? she asked.

"Please," we both said, almost simultaneously.

"Oh, there is plenty of work to do," said Mally, "I go out, like Father Neil does, to out-clinics around the whole area most days. You are lucky to catch me in – I have just got back. Be warned Sam, you will not find this such a peaceful backwater as you think," he laughed, and shook his head.

"You have seen the stores in the village, about ten or a dozen of them, eh? Well, they are all general stores and fighting for the same custom, so they are always undercutting each other. This goes on until one goes bust. Then, after a while, he starts up again, under a slightly different name. So you can imagine that they do not all love each other like brothers, even though some are related. Then there is another division -about half are Muslim and the other half are Hindu. So there are all sorts of invisible under-currents. It is even reported that one shop-keeper tried to kill his neighbour the other night. The alleged killer was driving his truck when he recognised his rival walking along the road in the dark. There was no one about, or not near enough to be able to see clearly anyway, so, the story goes, the one in the truck deliberately ran the other one down. I was called and he was certainly quite badly injured: broken leg and arm and one lung damaged. The other, the driver, was full of concern and regret at the unfortunate accident, while the injured man lay there making accusations against him. Of course, there is no way of proving or disproving either and frankly the police don't care to get involved."

"Ah, well, you have shattered my image of the quiet country village, but I suppose where there are human beings, there will be disagreements and quarrels even in the most idyllic conditions."

"You'll have to convert them all, Sam," Mally laughed, as he teased me. "And actually there is nothing very idyllic about this area from the point of view of making a living. The valley with the mountain backing has a wonderful rugged grandeur with the giant boulders and outcrops of rock, but it is very difficult land to work. There is very little grazing for the cattle and water is always scarce."

"Oh, dear," I said, "I had better get rid of my romantic ideas, hadn't I?"

Lindy came in with the tea. She had boiled the milk, as was their custom, we discovered. We told the Malardi's about our plans next door and Lionel outlined his ideas about extension work and asked Mally's opinion about his prospects for success.

"One of your troubles will be that the government, and that means the local police too, are very suspicious of who goes into the reserve. Of course, the main road south, passes through the reserve and they can't really stop you travelling on it, but they get very suspicious if they see you stopped by the road. They assume you are inciting the Africans to something or other. But I think you will be able to get on quietly with such work you don't need to broadcast your intentions and the local police aren't exactly quick off the mark."

As we got up to go, Mally insisted that we must keep in touch and see a lot of each other. About his being doctor for the boys, there was no problem at all.

As we were walking away from the house a car turned in from the road. It was occupied by three stern-faced men, one of whom reluctantly returned our salute as the car drew up by the house.

"I have a funny suspicion, they are officials of some sort. I don't think they have come to wish Mally a Happy New Year," said Lionel to me, out of the corner of his mouth. We went back to the mission.

The next afternoon, we had just come out of one of the stores, when we saw Mally getting out of his Land-rover, higher up the village. He hailed us and we walked over to him. After friendly greetings, Lionel checked out his worries.

"Mally, I didn't like the look of your visitors who arrived as we left yesterday. They didn't really look like travelling drug salesmen."

Mally laughed easily, apparently unoffended by what seemed a prying remark.

"Listen, come back to the house. It's a bit difficult to talk here."

When we arrived, Mally led us round to the back of the house. It perched on the edge of a hillside which fell away almost immediately into the smaller valley, running parallel to the main road. Only when we were standing at the edge of the drop did Mally speak.

"The older man you saw in the car yesterday was a Mr. Odendaal. I don't know who the other two young ones were. I did hear their names, but I didn't really pay much attention. Mr. Odendaal belongs to the Special Branch of the police. They have some weird notion that I am involved in plotting against the government and they raid us periodically."

"Good God," I said, "Do you mean they continue to pester you, just because they have this idea in their heads that you are a subversive?"

"Sam, I would love to subvert them and their regime, wouldn't you, given the opportunity of half a chance of success?" asked Mally quietly. "You can't be what you are and do what you do and still think there is justice in this apartheid system, can you?"

"No, of course not, Mally." I had been caught in a dilemma. It did not take very long for anyone working with Africans in South Africa to see the massive injustice of a totally abhorrent system, but to be actively involved in trying to overthrow it...

"Do you mean to say, that you are actively engaged in trying to overthrow the system?"

"It depends what you mean by 'actively involved'," replied Mally. "I'm not making bombs if that's what you mean. I brought you round the back here for a good reason, it is private and the open air cannot be bugged easily like a house. Myself and my friends from round about – and 'round about' means quite a wide radius in North Natal – get together regularly and discuss the situation. When the police come in by the front gate, my friends disperse over the edge of this hillside and disappear into the bush, while I go out and am pleasant to the Special Branch to give everyone time to get away. It has never failed yet. They always want to search the house for papers. They never, and never will, find any because there aren't any – not here anyway. We meet because we hate the system and it helps to talk about it. It is good to feel there is some organisation ready for when, we hope, things will change. We also get people out of the country when it's too hot for them to stay, so we have contact with expatriates overseas."

Lionel was slowly shaking his head. "Mally, you realize Sam invited me down here to teach in a sleepy little village, where nothing happens." Mally laughed heartily.

"Come inside," Mally invited.

"Lindy," he called, as we went in, "the Catholics are here again."

Lindy came in, smiling. There seemed to be none of the reserve of the previous day in her manner. We must have passed some test. Lionel looked puzzled.

"Mally, why the devil are you saying all this to us? You hardly know us. We might be police spies, or at least in enough disagreement with your views to report what you have said to the police."

"Well, to start with you come from the mission. Joe Banks knows of my views and a little of my meetings. I had supposed that he might have told you about your new neighbours. But anyway," he seemed slightly embarrassed, "I have been able to find out a bit about you. Lionel, you come from Volksrust, from a good white family, from the African point of view. Your workers on the family farm are treated as human beings and, within the confines of the system, your family makes sure that none of them starve or lack medical treatment or schooling. And my information is that you have been heard making more openly hostile comments about the regime in recent years. So you see, we are not really rash. Sam is from overseas and I have less fear that he will be a police spy for that reason. Also he is a Catholic priest and, while there are Catholic priests who seem to be at least partially pro-apartheid, Sam has been working in an entirely African area for three years and my bet would be that he has seen enough to make him anti-government. All this I knew before we even met you. You see, if we have our meetings alongside your mission, I want to know who's living there and what their attitudes are."

"Well, I am impressed," I told Mally, "eh, Lionel?"

"All this in Pomeroy," said Lionel, still shaking his head in disbelief.

"But you were going to tell us about Odendaal," I prompted.

"No, before you start," said Lindy, "do you like curry?"

Lionel and myself looked uncertainly at each other.

"Well, I do," I said. I could see Lionel nodding his head in agreement. "But, please, you mustn't start cooking for us, we..."

"It is all ready; please stay. Listen to Mally while I get things onto the table."

"Mr. Odendaal is a bankrupt farmer from the Free State, who found a job with the Special Branch. They want to recruit men of a dogged sort of denseness and he is an ideal candidate. But don't misunderstand me, they are not all dense; the top brass are very shrewd. But Mr. Odendaal is only the local Special Branch flatfoot and he blunders in here with two of his thick young men about once every three weeks and makes a search. He never tells me what he is looking for. In fact he gets quite embarrassed now. Lindy follows him round with a poker face and watches him without saying anything. And of course they never find anything, which is half their embarrassment."

Lindy came in from the kitchen with things for the table.

"Lindy, have you heard what Mally is saying?" asked Lionel.

"Yes, I can hear from the kitchen."

"But you must offer Mr. Odendaal tea. That would be even more of an embarrassment to him than being watched and followed. I can assure you it is worth a try. A friend of mine did this to the Special Branch after they had been turning his house over for more than an hour and a half. He brought them a tray, saying, 'I'm sure you must be getting thirsty' and they didn't know what to say, and one of them actually blushed. They drank their tea and left very soon after, thanking him profusely."

Lindy laughed and a glint appeared in her eyes.

"It's interesting you should say that," said Mally. "About six weeks ago Odendaal was apologizing after finding nothing again. As he was getting into his car, he turned to me and said, 'We are only doing our job, you know, Doctor'. So I replied 'Oh, I realise that Mr. Odendaal and you would still have your job to do, even if the opposition United Party were in power'. 'That's right, man', he agreed. 'And who knows, Mr. Odendaal, when we get into power, we might give you a job as well,' I told him. "Poor man didn't know what to say. He just got into his car without another word or look at me and went."

The curry was ready, we abandoned conversation and concentrated on the delicious food. Not too hot for the European palate, but definitely curry.

Daniel came on the nineteenth. In his undemonstrative way he was eager to see what this new venture would be like. He probably came back a day early because he was a thoroughly professional teacher and wanted a day to get acquainted with his new colleagues. Lionel and I had discussed what subjects we should all be taking, but we could obviously not finalise things until Daniel arrived. Who was doing Zulu needed no discussion, I declared. Daniel laughed. He offered to teach history. Lionel would do geography and a broad subject we called science which would include biology, botany and anything else Lionel could think of to make use of the bits and pieces of scientific equipment he had salvaged from his practice. I grabbed English, and logically I suppose, religious instruction. Maths we divided between Daniel and myself, he for the lower class, because they would still be taught in Zulu and the upper class for me, in English. Lionel would also teach Afrikaans. All this was done surprisingly quickly with no acrimonious disputes and we felt ready for the morrow.

Daniel wandered over to see the progress on the new building and reminded Jack of his optimistic promises prior to Christmas that the building would be ready for use when he returned. Jack exploded into a long explanation of how the fates, the holiday season and delays in getting supplies had held him up – this problem had been intensified by the reluctance of the Fathers and Dr. Steel to help by running into Dundee for a dozen packets of cement, or fetching sand from the river bed. We had decided to put our feet down firmly with Jack. It was clear that he would use any labour he happened to find about the place and that included us. We had brought back loads from Dundee for him when we had been going in for supplies for the mission. But his next step was to beg us to go on special trips just to fetch his supplies. When Jack had seen we were aware of what he was up to, he laughed:

"Well, you got to try, Father, we are all working for the same thing."

Over tea one morning, before the descent of the boys, I had told him there would be times when the boys could do a little work for him, but only at specified times. We thought it would be good for the boys to get some idea of what Jack was doing and how he did it. Realistically, in South Africa, the vast majority of Africans were destined for manual work and a little expertise in buillding might not go amiss in the future. Apart from that the involvement in building their own classrooms and dormitories would involve them personally.

The twentieth was a chaotic day. The boys were brought to Pomeroy by their respective parish priests, all of whom wanted to have a look at the new seminary. Most had never been to Pomeroy before, situated as it was in one corner of the diocese, and a long way from the main north-south road which ran through the province. And, having found their way there, they wanted a meal. The boys I had no worry about. I knew them all well by this time. They wandered about in small groups, getting used to the new place, talking excitedly waiting for the next arrivals so they could show them around.

"Father, where is the school? Father, where do we play football? Hey, Father have you seen the people here?"

The last question was the one that amused me most. The people they were speaking about were their own people – Zulus – but they did not live in towns, but in the huge reserve stretching away to the South. They were not westernised in dress and what made the boys talk about "these people" was not their dress, but rather their undress. In an area as hot as Pomeroy – and it became hotter as the country fell away towards the great Tugela River – their clothing was minimal. Both men and women wore animal hides covering their lower limbs. From the waist upwards both men and women wore only ornamentation. The women wore marvellous beads and sometimes a cloth shawl about their shoulders. A married woman's hair was coloured with red ochre and built up in cylindrical form about twelve to eighteen inches high widening out to a flat top about the size of a dinner plate. This hair-dressing was coloured with a red ochre. There was no doubt the boys found it as strange as any visitor from Europe might. They gazed in frank amazement for the first week at these "strange people".

My experience of teaching had been very much a part-time affair at Besters. We started the next morning sorting out books and by the end of the week we were in full swing; boys got used to the new teachers and the new teachers got used to the boys. Daniel was delighted with the small numbers in his classes which gave him the first opportunity of really personalised teaching – Lionel took to teaching like a duck to water.

By the end of the second week crammed full of classes; marking books; attending to preparation in the evenings, I knew what teaching was about and was ready to strike anyone who talked about teachers getting long holidays. By Saturday I was tired and ready for two days off. But for all that, it was thoroughly enjoyable. Lionel and I compared notes with Daniel sitting on the sidelines and chuckling at the enthusiasm of the student teachers. I even tried teaching Bible instruction in Zulu. At least a lot of the vocabulary I already knew from the sermons which I had inflicted on the congregations at Besters.

It was not long before Lionel was marching through the bush with bands of boys, studying the local terrain. They would return and try to put it all onto paper. But that was not graphic enough.

"Torkington," he said one evening barging into my room, disturbing me as I read English essays, "we must have sheets of hardboard and plasticine – we are making contour models. Oh, and paints – probably poster paints will be O.K. plus brushes, of course."

It was quite evident that none of these things was available in the village. I said yes and went on with the marking of books.

By dinner the next day Lionel was berating me because his requests had not yet been met.

"How can I possibly teach without the necessary equipment," he moaned. He was marching up and down my room.

"Yes, but I cannot be in two places at once, Steel, I shall endeavour to zoom into Dundee after school today and obtain the required trivia." I was pacing the room too. It had become our curious way of working things out. We were both room-walkers unfortunately. This was fine when we confined it to his or my room, but in a more public room it caused Fred to become agitated and unsettled, until he bellowed at us to sit down.

"Trivia?" said Lionel stopping in his tracks. "Essentials! we are at a stage when we cannot carry on without them"

"O.K. then, this afternoon. I can combine it with some other shopping."

"And another thing. We really ought to have a deep freeze to save on costs", insisted Lionel, "You can get paraffin-powered ones, just right for us". So another special trip to Dundee.

After we had installed the deep freeze, Lionel, our animal expert, went off to seek out sheep. He came back with two in the back of the Kombi, held fearfully by four boys he had taken with him. I imagine the sheep were also fearful, as well they might have been. They were slaughtered the next day with the interested assistance of all the boys -it was a Saturday morning – skinned and butchered into joints and

126

chops and miscellaneous bits for the pot. The boys were delighted at the prospects of meat dinners to come. That weekend we had a minor feast to celebrate.

By Easter it was apparent that Prisca, our cook, though battling valiantly, was getting worn down by the constant demands of, what was for her, large scale cooking. One day I caught her in the kitchen sitting down after preparing the dinner, looking very weary. I kicked myself for not keeping a more careful eye on her. She jumped up as I came in, as if I was about to upbraid her for slacking. I decided to leave out any subtlety.

"Prisca, you are tired," I stated.

She looked down shyly, and murmured, "Yes, Father".

"Now, please tell me, is all this a bit too much for you?"

"Perhaps, Father, but I do not mind carrying on, because who will cook for you all?"

"Well, that depends. Suppose that I find someone else who can cook, would you like to work with her, or do you want me to find someone just to assist you."

"Father," she said apologetically, "if you could find someone to be cook, perhaps I could help and also do some house work."

"Well, alright, we'll try that. Now, there is only one more week before the boys go for the Easter holiday, you can manage until then?"

"Oh, yes, Father," she agreed brightly, now that the burden had been lifted.

In fact, I already had heard of someone in the village who could help us out. Mally had asked some time ago if I needed a cook, as he knew a girl who could fill the post. She was half Indian, half African and stayed in the Indian community. I had asked Mally if she could cook for us during the holidays and continue when the boys returned from holidays.

Some ten days before the holidays, Jack announced proudly that the first room was completely ready. We decided that we should do a little moving round in the holidays rather than disturbing the existing arrangments. The boys went home, Daniel went home. We helped Fred with the Holy Week services, and then got down to reorganising the seminary. We decided to invite the Bishop down at the beginning of the new term, to show off our progress. He had kept away so far. I rather think he had been nervous about coming down, in case he was worried by all the problems we were facing. I had tried to reassure him over the phone, but I think he really believed I was hiding something.

We were conscious we had seen very little of the Malardis during the term, but then we had seen very little of any outsiders. We had become thoroughly unwelcoming to any visitors that turned up. We soon realised that a night chatting left us tired for school the next day. So Lionel and I took to leaving Fred to cope, wishing people a cheery good night about half past nine, or ten at the latest.

We popped in to see the Malardis late one afternoon to say hello. They were sat with their two young children and a couple of visitors we did not know, eating curry. Our envy must have been transparent.

"Come in, come in," Mally gestured at us with a ricey hand. At their table they ate traditionally using their hands "You must have some curry."

We sat down expectantly. We tasted, we gasped. It was burning hot. We cried at the experience and Mally laughed, but contritely.

"My friends, I am really so sorry. I should have warned you. Another friend has cooked this one. She is a Hindu and makes a much hotter curry – not that she can't make it more gentle, but this one is truly hot. Look, some poached eggs, alright?"

Reluctantly and tearfully we agreed. As we talked after eating Mally suddenly realised something.

"But you do not know that we are moving."

"Moving?" we asked, "Where to?"

"We are going to Durban. I'm moving for my career and also, between ourselves, for political reasons, I would like to move now. But there is some delay, because I have to have my banning order changed to the magisterial district of Durban."

"We didn't even know that you were under a banning order," said Lionel.

"Well, it confines me to the magisterial district of Dundee, but the supervision is not very strict here and I have taken many chances and got away with them. I shall have to be more careful in Durban."

"Well, we are glad for you, but sorry you are leaving Pomeroy. When do you hope to get away and what will happen to the clinic?" I asked.

"We really don't know. As you know there is a district surgeon who comes out this way once a week and deals impatiently with anyone who asks for help and can pay for it. So, whatever we may think of him, there will still be a doctor available. Of course, I should love to see another doctor here, but there are not many who would consider coming to this, what did you call it, Sam? – peaceful, sleepy backwater" he laughed, "I am trying to find someone as I should, of course, at least like to be able to sell the house, if not the practice. Ultimately we have decided, if all fails, we shall reluctantly have to go without getting a replacement for the practice."

As an after-thought he added with a laugh: "You wouldn't like to buy it, would you, Sam? Make it a hall of residence for your University."

We were depressed by the proposed departure of our neighbours. We had seen all too little of them. Although we were not part of their political circle, we had almost unconsciously been elated to think that in little out-of-the-way places throughout the country there were centres where, even if nothing else were done, men and women met together to give each other hope. Groups that changed the isolated dreaming of one man that 'if only...' to the group conviction of 'when'.

"Lionel," I said as we walked slowly back the few yards to the seminary, "do you think that there is any possibility that the Bish would consider buying Mally's place and try to get a doctor here, even perhaps someone from overseas?"

"Oh, Torkington," he began with a dismal sigh, "he will cry poverty you know that. I suppose to be fair, it would cost rather a lot of money; but then perhaps Mally might let it go for a reasonable price, as he's had difficulty finding a buyer. You know, Sam", he was warming to the idea, "you might at least tell him about it."

I went to the phone as soon as we got in.

"Yes?" enquired a tired and bored voice. He would not learn to answer the phone properly.

"Me," I told him. "Now, the Malardis, our next door neighbours, the doctor, you know, they are moving to Durban and he is looking for someone to buy the place, and the practice as well if possible. I thought that I should tell you in case your ambitions ran in that direction. Mally suggested it as an adjunct to your 'University'".

That raised a chuckle from him. Cos and I had learned at Besters that it didn't pay to argue with him. The issues became so muddled – on occasions we found that at the end of a couple of hours' discussion we had even changed sides. The strategy was to sow seeds and hope they germinated. So I left him with the information and didn't try to argue one way or the other.

"We haven't got any money," was his immediate and expected reaction.

"No, I realise that," I agreed, "Just thought I ought to tell you, in case .. you know."

"Yes, yes, dear boy. Wish we could see our way clear. Really it is an area crying out for a medical centre of some sort." He was musing sadly.

"Everything alright with you, there?"

"Oh, yes, the boys are off for the holidays, but we are reasonably happy with the first term."

"Good. Well, thank you anyway, old boy."

"Any use?" asked Lionel when I re-appeared.

"Not immediately. But you never know with his lordship."

We did know by Sunday evening; the Bishop phoned.

"Sam, I'm coming down to talk to you about the next door place in the morning, is that O.K.?" He sounded chirpy and business-like. It looked as if he had made a decision.

"Sure, we'll be here."

"O.K., old boy. See you tomorrow."

I told the others the boss was due to arrive the following morning.

"Good," said Fred, "I have a couple of things to see him about."

"And I have not yet been given a contract," complained Lionel, "I want to see him too."

"I think you'll have to get in line. He seems to be taken up with the next door project and if I am any judge of his moods, he is now hell-bent on having it. He has probably spent the last three days reshuffling his projects, putting Mally's place at the top of the list."

We were having a quiet beer, prior to sampling Fred's cooking. I had found the cook Mally had recommended and Lilly was starting the next day — to practise on us before the boys came back. Fred had announced he would treat us to omelettes that evening. We offered our help, but were thrown out of the kitchen. No, we could not beat the eggs — it had to be done very carefully — just go and sit down. We admitted later that his fluffy creations were delicious, but in order to enjoy them at their best, fresh from the pan, we had to have an anti-social meal, eating in relays. Fred was exasperated by our minor criticism and only mollified when Lionel went to his room and appeared with more cans of beer.

The Bishop was with us before ten in the morning, obviously determined to do business. He was agreeably surprised at his tour of the nearly completed seminary, but nonetheless took the opportunity to urge Jack on.

"Lying down on the job again, Jack, what?" he roared, his voice echoing round the empty room we were standing in.

Jack was undismayed; he knew the Bishop well enough to take no offence at his comments.

"Monsignor, I get no help from these priests. They do nothing for me. Everything I do myself. No proper sand, no cement, not enough water..." Jack started his usual litany.

"Yes, yes, yes, I know, I know," the Bishop cut in on him. "I just want to see it finished before the winter, d'you see?"

"Of course," beamed Jack, this time with reason for his optimism, as he was near completion.

"Now, dear boy," said the Bishop confidentially, as we went into the house, "How about a cup of tea for your old uncle, eh?" He was evidently in a good mood.

We were passing the kitchen door. He looked in, hoping no doubt to see a cockroach, to confirm his worst fears about my inability to run the place properly. Instead he saw Lily.

"Ah, and whom have we here? I don't think I know you, do I?"

"Monsignor, this is Lilly, our new cook. She has just joined us today."

"Really?" Well just see that he pays you well, Lilly. Now, are you going to be so kind as to make us a cup of tea."

"Oh, yes," said Lilly glad to have some thing to do. She would not be too busy until the boys returned, and on her first morning she had been standing in the kitchen, not quite sure what to do.

We had, of course, already guessed the Bishop's interest in the next door property. His main point was that its proximity to the seminary made it very desirable, even if we could not immediately get a doctor. We could perhaps have a nurse calling there a couple of times a week and find a doctor to hold a weekly surgery. In view of the huge population of the reserve, making provision for services for the people was of paramount importance, he said as if trying to convince the board of directors.

We pointed out we were already convinced of the potential in the place. He was a bit deflated, his fine oration cut short, but then he got down to practicalities.

"Now, Lionel," he approached somewhat gingerly. "I wondered if I could ask you to be a kind of overseer of the place – always supposing that we get it, I mean. I realise you are a veterinary doctor, but you would be more acceptable, and of course more knowledgeable than," he paused looking round, "er – Sam, for instance. D'you see what I mean?"

"Hang on a minute," I said, wanting to have my say before Lionel possibly sold himself into another job. "Lionel is very much full-time at teaching at the moment and anyway you seem to have forgotten the commitment to let him get on with his extension work."

"Thanks, Sam, I am content for the moment to shelve the extension work – and anyway I am getting to know different local people and laying possible foundations for all that. As to the clinic next door, I don't mind acting as agent on the spot, but I don't want to be totally in charge. As Sam says we have a lot going on here and that takes most of our time. Having said that, as we get more accustomed to teaching, it will not take so much time to organise ourselves. There should be more time in the coming terms for other projects."

"Thank you, Lionel," said the Bishop.

Lionel continued, "I should like all this written down – what my duties would be, in the event of any of this happening, I want terms of reference, and a proper contract – a thing I have not yet had, Monsignor."

"Oh, yes, yes, we can go into all that later. Heavens above, you speak as if I would cheat you, or something, what?"

"Monsignor, I'm sorry, but I don't trust the Church," Lionel pressed on, now getting into his stride, "I've seen so many laymen trust the Church and be let down. The Church uses people and then drops them when they are no longer any use. I want some security out of this job. I have nothing personally against any of you here, but you will not always be the Bishop or the Rector of this minor seminary and I want something on paper to prove that the job I am doing is the one I was taken on to do."

The wind had been taken out of the Bishop's sails a little.

"Alright, dear boy, you have a point and I don't doubt there is some validity in it. You will get your contract, I'll see to that." He paused to let the dust settle. "Now," he said briskly, stirring for action again, "can we see the property?"

"Well, I haven't told them you're interested, but if they are in, I am sure they will be delighted to see you," I said.

We all walked down the road to Malardi's. They were out. They had left, said the housekeeper, for Durban on Saturday. Mally had got a four day permission to leave the magisterial district to make some arrangements for moving down to Durban. They would be back tomorrow evening. I told the housekeeper, who knew us well, why we wanted to look round and to see Mally. She said we were most welcome to look round and that the Malardi's would not mind at all. So we had a thorough-going look at the whole property: house, surgery, small clinic; we paced out the measurements of the area and wondered what was in his lordship's mind as he viewed the whole site and pondered, without revealing his thoughts.

"Yes," he said slowly after about three-quarters of an hour, "I think that will do for the moment."

We thanked the house-keeper and strolled back to the seminary.

"What have you in mind for the place?" I ventured.

"Nothing really yet, dear boy. Let's see if we can get it at a reasonable price first of all."

Fred drove up as we neared the house and jumped out in front of the Bishop.

"Ah, just the man I want to see. Can you spare a couple of minutes" he asked.

"Oh, crumbs, that sounds ominous. Well, just a couple of minutes, because I must get back." They disappeared inside.

On Wednesday Lionel and myself treated ourselves to a short outing. We went over the small valley to see an African wood sculptor we had heard about. He was a very old man, but with bright alive eyes and a fund of stories about the old days. He worked with any local woods, some of them very hard, and one a very striking redwood, which at times looked as if it had been smeared with blood. While we watched, and he talked, he took an unlikely looking branch of a tree and methodically and sure-handedly fashioned a big wooden cooking spoon out of it. He used an axe which had been honed so often that it was now only about half its original size. It was very sharp and the old man's aim was unerring. He made brisk, accurate passes at the wood with the axe and the spoon magically appeared in only few minutes. We wanted him to show the boys how this sort of thing was done and to teach them some of his expertise. We told him we were very interested in his work and any other craft work done on the reserve. To his delight we bought a few articles and walked back to the village.

As we were passing Malardi's, we were hailed by Mally from his front door. He was standing there with an elegantly dressed African. A 'beetle' Volkswagon was parked outside the house and, as we approached we noticed the number plates were not like South African ones.

"So you got back, Mally," I said as we drew near.

"Well, wait till I tell you, Sam," said Mally, "But let me introduce you to Dr David Molefe; David, this is Father Sam Torkington and Doctor Lionel Steel. You now see in the flesh the gentlemen I have been telling you about. David a co-religionist of yours, Sam."

"Oh, really? Where are you from Doctor?"

"Oh, please Father, my name is David. I am from Botswana, though of course originally I was from Johannesburg." His English was very smooth, with almost no African accent.

"This is a beautiful place," said David. "But I am taken aback a little. Here we are, two white men, an Indian and an African chatting and passing the time of day in full view of anyone who cares to see. Have things changed so much since I was here last, has apartheid gone?"

We all laughed.

"Not if Sergeant Wessels can help it, it hasn't. He would probably crash his truck, if he passed at this moment," said Lionel, grinning.

"Have you got a few minutes?" Mally asked.

"Certainly", I said, "as a matter of fact, we wanted to see you sometime – but that can wait for another day."

"Come inside. I want to tell you how I met David." He gestured towards David's car at the parking area around the front of the house as we went indoors. "You will notice I have no car. My car broke down near Pinetown and I was stuck by the side of the road, with the bonnet of the car up and no idea what was the matter with it. I was just about to find a phone box and call a friend in Durban, when David pulled up and asked if he could help me. I said I'd appreciate a lift into Durban if he was going that far. So Lindy and myself went with David into Durban. We got talking and I discovered that David was from Botswana on holiday, but also looking for a job. He had no rigid plans, so I invited him up here. He's never been to this part of the country before. So he's staying for a few days."

Then Mally said: "I hear the Bishop was here while we were away."

"Yes, that's what we were going to see you about. But some time later this week will do, Mally, no hurry."

"Is he interested?" asked Mally, unable to wait.

"Oh, yes, he is, but I think there would have to be a lot of discussion before he would make any hard decision.

"Of course," conceded Mally, "but at least we can talk about it."

I suspected I knew how Mally's mind was working and wanted to get away before he put us in an embarrassing position. He obviously thought he had found a likely candidate for the practice in Dr Molefe, but one who could not buy it himself. The Bishop offered the possibility of an employer for the Doctor and the continuation of the practice. At this stage I did not want to get into a discussion about it. We pleaded the need to get back to the seminary, and promised we would tell the Bishop Mally was interested in talking with him.

A week later Mally came round to see us, alone. David was still staying with them. He was going about with Mally to the clinics and getting to know the area. He came to say that David was fascinated with the area and would love to take over from him. Not only that, he told us, but he had watched him very closely in his dealings with patients and was very impressed with his manner and with his clinical skill in diagnosis and treatment. His background, he said, had been in hospital work, but he wanted a change and hence his expedition to South Africa.

We explained to Mally that we could not make any decisions about either buying the practice or employing David. But if he was willing to stay, a meeting could be set up with the Bishop. We gave Mally the Bishop's number and he promised to ring and fix a mutually agreeable date for a meeting.

We reported all this to the Bishop, who was delighted and looked forward to hearing from Mally.

Chapter Ten

The boys came back the next day. It felt much easier re-starting than it had in January when we were so new to it all. Lionel and myself had become old hands in one term. I began to be gratified by the alacrity with which some of the boys learnt English. One or two of them appeared to be very bright and wrote good English in their essays, even if the language was a trifle florid at times.

Within a couple of weeks negotiations between Mally and the Bishop seemed to have progressed very quickly. It appeared Mally had reduced the price in consideration of the difficulty in selling the practice and because he was anxious that the service to the people of the district would continue. With regard to David, the Bishop was prepared to accept Mally's recommendation – David, had now been working with Mally for about three weeks. He had no job to rush back to and was content with the situation as it stood, especially as Mally was now paying him. If a job materialised he would stay, if not he would travel on with no regrets. He would, at some point, have to go back to Botswana to tidy up his affairs and collect his papers and luggage if he was staying.

Mally now planned to leave in a fortnight and had given the authorities a date at which his banning order could be changed from Dundee to Durban. He said he would not be giving a farewell party, because he felt that he did not want to gather all his friends together in one place, as it would give the police an excuse to raid the place.

So they slipped away quietly one morning with a brief hand-shake and an invitation to call on them when we were in Durban. We readily accepted that.

Lionel was now acting as the Bishop's agent for the practice next door. He found David was a very pleasant man to work with. He seemed to be conscientious and hardworking and remained cool and unflappable under pressure. A nurse had been employed to help in the out-clinics and the main clinic seemed to be working well. David had the most charming manner and his engaging personality seemed to draw as many patients as we had seen there in Mally's time.

One day after school, Lionel came in, and as was his wont, fell into an easy chair, apparently exhausted. This always seemed to amuse Daniel, who remained unaffected by his day's work, coming through it all quite unruffled.

"Torkington, I'm finished, finished, man," he insisted. "Look here, these boys have no conception of what an ocean-going ship is like, the Transvaal crowd have never seen the sea and only one of the Natal boys has. We must arrange a trip to the docks at Durban."

"Good idea, Steel," I agreed absently, sipping tea and reading an article in a magazine.

The next day the idea had grown on him. At mid-morning break he revealed his plan.

"Torkington, we shall take them South for a few days. We can camp somewhere."

"Oh can we?" I asked weakly, "What about equipment?"

"I've thought of that," He said. "All we need is a few pans from the kitchen, a blanket each and we can buy food as we go."

"Beds?" I asked.

"My dear Torkington, we don't need beds. We sleep on the beach, we scoop out the sand to make a comfortable position and one blanket is ample in the summer on the coast."

"Oh, well, if you say so," I capitulated.

About the end of September that year I thought I ought to remind the Bishop I was due to have home leave the next March. The reason for the leave, some time before I was strictly due for it, was the ordination of my brother. I had in my own mind worked out a scheme which would keep the seminary going without me, so that I could take up my duties when I returned. I rang him that evening.

He hadn't forgotten. In fact he had already his own ideas about how the seminary would manage in my absence.

"Well," he began, I thought a little diffidently after I had outlined my plan, "I haven't told you before, old boy, but there may have to be a different plan. There is a priest, whom you won't know, he has been in the Holy Land for years, who is willing to come out here. But he fears that at his advanced age he will not be able to manage the sort of rough travelling we have to do to cover the out-stations and I have offered him the seminary, knowing that you will be away from the beginning of next year. That way I could use a young man like yourself on one of the more difficult missions that the older priests can't cope with, d'you see old boy?" In the silence which followed his remarks he tried to soften the blow, "Of course, it isn't certain he will come. In which case you will continue in post as you are now. I am, as you know, most grateful for all that you have done, and always shall be. You do see it from my point of view, don't you, dear boy?"

"As of this moment I find it difficult to see your point of view, but I suppose I shall, given time," I told him disconsolately.

"I do appreciate how you feel, Sam, but I am trying to consider the needs of the whole diocese. Anyway, let's leave discussion of it for the time being. Is Fred there, I'd like a word with him?"

I called Fred to the phone. Then I slumped into a chair and told Lionel what the Bishop had just said.

"You're joking, Torkington," he said, but he knew I wasn't.

"Do I look as if I'm joking?" I asked him. We sat in silence. Fred came back from the phone, looking ruddy.

"He told me what he had just told you," he said to me, "and I told him what I thought. He said you sounded a bit upset. I asked what he expected you to feel, after getting this seminary going, working it up from nothing for the last four years and just when it is beginning to really get going, he drops you."

136

"What did he say to that?" I asked.

'Oh, crumbs' is all he could manage," said Fred.

I managed to laugh.

Of course, this was all right up Lionel's street.

"This is so typical of the way the Church works. They don't see you as human beings; they pick you up, use you and throw you down when they have finished with you. Who is to be your successor anyway?"

"Bloke called Eustace, who has been in the Holy Land for many years, he said. We don't know him. "Right," said Fred, "We need a drink, I happen to have a bottle of brandy."

By the end of the evening I could see the logic of the Bishop's position and his thinking, but that did not make me any more enthusiastic about it. I knew that in the long run I would do as I was told and even remain friends with the great man, even though I cursed him roundly that night.

Lionel started to organise the camping trip over the following weeks. He wrote to Mally, knowing he would have contacts along the coast north of Durban and that we could find help from his Indian friends. He also wrote to an old school friend who was a school teacher near Durban and asked if we could find accommodation for a night at his school. We could pack as many boys as possible into the Kombi and some could come in the small Volkswagen which Lionel had recently acquired and thus, packed solid, we would travel very slowly to the coast.

In November we had the end of year examinations and were highly delighted with the results. There were occasions, especially for some reason on Monday mornings, when the boys were dead and unresponsive, but normally teaching them was a joy. They were very keen to learn. I recalled how I had wasted my time at school, for the most part avoiding work and saving my energy for the rugby field. With the African boys there was no playing in class; there was an eagerness, which unfortunately was a little blunted, as I say, on Monday mornings. On such occasions I would declare a general knowledge period. I recall a revealing question one Monday about who does the manual work in England, if there were so few black men. And another embarrasing one about how the questioner could get a job as an airline pilot. Of course, in the country he lived in, he couldn't. I floundered about trying to break it to him.

The day for the start of our expedition to the coast started with excitement as the boys dashed in all directions. A harassed Steel gave orders and contradictory orders. Daniel Makhaya stood by laughing, secure in the happy knowledge that he was free of boys till the start of next year. Nor would he be compelled to endure the rigours of rough camping with the lunatic white men. The convoy of two vehicles got under way, only an hour or so later than planned. Lionel so often said, when we started to get hot and bothered about plans going awry,

"Torkington, does it really matter?" He was right of course, but by the time he said, it had invariably worried himself to a headache.

We arrived at Stanger about four hours later. We parked alongside the memorial statue of Shaka, the great chief who united the clans into the Zulu tribe and led them with unchallenged success in battle at the beginning of the last century. I think I was more impressed than the boys. But then having spent the journey packed in like sardines they were a bit subdued. Lionel went off to find the Indian gentleman who was to allow us access to a beach, through his farm. The sand was secluded enough for white men and Africans to stay together without much fear of detection. Lionel returned with instructions and we blindly followed him over seemingly interminable, bumpy roads. Suddenly, through the lush sub-tropical coastal undergrowth, we came upon the beach, and down a small escarpment, the sea itself. Without more ado, I stripped down to my underpants and plunged in. The last fifty miles had been gradually getting stickier and stickier as we neared the humid coastal area. The sea was marvellous. I turned after a few seconds to see if anyone was following me. The boys were standing looking at the sea in some awe, some actually gaping open-mouthed. Slowly, one by one they followed Lionel and I into the water. It was mid-afternoon and we stayed in the water, on and off, until the sun went down. It was delicious. I kept going in and out, getting wet and then drying and diving in again. Once the boys had become accustomed to being buffeted by the rollers and got used to the idea that the water was salty, they loved it. They asked questions like:

"What about sharks? How far does the water stretch? Where does so much water come from?"

Lionel, I could see, felt justified in bringing them down to the coast, if only because they asked these questions.

When I got out finally and allowed my skin to dry, I felt it getting tight and sore. The sun had caught me unawares and I was badly burnt. As the night came on and we had our simple meal of sausages, bread and tea, I began to be feverish. The boys started to feel a bit apprehensive about sleeping in the open air. They had questions about snakes and we could hear monkeys chattering nearby in the dense undergrowth. Eventually, we satisfied them by arranging to sleep in a long line, boy next to boy with Lionel at one end and me at the other. I spent the night alternating between burning and shivering. I got up the next morning feeling tired and tender. Before the sun rose high I went for a bathe in the sea and the salt at first bit into my tender skin, but it soothed it somewhat after a time. I got out and dressed, determined to keep covered that day.

We had some breakfast and bundled all the bedding into the cars. Soon after nine o'clock we started off for Durban, going south down the coast road. To the boys it was all new and exciting and they suffered the cramped conditions well until we got to Durban. We drove through the city and saw the white tourists from the Transvaal, the Free State as well as inland Natal disporting themselves on the beach, where of course we could not take the boys. We drove right into the heart of the docks and again had the satisfaction of seeing the astonishment on the boys' faces at the size of the big ocean-going ships and liners, being loaded and unloaded, in the harbour.

Obviously we could not all go into any cafes together. We solved this problem by going into a 'take-away' place and coming out, to the astonishment of the owners, with two large cardboard boxes full of food. We sat and watched the busy activity of the docks while we ate.

Later we parked and wandered about the shops of the city. In the middle of the afternoon we made our way to the school where Lionel's friend taught. The boys of the school had all gone home, and most of the staff, so there was no great fear of embarrassing our host in front of his colleagues who might well disapprove of this racial mixing. The boys were shown to a dormitory and found beds, which delighted them. They had not been entirely at their ease the night before on the beach.

Ben, the chief cook of the school, who was an African was highly amused at the idea of two white men and twenty black boys, travelling round southern Natal and staying together for a holiday. He kept shaking his head and laughing every time we saw him. After our meal most of the boys confessed they were looking forward to a good sleep. We chatted and had a drink with Lionel's friend, Gerry, for a short time. The pair of them were waxing idealistic about the possibility of a link-up between his school and the seminary, including exchange visits. I had no wish to pour cold water on this, but I had to point out that though we might think it an excellent idea, the parents of at least some, and probably many, of the boys would object. They might even inform the police of such activities, and we should all get a lot of unwelcome attention.

"But don't you think, Father," asked Gerry, "that we should be taking the initiative and not let ourselves be held in thrall by government regulations?

"Oh, Gerry, I agree with you. I can do it, because I am white and have nothing to lose. I have no family to support and, as an Englishman, all they will do is throw me out if they don't like the way I conduct myself. They don't always make direct attacks on people like me. They attack the more vulnerable, don't they? The more impressionable? They might well not attack you directly, but they might go and see the parents of the boys at your school and harass them, ask them if they mind their boys being mixed up with black boys. And then you start to lose children from the school, discreetly withdrawn, after parents have had a visit from the Special Branch, until you go out of business and they have won."

"Okay, but I think perhaps we could work out something if we were discreet."

"Of course, we could, Torkington" Lionel burst in, "you get too fearful altogether. We shall do it," he proclaimed dramatically and defiantly. "But not tonight, I am too tired and am going to bed."

"Yes, me too," I said, "Pardon us, Gerry, but we are sore – well I am – and need rest. But before you go, Steel, I want cream applied to my back."

The next morning, after a leisurely breakfast, we wandered round the grounds. The boys marvelled at the sports facilites and acres of space to play football, rugby and cricket. Then we started for home. We bought fish and chips for everyone on the way back, which was very well received, and arrived back, thankfully, about five in the afternoon.

The next day the boys went home for the Christmas holidays. I rang up the Bishop to announce the end of term and report all had gone well with the camping trip. The Bishop appeared to have a pessimistic mind, though I suspected his pessimism was mostly verbal. He presupposed that with such a venture -he would call it a reckless adventure – as taking boys camping, one would expect to lose at least one or two. In this case his alarm had taken the form of supposing, when he heard that we would be sleeping on the beach, that several boys would inevitably be drowned. Hence his question:

"Did you bring all my boys back with you?"

Cos and I had found this constant fear that the worst had happened irresistably tempting. It took so little to start him off. Cos told me of one conversation, which went like this.

"Hello, old boy, you O.K.?"

"Oh, yes, thank you."

"And Sam?"

"Not too bad, considering."

"Considering what, dear boy?"

"Well, the accident, you know."

"The accident?" echoed the Bishop, with a tremour in his voice.

"In the car, you know," as if reminding someone of something they really ought not to have forgotten.

"The car?" repeated the Bishop, fear gripping him. He was, no doubt, worried about a large garage bill as much as my health.

"Yes," continued Cos, "happily he's not as badly hurt as was at first thought."

"Oh, crumbs, what's he done now?"

At this point Cos was unable to contain himself any longer and the deception was revealed as he burst out laughing. It did not seem to matter how often we did this. The Bishop nearly always began by believing it, though latterly he took more salt with such stories. He himself admitted this tendency to credulity. "I always", he said sadly on one occasion, "believe every travelling salesman who comes to the door".

I reassured him. All had gone well and had apparently been enjoyed by everyone except myself. I had gone through most of the trip in extreme pain as I lost the vast majority of my skin. This was the first time we had spoken on the phone since he had mentioned his proposals for my replacement at the seminary. He had written me several notes about different matters, but had not talked. He was cautious and a little formal, but then he ventured timidly:

"You still cross about future arrangements, Sam?" What was the use anyway it was nearly Christmas.

"Certainly," I told him, "nothing has changed. I have in fact spoken to my solicitors."

"Oh, crumbs," he said. But he knew he was off the hook and was pleased that relations could be resumed as before.

"Anyway," he was careful not to be too business-like, "I believe Eustace will be here in February." You might have supposed from his tone that someone else was imposing Eustace on us and there was nothing either of us could do about it.

"I have big plans for you, dear boy, when you get back from overseas," another fear gripped him, "you are coming back aren't you?" he enquired anxiously.

"Well, that depends on what you are offering."

"I don't know yet – or rather" he hastily corrected himself "I can't divulge it at this stage."

"I see. Well, I'll give it some thought and let you know."

"O.K., old boy." He rang off, knowing all was well again between us. I still hated the idea of leaving the seminary, but I saw no point in going about like a bear with a sore head. And anyway that was difficult to maintain; being angry burnt up too much energy.

Chapter Eleven

Lionel came back from next door for his lunch. Since his appointment as superintendent of the clinic and practice, Lionel had been calling in there at least twice a week for friendly checks and discussions. He reported that all was going well, David was industrious and regular in his attendance at the out-clinics. The nurse, Angela, had settled down very well was co-operating well with the doctor, was liked by the patients and certainly apeared to be a very cheerful and agreeable person. It all sounded too good to be true. He announced that David was to throw a Christmas party, a couple of days before Christmas and we were all invited. He was inviting one or two of the staff from Tugela Ferry Hospital, situated about twelve miles from us, and some friends from Ladysmith and from the village itself. Lionel had accepted for himself and suggested that Fred and I would not want to miss it.

I decided I ought to make an effort to look a little less disreputable than usual for the party. Usually I went about in my religious habit or more often, since the summer had started at Pomeroy, in a pair of old shorts and a shirt or a T-shirt. I took out my suit, a plain dark grey, brushed it off and pressed it. I borrowed one of the red seminary ties to wear with a white shirt.

David was deeply impressed with my unexpectedly spruce appearance.

"Sam," he said looking me up and down, "I never thought..." he stopped short as he realised that he was about to be rude about my normal appearance. "You look very smart".

David always looked elegant, even when he arrived back from a day clinic in the bush. He dressed well and obviously took care in his choice of clothes. Predictably he was a perfect host, courteously passing among his guests making sure that no one felt left out, or was without a drink, or something to eat. It was a multi-racial party, and the possible intervention of the police must have given him a little concern. Not that such parties were in themselves illegal, but they were very heavily frowned upon. Any whites attending were likely to be regarded as socialising beneath themselves and open to harassment by the Special Branch. It was simply assumed that there must be something funny, if not actually dangerously radical, about whites who mixed with any of the other race groups. Fortunately, David had been reluctantly called in, by one of the police whose child had taken a nasty fall the previous week; there was no white doctor within thirty miles. They had seen their own doctor the next day, who had reassured them the child was in no danger. But they were grudgingly grateful to David, though at the same time not anxious that it was widely known that they had consulted an African doctor.

In the event there was no intrusion by suspicious police, despite the party continuing until about three in the morning. We danced and sang, and in between bouts of these noisy good times, we talked. Odd pairs or threesomes would be seen in corners having serious discussions about race situation and how wonderful things might be; if only life could be like this party with different groups all mixing so easily together. It was pleasant to forget for a while the racial barriers that soured people's minds and behaviour in South Africa.

After Christmas Lionel and myself decided to escape for a week's holiday. Gerry, his friend at the school near Durban, had told us we were welcome to stay at his house on the South Coast below Durban, while he was away during the summer holidays on a trip to Mozambique. We called at the school to collect the keys to the house and met Ben, the cook, who was delighted to see the strange white men again. He told us he was going home for a wedding in ten days time and that, if we wished, we would be most welcome to attend. His niece was to be married. We told him we should be very interested to come along, we had never seen a Zulu tribal wedding.

The stay at the house on the South Coast was distinguished by nothing at all and was wonderful. We slept a lot, read and generally had a good rest. We went back to the school after a week. Ben made us a meal and invited us to go and meet some of his friends. We gladly accepted. We felt honoured by the invitation and eager to see how his African friends enjoyed their time off in the evenings. It was dark when we set out with Ben. He took us to what appeared to be a small garage, attached to the house of a white resident in the area. The owner of the house allowed his servants to entertain their friends and to hold social evenings for their fellow domestic servants from time to time. The area was a residential district on the out-skirts of Durban and all Ben's friends worked as house servants, cooks or garden 'boys', in the white men's houses. During the day they slid about the house or garden, silently doing their jobs for their white masters and mistresses. We were a little fearful that our presence would put a damper on the evening. Ben, however, delivered a short speech of introduction telling his friends in embarrassing terms how we had given our lives to teaching their boys, rather than giving ourselves to the pursuit of money like so many of our white race. We received friendly nods and smiles and were made welcome.

Although these men were dressed in clothing that distinguished them as domestic servants – the ridiculous, and demeaning long short trousers, reaching to about the knee-cap and a loose collarless jacket above – they no longer behaved as they did in the white man's house, moving about with demure downcast eyes. They discussed the affairs of their families, or told with disgust, or sometimes amusement, of the behaviour of their white masters and mistresses. We were intrigued by the transformation. After a while one of the men started a chant, which was gradually and amiably taken up by the others. They clapped their hands in accompaniment and one or two found pieces of wood about the place and beat those together to emphasise the rhythm of the tribal

143

music. One at a time different men would get up and perform steps of ritual dances to the music and after a few steps would sit down and give way to another. They were relaxed, remembering and talking about their homes, enjoying each other's company, without the restraints under which they lived during their long working day. At about ten o'clock we slipped quietly into the night.

The next morning we started out early. We were travelling with Ben to a huge African reserve in the Valley of a Thousand Hills situated South of Pietermaritzburg. We were directed by Ben to the top of one of the hills in this magnificent valley. The journey through the valley lived up to its name; we dropped into the valley only to rise up again to a new peak and a different view of the many hills of the valley.

When we arrived at the wedding the ceremonies had already begun. Ben rushed off to see some of his family and doubtless to join in the ceremonies. Lionel and myself stood at some distance watching and attracting curious glances from time to time. After about twenty minutes Ben reappeared in tribal attire, very much like the men of Msinga. He was followed by two boys bearing two old fashioned dining chairs, which were set down at the scene of the wedding ceremony. Ben beckoned to us. Although we did not like the idea of being seated as guests of honour, we took the chairs. At least they signified to the rest of the gathering that we were accepted viewers and therefore acceptable white men. Ben put our minds at rest on one point. We were not really guests as this was very much a tribal and family affair but we were welcome, as his friends, to watch the proceedings.

The wedding ceremonies consisted of a series of songs and ritual dances or movements towards and away from each other by two groups – one with the groom and one with the bride. According to Ben much of the symbolism was centred around the fiction that the bride was reluctant to leave her own home and the groom and his group had almost to take her by force from her kinship group. Thus there were fierce gestures and menacing sorties enacted by the groom's party, while the whole time the bride looked downcast and reluctant. There was nothing of the European blushing, radiant bride in a tribal Zulu marriage and the groom looked much more bellicose than love-smitten. The morning wore on with no break, as first one party then the other would take it in turns to dramatise the struggle to wrest the bride from her home, until quite suddenly an elder, or perhaps it was the local chief stepped forward and the actual marraige had been accomplished. Thereafter the bride joined the groom's party, but still with no visible sign of elation or joy at the completion of the ceremony. I imagined they must be exhausted, perhaps they were just physically incapable of showing anything else but fatigue.

Soon after the actual completion of the marriage we thanked Ben for allowing us to see what so few outsiders had seen and said goodbye.

144

We drove to the bookshop in Pietermaritzburg to buy some texts for the next school year and then on to Pomeroy through the Msinga reserve. Leaving the District of Greytown it was very apparent where the white farms ended. Entering the reserve is like entering a different country. The terrain changed immediately from lush green to barren brown where, as one commentator on African affairs put it, stones grow. The reserve is grossly overpopulated by people and by cattle and goats and the rainfall is very low. In consequence, erosion increases year after year and as it does the stones appear on the surface of the hillsides. In this arid land the tribal people tried to cultivate what little arable land remained. This hardship broke up many families as many of the men were forced off the land to work in Johannesburg or Durban. In spite of the social havoc wreaked by the policy of confining the Africans into an area insufficient to provide them with a livelihood, the scenery is superb in its grandeur of sweeping steep mountain slopes, covered with flaming red aloes and massive boulders under a blazing hot sun.

We were within about two miles of the Tugela river when the car started to make strange noises, then to splutter ominously and after another five minutes struggle up another daunting slope, it coughed and was silent. We looked at each other with an air of resignation. We got out and I did what I usually did on these occasions. I threw open the bonnet of the car and looked inside. The engine was as incomprehensible as ever. Lionel was as ignorant of mechanics as I was. We looked around, the nearest houses were hundreds of feet below us in the valley. I had no inclination to climb down there. There would certainly be no telephone.

"Well, here we are, Torkington, what do you suggest?"

"It's a long way home, isn't it?"

"Yes," he said with an air of finality. We brooded silently for some three minutes. At the end of this time a cheerful smiling face appeared through the bush, which fell away to the right of the road.

We greeted him in Zulu. He looked at the car and enquired after its health. We told him about its health, or rather its illness. We were unable to be specific because we had made no diagnosis.

"Perhaps I could look?" asked the stranger. What had we to lose in our reprehensible ignorance? As he looked he explained that he had worked in a garage in Pietermaritzburg and maybe he could help us. Whatever it was that he did, he had the car roaring with power in about ten minutes. He smiled happily. We thanked him profusely; what was his charge, we asked. He declined to take anything, laughing that he had not used any tools or new parts, so how could he charge? To him it was just part of daily life. We drove along gingerly, but he had done a good job and we arrived back at the seminary before dark.

We swung into the new term with enthusiasm. I would be gone before the end of term and I was determined to leave it running well. Jack had finished the whole building programme and we had effected all the necessary changes. He was now working on another job which was waiting for him in another part of the diocese. But happily Jack lived in Pomeroy and we were able to call him in for any minor adjustments necessary.

The Bishop – I think partly to placate me – decreed a special ceremony of blessing for the completed seminary building. It was dedicated to St Augustine, an African saint from further north. To the delight of the boys and local people, an ox was slaughtered and cooked for a feast after the ceremony.

The Bishop and I sneaked inside after the feast had been going for some time. He told me Eustace was on his way by ship and would arrive in less than three weeks. He asked me to make sure he was shown the ropes for about a week before I went off on leave. He said he realised I would suffer a certain amount of pain in leaving and so he would keep the change-over to a minimum of a week. Anyway Daniel and Lionel would be here to see he did not go too far astray.

When Eustace did arrive, he had been informed that I was not over- happy at being supplanted. He made it clear he had no idea if he would be able to cope and that if he could not, he would certainly let the Bishop know before I came back in a few months time.

I had decided, given the option, to take the ship home and arranged to sail from Durban at the end of February. The Bishop and Lionel took me down there and saw me aboard. I had worked to get things in order before leaving and was tired enough to enjoy three weeks of doing nothing but eat, read and sleep. I did that, and put on a stone in weight.

Chapter Twelve

Interlude.

The sea journey had made it possible for me to readjust by the time I arrived in Southampton. I travelled to London first to see my superiors briefly, before making my way home to Manchester. My parents were both well and we were mutually delighted at our reunion. A week later we travelled south again for my brother's ordination. It was good to meet so many old friends and colleagues. After the ordination he had three weeks holiday at home, and we spent a lot of time, between visits to family and friends, discussing the state of the Church. It was apparent that his training had been of an entirely different kind to my own. I had been taught under a regime that was far less questioning; it was based on authority – establish the authority of Rome and the papal pronouncements and all we had to do was learn, listen and follow. A more open and questioning spirit was evident among my brother's contemporaries, who would not merely accept because someone in authority had spoken. The same ideas had been filtering through to some of us in South Africa though there we did have greater freedom from hide-bound Bishops, fearful of change and of the possibility of the loss of their status and power.

After my brother David had gone back to complete his studies, I received letters from Lionel. The first ones were dated April 29th. They carried shattering news.

"Dear Torkington,

You will doubtless have settled into a life of ease and comfort and never a thought for the hard-worked teachers at Pomeroy. Eustace has settled fairly well into what must be an entirely new departure in life for him. With no disrespect to him, I had got used to you and all your miserable failings. Frankly things are not the same. For one reason or another I am now teaching somewhat less, I have moved next door and just go up to the seminary each day for classes. I have become very much involved with the running of the clinic and practice because David has gone.

This will shock you, as it shocked us. David was not even a doctor. He has no qualification at all to practise, the only contact he seems to have had with a hospital is some time he spent as an orderly. It turns out he has impersonated a doctor before in Gaberones in Botswana, and had to get out when things were getting a little bit hot for him. The Bishop had been swayed by Mally's estimate of David's ability -I have been in touch with Mally, who is very upset by it all and astounded that he could have been hoodwinked like that. Admittedly he had never received any proof of qualification from David, though he had asked for them. David kept saying he must go and sort out matters in Gaberones and bring his belongings over here but he never did.

Unfortunately, he gave far too strong a dose of some drug to a very sick child, who died. It is not really possible to say whether the child would have died anyway. Angela, the nurse, had warned David that it was too strong a dose and she had refused to administer it. So David did it himself and then when the child looked worse, he panicked, drove down to Tugela Ferry hospital, and asked for help. They also thought it was too strong a dose, and when the child died, they began to ask questions, about where he trained and things like that and David's goose was cooked. He is at present in prison, while letters are sent to Gaberones and replies come back with more of his history.

Oh dear, Sam, it is all very sad and a great upset here. The patients at the clinic are remarkably forgiving; they liked him so much. And you will remember what a charming person he was. It's all an appalling shame that such a man could not have been properly trained. I had to try to pacify the parents of the child, which was quite awful. I didn't know what to say to be of any comfort – I don't think there really is anything that one can say; the child is dead.

Of course, the Bishop nearly went through the ceiling, or the clouds or sky high anyway, and has come down only to clutch his head. He has asked me to sort out what I can and has given me a free hand. Which sounds marvellous, until you think about it. It means a free had to sort out chaos. We are carrying on as best we can. Angela is coping wonderfully, and a Dr Moya is coming up a couple of times a week from Tugela Ferry to hold surgery. Of course, I'm looking for a doctor, so if you happen to meet one who wants to do mission doctoring... I also have hopes of getting another nurse. I have advertised for one.

You really are missing all the excitement. If it wasn't so tragic about the death of a child, it would be hilariously funny, and I suppose in years to come we too will see the comic side of it – all being hoodwinked like that. David really is a superb con man, Torkington.

I hope all goes well with you and that you are enjoying your holiday. We all send regards and hope to see you in the not too distant future.

Lionel."

This letter was contained in two air letters which came together. I heard again from Lionel after another month.

"Dear Sam,

Things have calmed down here since I last wrote. I have made contact with a new doctor – I have actually seen his qualification papers. He is a coloured doctor and originates from the Cape. I am hoping that he will be starting in about three weeks time. I have also interviewed a young nurse, who is qualified as a general nurse and is just completing her midwifery course in Zululand. She came over to see us a week ago and seems to like the idea of working here rather than in a Provincial Hospital. I think this is a point in her favour. I told her she would not be working regular hours like a state hospital, but she seemed to like the idea of the freedom this job would offer, rather than being under a matron and sister in the wards. Anyway, we shall see.

She is also, though this will mean nothing to a confirmed celibate like yourself, pretty, and will add glamour to our miserable existence. She comes from the borders of Natal and Cape, but she is a Zulu – Protasia Mayeza. I am sure that you will approve.

What else? I am still teaching but I am more and more involved here at the clinic. I have taken over the running of the old shop on the road at the corner of the property. It always was part of the property but had been leased out. Well, the lease ran out and the lessee did not want to renew it. So I have got a manager in and we are running it, we hope, for some profit to finance the other ventures here. Mind you, I am very conscious of the problems of competition.

Do you remember the little one up and one down house at the gateway to the clinic with the outside stairway? I am living in that. I feel a bit like an anchorite, but it is quite pleasant.

By the way, David and a number of others escaped from the prison down at Tugela Ferry. This was at night and by early morning they had headed south and must have arrived at about the place we once broke down in the reserve, if you remember. They were met by local people driving cattle to the dip and the locals recognised three of the escapees as goat thieves who had stolen their animals. So the locals surrounded them and gave them all a sound beating then drove them back to Tugela Ferry and handed them over. David had apparently not realised the danger of being in such company. He has now been transferred to the small jail at the police station here and has his ankles manacled in case he makes another break for it.

I heard yesterday, from a very reliable source – I won't say who, you never know what prying eyes read letters – that Mally has got out of the country. Things had been getting more and more difficult for him and it looked as if the police would put him inside on the ninety days no trial thing. Very typically when the police were looking for him – he had been hiding at different places for a number of days – he drove up to Louis Botha Airport in Durban and calmly got onto a plane for Salisbury. He is now in West Africa somewhere. Once Lindy learned he was safely away, she followed. We live in exciting times, Torkington....

Surely you must be coming back soon? It seems ages since we saw you. I met that dreadful man Cos last week and he asked to be remembered to you. He asked if you have been to see his family? They have been swopping round a few of the clergy here and Cos has been moved to the old German farm mission at Washbank. Heaven knows what is in store for you when you get back.

All the best,
Lionel".
P.S. I still have got no contract from his Lordship.

I was entitled to six months leave, on the understanding that I would do a bit of fund-raising round the parishes while home. After five months I made arrangements to fly back and sadly left my parents.

149

I wondered, as they must also have wondered, if in five years time they would still be alive. I urged them to come out for a visit, but they would not commit themselves and I had to be content with a 'We'll see'.

Chapter Thirteen

I arrived at Jan Smuts Airport, Johannesburg, on the morning of August 21st to be met by the Bishop and Cos. I was weary after my sleepless all-night flight, but excited at getting back to my place of work. They were bursting to tell me all the news. I was getting the Bishop's view of what Lionel had already told me. He was in a very chastened mood about it all, but beginning to laugh at himself for being fooled by a 'con' man.

"It's the same principle as with the travelling salesman, Sam," he reflected ruefully, "I believe too easily and trust people's claims about themselves. Oh, dear, we do learn the hard way, don't we?"

Cos was getting used to his move but admitted he had argued with the Bishop when he had been told of his new appointment. Cos had pushed the value of continuity while the Bishop insisted that a move was often a good idea, both for the priest and the people. Cos was retelling the episode with some amusement now.

"The trouble with you young fellows is that you think that you are God's gift to the people of the parish you happen to be in. You don't consider the people might like a change from you, do you."

"Oh, so you had complaints about me, did you? In that case I think I have a right to know about them," said Cos, retaliating.

"No, no, no, dear boy. I've had no complaints at all, and I make no complaints about your work, except the bad advice you give me from time to time, what?" he grinned mischievously at Cos.

"It all sounds entirely typical" I said, "anyway where are we going now?" I hoped to find out as soon as possible where I was being posted.

"Well, we shall all go to Washbank for the moment and stay with Cos for a few days while I make certain arrangements. Then I shall let you know where you are going."

"Why not tell me now?"

"I can't do that, dear boy, until I have had a chance to sort out matters with other people and make certain moves, d'you see?"

"Not really," I said, "We'll have to be informed, why not start with me?"

"It's not as simple as that, dear boy, just trust your uncle."

And I had to be content with that..

It was only when we pulled in at a garage that Cos had the chance to brief me a bit more. The Bishop got out, as always, to supervise the whole business of petrol and cleaning of insects off the windscreen.

"I reckon you're going to Newcastle," he said, and grinned malevolently.

"Newcastle?" I thought about it. Newcastle was a small town in north Natal, just off the national road, not far from the Natal/Transvaal border. It had a white population, two or three thousand at the most. I had been there once or twice for meetings of clergy, and from what I had seen, I was not overjoyed at the thought of it as a prospective parish. I had been used to living in African areas and did not relish the problems of trying to serve white and African, a foot in both camps. I suspected Cos of trying to frighten me.

"I don't believe you," I told him, "What's wrong with Alexander anyway?" Fr Alexander was the present parish priest at Newcastle.

"Alexander has not been very well in recent months and the boss is thinking of moving him out to a smaller, place."

I remained unconvinced. "I don't trust you, Cos."

"Well, you wait and see. But don't say anything to the boss, he hasn't said anything to me. On the way down I tried to pump him for information but with no joy. All the same, I have watched the recent moves, I reckon you'll find Newcastle is the place," he said, "Try to regard it as a challenge."

I cuffed his head and sat back to think about it.

The Bishop was back again, after ensuring we were road worthy. The African pump attendant must have been getting a bit fed up with the demanding clergyman who wanted every possible thing checking. He looked weary of his customer, though his expression changed to happy astonishment when he received an ample tip for his trouble. The Bishop's policy was to compensate for the pitiful wages paid to the black man. He always tipped heavily and brushed away the extravagant gratitude he invariably received. He considered he was simply distributing a small part of the justice due to the Africans in their own country.

"Well, now, Sam," he said as he clambered into the car, "Eustace is doing very well. It's the feast of the seminary on the twenty-seventh of this month. We shall be having a big sung mass in the open air and I want you to be the deacon to me, alright? It would be nice for you to be there to make Eustace feel better, he feels as if he has unseated you and you must bear him a grudge."

"True, Monsignor, I do," I told him with great seriousness.

"Oh, crumbs," he said dejectedly, "you are still like that, are you, you misery?"

"No, not really," I laughed, "you take me too seriously."

"I never know where I am with you two. You're such a moody pair."

"And that's the thanks we get, for our unstinting loyalty", complained Cos.

The Bishop laughed his hiccoughing chuckle. "Alright, I know we do think the same way on many matters, but it's not always easy to tell."

We did not see much of the Bishop during the first two days. He was out and about arranging all his clergy's moves. I spent the time with Cos discussing the news the Bishop had brought from his visits to the Vatican Council. We ended up with some hope, but also a realisation that the Church did nothing in a hurry. On the day before

152

the feast at Pomeroy, Cos came into my room about eleven in the morning and told me the boss wanted to see me. He grinned wickedly at me.

"Come in, old boy," the Bishop called out as I knocked.

"Sit down. Now," he pronounced the word portentously, "I have a very special job to entrust to you." It was made to sound like promotion, but just as could well disguise a dirty job of clearing up someone else's mess.

"It's something which might be a little difficult to start with, but I think I know your abilities well enough by now to realise that Sam Torkington rises to the occasion and meets all challenges, what?"

Oh, yes, I decided, I was about to be dumped in it.

"Excuse me," I said, "let me guess. I'm going to Newcastle."

"How did you know that? I haven't told anyone, but Alexander. Has he been on to you? He promised me that ...."

"No," I reassured him, "I haven't heard a word from Alexander. I'm just psychic that's all."

"Well, you're right. Alexander hasn't been at all well and frankly has not been able to keep things going properly for some time. So I want you to sort out and ginger up, if you see what I mean. All sorts of things have, of necessity, been neglected, I think the people there have understood and coped very well, but they do deserve a better deal. D'you see why I want you there, dear boy?"

"Do I have a choice, Monsignor?" I asked embarrassing him briefly into silence.

"Well," he said, drawing the word out, playing for time. He hadn't expected that question. "I don't see how you can offer your resignation before you actually take up your post."

We both laughed. He put me in the picture about the parish and promised that in the near future he hoped to give me an African curate. He would take me over there next Monday so I could have a few days with Alexander before he left.

I suffered all sorts of strange emotions as we neared Pomeroy the following morning. There was still a lot of my heart here, I thought as we came down the steep hill and entered the mission area. Some of the boys saw me and greeted me with mock formality, then we all laughed. Eustace came out and was effusive in his welcome, eager to make sure that the first Rector of the seminary was accorded full honours on his first return visit. After the initial tense minutes, I relaxed, happy to be back so soon.

There must have been about two hundred people at the mass, including the boys and many familiar faces of local parishioners. As we came out in procession I saw Lionel just arriving from next door, with him was Angela and, I presumed, the new nurse, Protasia. The Bishop gave a stirring address about the future of the Church in Africa – it was in African hands, and that was the whole raison d'être for the seminary. He told us there were signs from the Vatican Council that the Church was prepared to change and adapt to conditions in other parts of the world. It was up to the Church in Africa to tell the Pope and his advisers what was really needed and not to accept meekly absolutes, rules and regulations made in Europe. We are coming, he told us, into an age of more active participation in the running of local churches; we must prepare ourselves for this; and indeed start to do it.

This was all pretty revolutionary stuff and I suspected that not all his clergy would be one hundred per cent behind his views, but Cos and myself thoroughly approved. After the altar had been taken away from the open land in front of the new buildings, tables were erected and filled with meat, bread, fruit and several different cheeses, provided particularly with the Bishop in mind. We all mingled together, chatting. It was good to renew old friendships and hear everyone's news.

"Ah, Torkington," sounded from behind me. I turned round, laughing.

"Ah, Steel," I countered, "Thanks for your letters, Lionel. I'm, glad the scandal happened while I was away. How are things looking now?"

"Not too badly, Sam much more settled now. Cos tells me you're going to Newcastle."

"Indeed, yes. I tried to resign, but as I'm not yet in post, I can't technically. I shall try again later."

"I don't really see you there," said Lionel, "but you might just survive. Anyway, say what you will of Eustace he can organise a bun-fight. A good spread don't you think?"

"Very good," I agreed. Lionel was peering over my shoulder, "Come with me. I want to stop Cos annoying my nurses." Cos was talking to one of the Sisters from the convent at the top of the hill and the two nurses.

"Excuse me, ladies," interrupted Lionel, "Is this man annoying you?"

"We were in the middle of a deep theological discussion, before you came blundering in," Cos informed him curtly.

"Sam, I want you to meet Pro, our new nurse. Pro, you have heard me talk about, Sam."

"Hello, Pro," I said, to the pretty little nurse.

"Hello, Father," she replied. "Yes, I have been looking forward to meeting you. I wanted to see if the marvellous man who used to be at the seminary was really nice."

"Well, this could be a big day in your life, then."

"Torkington," Cos broke in, "enough of these idiot pleasantries; the ladies require meat and I commission you to go and fetch it."

"And why are you incapable of doing the job yourself?"

"You may remember that you and Steel just broke into a very deep discussion. Now run along, there's a good chap."

154

"Father," said Pro, looking at me in mock surprise, "do you allow people to speak to you like that."

"Cos is beyond redemption; his manners are appalling. But, tell me, do you want some meat?"

"Well....." she left the word hanging.

"I see. Then I shall do as I'm told and get some for you."

Pro laughed delightedly. She was very petite and vivacious. I could see why Lionel was impressed.

By early afternoon most people had gone away and the boys, granted a day off for their big annual feast, had gone off to play football. I marvelled at their ability to run about after eating so much. I wandered over to see Lionel's place. He had made it very livable, though it was indeed small. He said that this did not matter, because he moved about between the seminary, the clinic and the store on the other side of the gateway. He showed me around the whole complex of buildings that now occupied so much of his time. I was surprised to find the house at the back of the shop, furnished and complete with an office and bedroom, and a small kitchen.

"Who lives here, then?" I asked.

"Oh, of course, all this is new. Fred has moved as you doubtless heard and Joe O'Grady, who replaced him has decided that it's better and more convenient, for both seminary and parish matters, if they are in different buildings. So he has taken up residence here."

"Who has invaded my private quarters?" called a voice from outside.

Joe came in.

"Do you know, I never realised that there was a habitable area behind the shop."

"You should have seen it when we started on it," he said, "it was full of smelly old sacks and cardboard boxes. But it's very comfortable now."

It was obvious Joe and Lionel got on well. He was another easy-going, friendly Irishman like his predecessor, Fred. As the afternoon wore on, most of the visiting clergy made their way to Joe's rooms, demanding cups of tea. Joe professed himself unable to cope with so many visitors. Pro walked in accusingly, looking for a large pair of scissors that had disappeared from the clinic. He denied it indignantly and then tried to use Pro as a maid.

"Pro, nine cups of tea, please." This was pushing his luck too far. She stopped in her tracks and gave him a long look.

"I'm not your servant," she told him, "and anyway I have patients to attend to. Make you own tea."

"Shall we save you a cup?" asked Joe, "Are you coming back?"

"I might," said Pro, and hurried away to see to her patients. Lionel laughed as Pro went out.

"She might be small, but she can take care of herself. I don't think she's likely to be over-awed by the clergy."

155

The doorway was filled by the large form of the Bishop. He viewed his assembled clergy.

"And a lot of seditious talk going on in here, I'll be bound."

He turned to Cos and myself. "Are you two coming back with me or not?"

The Bishop took me across to Newcastle on Monday morning. It was about forty miles from Washbank, where Cos was based. Alexander was relieved, to be handing over control of the place. It had really proved too much for him latterly. The Bishop was going up to Volksrust for a couple of days and would call back on the Wednesday afternoon to take Alexander off for a holiday. Whatever else was the matter with Alexander, his voice was unimpaired. He told me about the parish and the various out-stations at great length. He had known the parish for many years having spent two spells there. One when he first came to the country some ten years before plus his stay for the last two years. Alexander was about fifty-five, but looked older. He suffered from a recurrent stomach complaint which caused him a lot of pain from time to time. He made apologies for the lack of book-keeping and records, but said that the bills and collections from church were about the place. He was right, they were. On the mantlepiece, on the shelves of the bookcases, on the window-sills and on the desk of the office. I viewed it all with a certain dismay. On the second day I gave up trying to understand everything Alexander was telling me. With such a welter of detail imparted in a totally haphazard way, I was left bewildered. I was determined to start afresh, I had no hope of sorting out all Alexander was telling me anyway.

I was relieved when the Bishop came to remove Alexander on Wednesday and I was left in silence to get on with my job. On Thursday morning I went up to the convent about a mile out of town to say mass and introduce myself. The convent was of the Sisters of St Augustine or the Augustinians as they were commonly called – they ran a day and boarding school for white girls. The school catered for girls from South Eastern Transvaal and Northern Natal, though there were girls from as far away as Johannesburg, Durban and Mozambique. I was expected, I learnt, to conduct religious instruction for the sixth-form girls twice a week, or at least for the Catholic girls among them. Among the Sisters themselves were immigrant Sisters from Ireland and England, as well as South African whites. The usual practice of the priests in the parish had been to eat at the convent. Since arriving at Newcastle I had lived on snacks at the house or been out with Alexander to parishioners' houses for dinner. After I joined the Sisters for breakfast, Mother Superior came in and introduced herself. She was from Ireland, but had been in South Africa for over twenty years. She asked if I would be able to spare some time for instructions or conferences for the Sisters. She was particularly keen on looking at the documents from the Vatican Council. I agreed we should start to study them once I had got settled in.

For the rest of that week and most of the next I attempted to sort out the paper work of the parish, so as to discover what sort of financial state we were in. I went round the house and gathered together all the pieces of paper and amounts of money from weeks of collections on the living room table. That was my starting point. I sorted and sifted and made a start on the book-keeping as well as I could. In a fortnight I was able to give the Bishop a statement of account, and beg two hundred pounds to keep the bank from being very rude to us. He had promised that if we were really in a bad way, he would give us a little sustainer. After that I was on my own, he said, fearful I would make a monthly habit of begging from him.

The main church and the priest's house were situated in the centre of the small town. The Bishop had bought the building from the Methodists who had built a larger church. The house was a typical single story building, with seven rooms and a bathroom in it; it more than met my needs. An African woman from the location came each day to keep the place clean. The location was about a mile and a half to the East of the town and there was another simple church building there, which held about four hundred people.

My first few months were occupied in getting to know my new parishioners, not only in the town and the location, but in the out-stations as well. As I only visited some of the smaller ones once a month it took some time before I began to know the people there. In the town and location I was in daily contact with people and got to know them more quickly, but I was also feeling my way in an unfamiliar situation. I was serving two communities, whether I liked it or not. There was virtually no contact between the white and African Catholics. I was concerned about this and after a few weeks I casually asked about it. I could almost hear the sigh of relief with which one or two of the white parishioners answered. It was the language problem, they were quick to point out, and now that the vernacular had been introduced into the liturgy by the good offices of the Vatican Council, I could no longer point to the universality or joint non-comprehension of the Latin language. There were always a few Africans at the mass in the centre of the town on Sundays and at times one or two whites would come to the location church. I also spoke to members of the St Vincent de Paul Society. This multi-racial group sought to help the poor and needy from their slender funds. We fenced each other guardedly, trying to see how radical each other's views were. This was particularly so with the white members; with the Africans it was enough for me to make my sympathy with their oppressed state known and then leave it to them to decide about me. I was after all a white man.

After six months I had established that there were two or three quite liberal whites in the parish who were acutely aware of the awful disparities between the lives of the African and white man. Over a pint of beer in a quiet corner in one of the local pubs one evening, the white man I felt most at ease with, Anthony Jeffers, put his position like this. He agreed with what I said about the basic equality of men as the teaching of a Christian church; that teaching ought to be taken seriously as a philosophy to be lived by and, as far as possible, lived up to. Thus, he would try to do so within the constraints of the situation. He wanted to do some more to bring about justice for the oppressed blacks in South Africa, but – and here was the constant stumbling block – he had a wife and two small children. If he dared to speak out, what would he achieve? Even if you argued that you could not just base action on achievement, but that sometimes things needed to be said, noises ought to be made regardless of success or failure. But what then of his duty to his wife and children? What if he got put in jail without trial for ninety days and then another ninety days and so on, who would look after them? For some this was an excuse, the happy dilemma that left them able to say there was really nothing they could do. But for others, like Anthony Jeffers, it was a real and painful dilemma. Who was I to disagree, to urge the extreme of outspoken criticism? The only fate awaiting me, a single Englishman, was deportation.

The Vatican Council had made some useful statements about racialism and I began to use these and comment on them in sermons. I felt sorry for those who were anguished by a statement of Christianity which disturbed their consciences and left them wondering how they could do something about apartheid. I felt angry when it was evident that many did not wish to hear or to have their consciences disturbed and certainly did not want to have their lifestyles changed. I was astounded at some of the Sisters at the convent. When I started to discuss the Vatican Council documents on these matters, I was told that I was going too far. This was mainly from the South African sisters. In order to get feedback I was not preaching to them in church, but discussing the issues in their common room. I got feedback; I got vociferous disagreement, I got anger. As a foreigner I obviously misunderstood the situation, they told me. Alright, I was an outsider, but I was saying nothing that Archbishop Hurley of Durban, the outspoken critic of the apartheid system and himself a South African had not said. He too came in for the same angry condemnation from the South African sisters. I was amazed to hear the usually, docile, quietly prayerful Sisters speaking out with such fervour against a prelate of the church.

I decided to beat a retreat and mull over these interesting developments. I rounded off the discussion by suggesting that one could not pick and choose the comfortable bits of our religion to accept and forget the more difficult parts. I promised we would pursue these matters further in our perusal of the Vatican Council documents. What they were accusing Archbishop Hurley and myself was of going too quickly. Crudely, they argued that the African was emerging from some primitive stage of development. It would take years to catch up with the white man. The barely hidden trap was that the white man was still moving ahead, so that the black man might in fact take a very, long time indeed to catch up. Their Christian spirit led them to kindness toward Africans; servants would be given gifts of food and clothing but the status quo was not to be upset. I was in some disarray. I had finished off lamely and I knew it. One of the first things that occurred to me was how often the congregation on Sundays wanted to shout back at me like some of the Sisters. How many of the ordinary faithful in church had I outraged and left fuming in frustration? Or, alternatively, how many just switched off when I jumped onto my different hobby horses? I was quite unnerved by the thought.

In that first year my experience of trying to manage a multi-racial parish forced me to conclude that there was no simple formula to solve the racial problem. It was evident that direct frontal attacks were not going to change hearts and minds; they merely engendered the building of stouter defences. I tried to be more subtle, to put Christian relationships and attitudes to other race groups in the context of the wholeness of the Christian community.

I looked back over my shoulder at the days at Besters and Pomerory with some regret. It was unpleasant to be seen as a disturber of the peace. It was tempting to conform and I don't doubt that for the sake of a false peace I was at times a coward and kept quiet. I was conscious that when I was paying social visits, hosts and hostesses would steer conversation away from dangerous areas such as talk about the laziness, untidiness or just typical stupidity of their African servants. These were known to be my blood boilers. To the local white residents they were the common daily talk, feeding and perpetuating the image of the inferior black race.

At the end of my first year of Newcastle Lionel phoned me to tell me he was moving out of Pomeroy and going to live at Washbank with Cos. He would no longer be teaching at the seminary, and he had at last convinced the Bishop that he should start to put into operation his extension work schemes. Cos's mission farm was to be his base for the work. He would continue to have a lot to do with the clinic, though now that a doctor was in residence it would need less supervision. Anyway the Bishop was in negotiation with some nuns who were both willing to buy the place, run it and supervise the medical side. Lionel was relieved at the prospect of losing that headache and the Bishop delighted at the prospect of losing a debt, the clinic had been eating away at his resources for a couple of years.

Cos was faced with a farm of seven or eight thousand acres. His only farming experience had been as a student when he was in charge of the rearing of the turkeys and the chickens, but he shrank from applying his meagre expertise to the farming of eight thousand acres. He also had to consider the seventy African families, living on the farm, many of whom had been there for at least three generations. They were threatened with removal as squatters creating a nasty 'black spot' on the otherwise pure white area. Cos put it to the Bishop that, just as with Besters, the only way that the farm was going to make money, was if considerable investment took place. Deafness immediately struck the Bishop until Cos made it clear that he was not asking for money. What he suggested was that the people living on the farm, be allowed to use the land for their own subsistence existence. The Bishop was doubtful.

"What will it cost me, dear boy?"

"Nothing", insisted Cos.

"Schemes cost money", stated the Bishop, looking at Cos suspiciously over his half-moon glasses.

"The money must come out of the scheme itself."

"And who may I ask is going to organise it?"

"They are," replied Cos flatly. "If they want it, they must do it. They are not helpless idiots, though admittedly inexperienced and disadvantaged when dealing with whites. But since we cannot use the farm, why shouldn't they have a go?"

"Yes," said the Bishop slowly; he removed his glasses and leaned back. "Why doesn't Lionel want to be involved?"

"Well, he will be," Cos told him, "but only if invited by the Africans, otherwise he is just another white farm manager."

"It's the sort of thing that Lionel wants to do," he mused. "Well, you can give it a go, dear boy, as far as I am concerned. But," he warned replacing his spectacles, "don't come crying to me for money, d'you hear?"

Lionel had recently met an ex-farmer from the South of Natal who had latterly been involved in a charitable organisation which provided cheap nutritious foods to the Africans. He was fascinated by Lionel's ideas and understood that the white man could only be involved if invited, or, better still, employed by the Africans. Lionel invited Neil Alcock to come and look at the situation, and to advise, in strictly farming terms, on its feasibility.

Two weeks later Neil arrived. He and his wife, Creina stayed for four days, thoroughly intrigued by the prospects of the farm. Neil was excited by the possibilities for the farm if it could be run as a co-operative. Had it been suggested to the people, he asked Cos, had they formed any sort of association, with a chairman, would they be willing to pool their stock? Cos had to calm him with some sober facts.

"Neil, there have been many parish priests in the past seventy years. Probably a new one every three or four years. Now, each one has a new policy for the farm and, needless to say, they never bothered to consult the people. The Africans have been allowed to live here; to have their little plots; to graze their cattle and, of course, to work on the farm. Can you imagine their reaction when the latest incumbent starts talking about yet another new scheme. They have seen it all before; you can't expect instant enthusiasm."

Neil calmed down. He appreciated the argument. He said "Mm"

160

some ten or a dozen times. Then he looked shyly at Lionel and Cos.

"I should love to be involved with this, you know."

"Well, with your farming expertise I'm sure you would be invaluable", said Lionel thoughtfully.

"Listen, Father," said Neil, "can you find us a place to stay for a bit. We are used to looking after ourselves. We don't want to stay in the house or eat your food – we want to cater for ourselves. But I should like to watch and view and assess .... you know?"

"As far as I am concerned you're welcome. There are plenty of buildings here, heaven knows. If you really insist on setting up your own place. But they are in pretty poor condition..."

"We don't mind that," said Neil "do we Creina"?

"Of course not," said Creina. She appeared to be used to living in odd corners.

"Leave that with us Father – I mean about sorting out and cleaning one of your old out-buildings."

"Willingly" cried Cos, who had no inclination to start making accommodation ready for visitors.

"Right. We shall have to do a lot of organising in the next three weeks but we shall return. We can easily continue to run our food organisation from here and do our trips to the North of the province."

I learned all this some ten days later. It was Lionel's birthday, and he was having a party to celebrate both his birthday and his arrival at Washbank. He was also using the occasion to entertain some of the members of the nascent farm co-operative committee. Two sheep had been slaughtered and a braaivleis or barbecue was prepared. I arrived after dark to find the place alive with music and laughing voices. The approach to the mission farm house was up a two mile drive-way from the dirt road. The driveway, at its best, was appalling and a danger to the springs and shock-absorbers on a car. At its worst, after heavy rain, it was quite impassable. There was no possibility that the local police could make a swift raid on the mission, so the multi-racial party was quite safe. It took at least fifteen minutes to travel up the driveway and the lights of a car were clearly visible from the mission house nestling under the wooded mountain.

Cos was busy when I arrived, trying to encourage indifferent and undiscerning drinkers to have a brandy or perhaps a glass of wine or a beer. I knew what he was about, and he grinned at me over his glasses in recognition that I knew. He drew me aside. "Shall we hide the whisky?" he both asked and suggested.

"You can't really do that. It smacks of preferential treatment."

"But listen, one bloke just had some and put orange cordial in it," Cos told me, as if it were some gross breach of decency.

"Well, try not to think about it," I told him, "anyway pour me one before the stuff evaporates." He poured a niggardly tot, as if he were giving away his life blood. "A bit stiffer than that," I bullied. He

161

grudgingly complied.

There was a bellowing behind me. It was Lionel, already fully in the party spirit, clutching a glass of brandy in one hand and a heavy stick in the other. The stick was smoking gently at one end, he had been tending the fire.

"How are you, Torkington? So good of you to come," and he went off into peals of laughter. "Now listen, Sam," he continued, calming down a little, "I am a new man since I came here to Washbank. Cos is a bit of an awkward bugger, but I can cope with him. How is dear old Newcastle, tell me?"

"Steel, the fire you have been chivvying is now burning brightly and singeing the meat."

"Oh, hell, water someone, water," he yelled, and off he went.

"I take it he has been preparing for this all day?" I said to Cos.

"Oh yes and worried like mad until he started having a little drink about five o'clock. But it's good to have him here." Joe had come over from Pomeroy and brought the two nurses, Angela and Pro, and two other workers from the clinic I had not met before. They had moved over to a corner of the verandah and were working on Lionel's roasted meat. Cos and I got ourselves a helping and went to join them.

Joe called out as we approached, "I want to tell you something that will make you laugh. These two simple-minded nurses think you are handsome."

"I can't say I find that very funny, Joe. True yes, but not funny. Good evening, ladies, are you being attended to? Enough meat? I see that you have, but just say the word and I shall send Cos to get you some."

Cos growled a refusal.

Lionel announced a short delay before the next round of meat would be ready, but there was bread and cheese in the sitting room and dancing for those who felt strong enough. The music must have been audible a mile away. We slowly moved inside, while I asked for news of Pomeroy. Pro told me that things were changing now that Lionel had moved out. I think she regretted this, because Lionel had employed her and she found the Sisters rather more rigidly organised than Lionel, so that her freedom to do things in her own way was somewhat curtailed. She was wondering, without any real plans, how long she would remain there.

"It hardly seems a year since we met at Pomeroy", I told her.

"No, it's a pity we don't see you more often visiting the mission there", she said.

"That must be true", I teased her, "especially, as Joe says, you find me so handsome."

She laughed, and made a gesture with her hand as if to brush the remark aside. "Joe is a tell-tale", she said.

"Ah, so you did say it", I laughed at her.

We had joined the party inside. There were about twenty people

162

shuffling about on the floor. They were not dancing together in European style, but separately while employing their hands to carry biscuits and cheese which they were eating while dancing. As more people came in, it became less possible to carry a glass or plate while shuffling. I was still near Pro, when a hand appeared and snatched off the red beret she was wearing.

"Oh," she gasped and looked round.

"I suspect I know the hand of the culprit", I went in search. At the other end of the room I found Joe doing what appeared to be a bucolic clog dance. He was wearing a red beret. I crept up behind him and repossessed it for its rightful owner.

"Thank you", said Pro, "that man is so rude." I agreed solemnly.

At that moment a crush of people entering the room pushed us together and Pro grabbed me fearful of falling over. As the floor cleared again, a hand propelled me out of the door.

"Torkington, what are you doing?" Cos's voice demanded. "I come into the room to find you clutching a nurse."

"Just sort of thrown together, as it were, you know," I explained.

"Well, it didn't look like that to me. Positively amorous, you poor sex maniac."

"How dare you," I remonstrated. "Though – and I say this speaking purely from an aesthetic point of view – she is a most attractive young lady."

"That does not sound like an entirely objective view, I must say. Come, I have decided I shall allow you another sip from the whisky, on condition that you behave yourself for the rest of the evening."

"I make no such promises, anyway I maintain my behaviour so far has been quite unimpeachable."

Later I had a chat with one or two of the proposed committee for the co-operative. I saw Cos's point about their cautiousness, especially perhaps when talking to me, a white priest, but there did seem to be a certain guarded enthusiasm. As if they had begun to hope and think 'if only....'

Joe and Lionel broke into our conversation to announce the departure of the Pomeroy crowd who had to be at work first thing the next morning. Angela and Pro waved from the car, and Pro called out, that I must visit Pomeroy more often. I laughed and promised I would, though I really had no intention of going back there. The comparison with life at Newcastle would only make me yearn to be back at the seminary again in that magnificent valley.

I left soon after as I also had to be up early for mass at the convent. Lionel was still in high spirits but Cos was morose, the whisky bottle was empty and he hated brandy.

Chapter Fourteen

About a month before the Christmas holidays of the convent school, Sister Roberta, the head mistress asked if I would mind giving advice to some of the girls, who were boarding. Being away from their parents there was no one to talk to them in loco parentis. I was a bit dubious, I thought I might end up spending my time as psychiatrist to a girl's school when I had many other places to visit. However, she said I could use some of the time I usually gave to religious instruction and she would teach what I had to cut out. I asked if they had not spoken to her about their problems, and she said that some indeed did do so, but that some seemed to want to speak to a man.

I really did not know what to expect. I rather expected girlish worries about coming exams or little quarrels among class-mates. I was therefore, quite unprepared for the first girl who spoke to me about a problem she had. I had noticed her as one in the class I spoke to on Tuesday mornings, but I could not remember her name and recalled her as a quiet girl who never said anything in class. She told me a harrowing tale.

Her mother had separated from her father and then divorced him. Her father had then left the country altogether and she did not know where he was. Meanwhile her mother had remarried – this some three years ago. She, the daughter, Maureen, did not really like or trust her step-father. He always seemed too ingratiatingly nice. I thought she had come to the core of her problem and I tried to explain that he might genuinely be trying to win her approval and perhaps she had to concede a point to him, even if she thought he was trying so hard to be nice as to appear objectionable.

She quietly assured me that that was at first what she had thought and had tried to make allowances. But there was more to it than that. They were supposed to be going away for a holiday in Rhodesia, now Zimbabwe, in the summer and he had made it clear that she could come, as long as she agreed to have sexual intercourse with him.

"Good lord, Maureen", I said quite bowled over by this twist to the story. I collected myself as quickly as possible, hoping that I had not shown the horror I felt. "But have you told your mother about this?"

She said she had not. Both she and her step-father knew her mother would not believe it. She would think that Maureen was merely trying to make trouble for a step-father she was known not to like very much, and he would deny it indignantly. He said that if she promised to go on the holiday he would take that to mean that she agreed to his terms. I was quite appalled at the calculated depravity of the man. I asked what she wanted me to do – to speak to her mother? No, she pleaded, that would not help. She wanted advice. She did so want to go on holiday to Rhodesia, but refused to pay the hateful price.

I told her I thought that her mother ought to know about this even if the present might not be the best time to tell her. As to the holiday, she had really already made her decision. She nodded sadly, and told me she had wanted to tell someone and did not relish telling the Sister who was her form mistress.

There were other girls who did not look forward to the holidays either because of broken marriages and being pushed from one parent to another to suit the convenience of each. They were often treated like pawns in a game, one parent trying to score off another. I came to dread being asked to listen to the girls' problems, not because I did not want to help, but because I hated to see these youngsters being forced to bear such misery at an early age. It was evident that the school was used as a dumping ground by some parents who wanted to get rid of children who were a burden of responsibility to them and inhibited them from leading the lives they wanted.

****

Just before Christmas the Bishop rang me to tell me he was sending me my promised curate, Fr Rupert Maluleka. He had only been ordained the previous Christmas and since then he had been helping at the seminary while getting a little experience with Joe O'Grady at weekends. The seminary had closed for the holidays and Rupert was to join me. The Bishop wanted him to stay with me at the town house for the time being, but with a view to letting him have a place near the church in the location later. It was illegal, of course, for him to live with me in the town house – there were servants quarters out at the back of the house where he could live legally pretending to be a house servant. We refused to play that game. Rupert was far too obliging and said that he would do whatever we thought best, living at the back if we felt that that would be safer. I told the Bishop I could not accept that and he agreed we could hardly accept such discrimination.

I had a long talk with Rupert about a mixed race parish like ours. He was a quiet man, but as an African he had no illusions about the problems he faced. He knew his easiest course would be to get out to the location and stay there. He also knew the whites in the parish would prefer him to do just that. It went without saying that the Government officials would see that as his only course. But he wanted to try to work for a church which would be able, if not now, then at some date in the future, to behave as if there were not colour lines to be crossed. He was prepared to be snubbed and humiliated in this cause.

"Sam, as a black man I am snubbed and humiliated every day anyway. At least if the white parishioners do it, it may bear some sort of fruit in the future. They may be ashamed of themselves when they think back on what they have done."

165

In fairness to the parishioners in the town they did not, openly anyway, snub Rupert; they were polite, they talked to him and told him he was welcome. That at least they did. They knew what my views were, but there had been those in the past year who had told me quietly, without having an open row, they disagreed with me. The only adverse behaviour to Rupert that I heard was a report that one parishioner could not bring herself to receive communion from a black hand.

Rupert preached his first sermon in English on the Sunday between Christmas and New Year. I was present at the back of the church and amazed at his apparent calmness and authority when speaking. I told him afterwards that my first sermon in Zulu had been given with the loss of about a gallon of sweat. He laughed and confessed that he had spent the half hour before the beginning of the mass in the toilet, feeling extremely sick.

When it came to socialising, I had to admit that there were only two white homes where I was sure I could go with Rupert and know that we would be welcome. There may in fact have been others, but I could not be sure and I would not risk subjecting Rupert to the indignity of being unwelcome. Rupert lived in the house for about nine months with no queries from police or Special Branch about our domestic arrangments. After that time he said he thought he was ready to strike out on his own and stay in the little house attached to the church in the location. We were only a mile and a half apart and still saw a good deal of each other. After he moved he said the bulk of the masses in the location and I most of the masses in the town church.

****

In March of the following year a one day clergy conference had been arranged for the whole diocese – about twenty-five clergy in all – to be held at Pomeroy. By that time I had got over my nostalgia and was happy to spend a day in my old home. Rupert had a funeral to attend to in the location and could not come. I set out immediately after breakfast in order to arrive in good time.

I was just coming up to the convent at the top of the Pomeroy hill when I saw a Landrover approaching. As it came near I realised it was the clinic doctor with Pro by his side. They slowed down and I did too, waving to them as I passed. I pulled up some yards further along the road and looked back. Pro jumped from the Landrover and ran back to me laughing.

"Hello, Father, are you going to Pomeroy?"

"Hello, Pro. Yes, of course I am." I remembered I had received a Christmas card from Swaziland and wondered from whom it could have been. I had puzzled over the small neat signature for two days before it dawned on me. Pro had told me she was going to Swaziland for Christmas. It had to be from her.

"I must thank you very much for your card at Christmas. Do you send all the clergy Christmas cards?"

"Oh, no, Father, not all of them. Only the very special ones," she said, laughing. "Father, I must go, I shall see you later, I hope."

"Well, I hope so," I agreed.

As I watched her leaving, I realised just how much I meant that casual phrase. She seemed so small and young, so alive and full of laughter. I suppose that for me she typified what I had thought so wonderfully African about my time at Pomeroy – a lightness of heart, as if infected by the constant shining of the sun, and the ability to bear with what we would have considered appalling conditions of life. Yet, Lionel had said, that for all her carefree appearance, Pro was most competent and reliable in her work and for all her youthful looks and slightness of build, quite capable of putting the doctor in his place.

I drove down the hill to Pomeroy.

Clergy gatherings were noisy, boisterous affairs. So many of us had been students together and saw each other so infrequently now that there was always a lot to talk about. We boasted like fishermen about our successes. Most of us lived alone in our missions and there was no one to disprove our claims. We lied shamelessly about the exploits we had been through, the dangers we had encountered and overcome. No one believed anyone else. The Bishop brought us together for meetings by calling 'children children' and he was not far from the truth when he said it. On these occasions we regressed and behaved like children at school let out to play. For all that the discussions were what are described so often in diplomatic circles as 'full and frank', as we quite violently disagreed about methods of our work; priorities for spending and so on.

By mid-afternoon we had argued into exhaustion and broke for tea. This had to be the end of the meeting, some priests had as much as a hundred miles to travel home. Some of us made our way to Joe's place to have a chat over tea. As we left for our cars I saw Pro over by the maternity clinic building and went to say good-bye to her.

"Father, you promised that we should see you this afternoon and now you are running away."

"Well, if you are too busy to come and have a cup of tea with us, I cannot interrupt, can I? You really must get away from here if you want to have a quiet cup of tea. Get Joe to bring you up to Newcastle some day."

"Do you know, Father, I shall do that," she said laughing, "Bye now".

****

When the girls returned to school after Easter, Sister Roberta

167

asked me if I could have a word with a girl from Springs, in the Transvaal. She argued disruptively in religious instruction lessons and professed not to believe any of it. I agreed to have a word with her.

Rose Duplessis came into Sister's office with an exaggerated carelessness in her walk, which suggested she would do as she was told merely because she had to, not because she was being co-operative. For half an hour I tried to talk to Rose and got monosyllabic replies to my questions. As far as I was concerned I achieved very little, if anything. I admitted as much to Sister, but agreed that I would try again next week.

I saw Rose once a week and occasionally twice a week for the next few months. At first she resisted all my efforts to get through her defences. She was very guarded though she freely told me about her scorn of belief in God. She was very loath to talk about herself and her family life and I suspected that her troubles lay in difficult relationships at home.

Slowly over the months there emerged the story of a broken marriage and the consequent unhappiness of Rose who loved both her parents and hated to see them fighting and unloved amidst their mutual hatred. She ended up with an irrational fear that she too would be doomed to make a tragic mistake in her choice of marriage partner. As it all slowly came out, the hard facade began to dissolve and fall away.

At last one day as she told me about her fears in greater detail, she cried until she could not speak clearly. Talking I could cope with, but I had no answer to the flood of tears. I looked round helplessly and saw a box of tissues on Sister's desk. I took one out and handed it to Rose but she merely sat and did nothing to staunch the flow. In exasperation I took another and dabbed at her eyes, she merely sat submissively and not even looking at me.

By this time – the end of the winter – I was seeing Rose twice a week. I told Sister there was some progress. I would cope with the tears for at least her problems were coming out in the open. Of course Rose had told me all she had in confidence and Sister appreciated that had to be so.

For the next two weeks Rose's crying repeated each time we met, but also talked more about her feelings and fears. At times when she sobbed she would stretch out her hand wordlessly for another tissue. Sometimes she would hold on to my hand for a moment, as if taking strength from the contact. And then one day silently she put her head against my shoulder and cried that there was literally no one in the world who had any affection for her. I told her I did and Sister certainly did and that, beneath all the fighting, her parents loved her.

"Do you really care for me?" she asked.

"Yes, of course I do. When you first started talking to me, or rather not talking to me, months ago, you were not a very attractive girl. But now I have got to know you and I understand your problems.

168

When you know people well you do have an appreciation and affection for them."

She seemed mollified. I put my arm round her shoulders and led her back to her class.

I did feel by this time that Rose was perhaps indulging in a little self-pity and prolonging the agony. She still said she could not believe and nothing I had said over the last months had given her any reason to see why she should believe. I was a little surprised as she had appeared to agree with so much of what I had been saying.

"But just latterly you seem to have been listening more and discussing matters of faith. So why?"

She shrugged and smiled. "To be with you," she said.

"But what for, if you have no intention of believing?"

She leaned across and took my hands. "Because I love you," she told me.

I gently released my hands. "You mean all this time you have been coming here just for that reason."

"No", she answered, "at first I did not want to come, but Sister said I must. But you listened and you seemed to care about me and I fell in love with you."

"Oh, Lord," I said, "I can't carry on under these conditions. How old are you, Rose?"

"I am seventeen", she told me.

"I am over twice your age."

"That does not matter."

"Matter for what?" I asked.

"Being in love," she replied, "you did say you cared for me."

"Well of course I do and you are very attractive when you are not being deliberately unpleasant, but that doesn't mean I want to spend the rest of my life with you."

Rose got up and gave me a scornful look and turned on her heel and went towards the door.

"Now don't go out like that ...." But she was gone.

I told Sister later that I did not think it a good idea for me to see Rose again for the time being.

Ten days later the Bishop rang and said he was coming to see me. He arrived looking weary and worried. We went to my office. He was brusque.

"Sit down, Sam. Now, I have had reports – I cannot tell you from whom – about an alleged affair between you and a girl at the school called Rose." He blew out air in a great whoosh, as if he had been steeling himself for this unpleasant task all the way to the house. At last he had said it.

"What?" I asked increduously.

"Dear boy, you heard me. The report I received goes on to say that it is your intention to go away with the girl and get married."

"Good God. Who told you all this? Oh, no, you can't tell me, you

169

say." I shook my head and thought about it.

"Well", asked the Bishop after a long minute, "is it true?"

"No, of course it's not true." I roared, quite angry now.

"Are you sure, Sam? Listen, I'm not setting myself up as the great judge. What you tell me will stay here in this room and in my head. So, I really would prefer you to tell the truth, just between the pair of us."

"No", I repeated, not roaring this time.

"You didn't have a little poke".

I laughed in spite of the seriousness of the matter under discussion. "Really, Monsignor, I do wish you would try to lose your old R.A.F. coarseness. But the answer is still no."

"Are you saying that there is no substance in these allegations at all? Did you ever lay hands on the girl at all?"

"Well, I'll tell you. She came to see me at Sister's request because of all sorts of problems with family at home, which I can't tell you about, as it was all in confidence. Eventually, she broke down and all the worries came pouring. I have probably at times patted her hand, put my arm round her shoulders or something like that."

"What is 'something like that'?" he asked suspiciously.

"Well, what I just said – perhaps wiped her eyes when she had been bursting her heart crying. But certainly not what you previously suggested."

"Are you still seeing her?"

"No, as matter of fact I'm not", I replied. "She told me she loved me and rather hinted we could make a go of it. So I decided against further interviews until she had got rid of that idea."

"Does she understand that?"

"I should think so. I made it pretty clear and I have not seen her for the past ten days."

He sat and thought for a full three minutes, not looking at me.

"Alright, Sam," he said slowly, "I'll believe you."

"Oh, thank you very much," I said with some disgust, "I had hoped you might believe me because I happened to be telling the truth."

"Well, yes, dear boy, perhaps you were, as you see it, but we are expert self-deceivers, all of us."

"True," I conceded, "but I rather think I should have remembered if I had, as you so crudely put it, had a poke. It would take a fair amount of rationalisation to avoid that fact."

"Do you care for the girl?"

"Whatever that may mean. In a way, yes, I do. Latterly I knew she was leading me up the garden path, but that doesn't mean she didn't have real problems. There was never the slightest chance I would even consider taking advantage of her or making a dash for freedom with her."

"Mmm, well, if you say so, dear boy. You see the trouble is that

170

she has told all her class mates, and apparently half the school, that you have been having sexual relations with her in Sister's office, and that you plan to get married when she leaves school for good at Christmas."

"Bloody hell", I said with feeling.

"Well, indeed," agreed the Bishop. "You will see that your name does not rate very high by this time."

I was beginning to understand just why there had been a certain coldness in the last classes I had given at the school.

"My first reaction is to fight this", I told the Bishop, "but I don't know where to begin."

"You don't", he said with an air of finality. "You get out of the way".

"Good grief, you mean run away?"

"Well, dear boy, yes and no. You get out of the immediate way of a slanging match which you cannot win. A case of heads you lose, tails she or everyone else wins. No smoke without fire. So you get away. It is all arranged, dear boy, I assure you. All I need is your co-operation. The girl will leave school in December, then you come back, d'you see."

"You seem to be highly organised," I remarked a trifle cynically.

"I have seen it all before. We're fair game aren't we? Celibates. All anyone needs to do is to raise the slightest doubt about how celibate we are. A breath of rumour is enough and it's almost impossible to fight. The more you plead innocence, the more people think you are protesting too much, or perhaps not enough, and the horrible suspicion lingers. No, dear boy, you get out of the way for the time being and trust your uncle, O.K.?"

"O.K. I'll do what you say."

"Right", he said and he was in business again. "First thing in the morning you go to Standerton. It just so happens that Malcolm is having an operation on a cartilage next week, so you can go there for a bit anyway. After that we shall see. But it should only be for about six weeks. Meanwhile I shall keep my ear to the ground and in touch with local feeling and opinion. I want you to come back and show them I have confidence in you; I think that should silence a lot of tongue wagging. Any questions, old boy? I am sorry about all this, Sam."

I proposed a meal of bacon, egg, sausage and fried bread at the house. I knew I could tempt his lordship with such fare. He promised to be back for a late lunch after he had been to the convent to tell them of the change round he was making because Malcolm was going into hospital. He was going to tell them I was being 'borrowed' for a few weeks; one of the older priests, Barney, would be coming to hold the fort at Newcastle.

We set off early the next morning to go up to Standerton. In view of recent events it was not surprising that the Bishop started musing on

171

the celibacy of Catholic priests. The subject had come in for a lot of discussion at the Vatican Council, he said, most of it unofficial and behind the scenes. Many of the missionary bishops wanted a change in the law, as many countries only regarded a man as fully adult when he had a wife and had a family. Married priests will be accepted sometime, but Rome moves very slowly was the Bishop's opinion.

"You find it irksome, old boy?" he asked, trying to keep it as casual as he could. I eyed him with suspicion.

"Are you bringing up the subject of Rose again in an oblique way?"

"No, no, no – no," he insisted, "but a young man like you, it is difficult. Not for me particularly at my age. I should hate to share my privacy now – I am too set in my ways."

"Well, of course it's difficult", I told him. "Ordination doesn't mysteriously blunt your natural instincts. I suppose we drift through for most part satisfying ourselves with non-efficacious and merely mental attachments to women. I mean, putting it bluntly, that I do see, desire, and even enjoy the desiring, while all the time knowing that there will never be any fulfilment. That being the case it is absolutely essential that the member of the opposite sex being desired never learns of it. I suppose that is less than ideal in terms of the recommended re-direction of all desires in a heavenward direction. Perhaps that takes a lot of practice, I'm still a learner."

The Bishop chuckled a little, probably thinking back to days of more intense yearnings in his own heart.

"Did you get the old nonsense about 'not taking pleasure in such thoughts' when you did moral theology?" He asked, and I nodded agreement "As if such thoughts are not innately pleasurable and then you tangle yourself up in knots trying not to think about them. Oh, dear."

We did little more than drop the bags in the house at Standerton before the Bishop was off again, taking the opportunity while this far north to do business in Johannesburg. Malcolm had already gone to hospital in Pretoria and I was greeted at the house by the old, gnarled cook, Peter, who cackled and crackled with laughter. He made my stay at Standerton enjoyable because of his irrepressible cheerfulness. He presented everything he cooked as 'very nice... eggs, meat, potatoes...'; to Peter everything was very nice, but he gave you pause for thought about his sincerity by the laugh which followed such announcements. It sounded like the traditional witch's cackle after presenting some hell- brew which she enticingly described as very nice.

Malcolm had left a list of minimal services he had arranged for his absence. With a proposed stay of only six weeks, there was little to do but keep things ticking over. The parishioners in the town made efforts to entertain me and I dined out about twice a week during my stay. Otherwise the only other noteworthy diversions were the sad plight of a confirmed alcoholic, who was in a far worse condition than ever

172

Graham had been, and a local hotelier who was a homosexual and made it quite clear he would like to make love to me. To him I made it quite clear that I didn't want to do anything of the kind and with the alcoholic I went to meetings of Alcoholics Anonymous. I had never met the association before and was very impressed with the strength of the members who had to fight alcohol for the rest of their lives.

****

According to plan, I was back at Newcastle by Christmas. I moved about gingerly for the first week or so, like a convalescent patient not too sure of his footing. But I found no trace of strain in the Sisters or parishioners, and I asked no questions.

Our crowd – Lionel, Cos and the Pomeroy set, including Jack – met for a get-together at Washbank after Christmas. They were a little curious about my temporary stay up in Standerton, but I explained it all as a direct result of Malcolm's operation. Of course, Cos just had to be logical and ask why Barney had not gone up to Standerton and left me where I was at Newcastle. However, they had all seen examples of the inexplicable way the Bishop had of moving his clergy around and were content to accept this as just another example of his idiosyncracies. I spent most of the afternoon talking to Pro. In view of recent events, I was very conscious of the care which had to be taken in relationships with the opposite sex. Pro was often in my thoughts and I knew very well how fond I had grown of her. I warned myself to take precautions. Happily and fortunately, it seemed to me, she had not sensed any of my feelings and appeared to be as friendly with all the others in the crowd as she was with me.

Before it got dark in the late afternoon we went down to see how Neil and Creina had renovated their out-building. The whole of the mission complex was set on the lower slopes of the mountain which rose up behind the priests' house, so every building had front doors and back doors on different levels. The Alcock's was no exception. We entered the old, substantial barn and in the middle of the floor was a staircase leading down to another level where they had two more rooms. They had worked very hard to make it habitable and we were all able to scatter ourselves about the large room on low seats and cushions. Neil spent a lot of his time making critical remarks about the Catholic clergy -they were Anglicans – which Cos eventually countered by threatening to throw them off his farm. Neil fell back, laughing uproariously.

"Which proves exactly what I have been saying, Father; you clergy are so insufferably authoritarian in your manner and expect us all to bow the knee every time you speak. When that doesn't happen, you resort to the use of whatever power you can lay your hands on -excommunication, or whatever – in Fr Cos's case his power as a

173

landlord. Really what hope is there of having a co-operative here when there is a man who vetoes what he doesn't like and claims some sort of infallibility in doing it."

Cos knew he had fallen into a cleverly set trap. In fact it was obvious to me that in the year the Alcocks had been there, relationships had formed that made co-operation, and the co-operative, a real possibility. I asked Neil in a quieter moment how things were coming along. He told me that it had taken a long time – many months -before the Africans even began to trust them and believe in the possibility of continuity and security of tenure, but it was happening. He, Neil, had merely been, pottering about, getting to know people, until first invited to advise, and then to be a sort of manager of the farm co-operative. He was an employee of the committee and answerable to them. His task was made a lot easier, because he spoke fluent Zulu which he had learned as a small boy.

****

During the next year I became very friendly with the Anglican and Methodist clergy in Newcastle. In an ecumenical spirit we took to visiting each other and talking about our differences and our many similarities. We began to arrange joint services, and to preach in each other's churches. In my enthusiasm for the ecumenism, as urged by the Vatican Council, I suggested to the others, John Langdon, the Anglican priest, and William Williams, the Methodist, that I should approach The United Reform and Dutch Reform Churches.

"Sam, man", said William slowly, "I think it might be better if I approached the Dominee of the Dutch Reform Church. How shall I put it...."

"I know, William. He won't take too kindly to being approached by the Roman danger."

"Well, yes," agreed William rather sadly.

Eventually we all met together at the Methodist hall, which William thought would be the most neutral ground. It was cordial enough, as long as we were all together and could let our hair down in private. Sadly I met the Dominee in the town some fortnight later and he refused to recognise me. He was standing with some of his own parishioners talking and when I hailed him I got no response. I told William about the odd incident, again William's tact and charity were hard pressed.

He looked over my head for inspiration, "Sam he is a good chap, but he has many parishioners who would want him out if they knew he had been talking to you. I hope this doesn't hurt your feelings too much...." He was most concerned.

"Not a bit of it, William. I am just sorry for him".

I tried preaching about ecumenism at one of the African out-stations. I explained how we should now be ready to get together with other denominations and work together on projects, even though there were still quite a number of doctrinal differences. After mass some of the parishioners talked to me about my sermon, asking for specific instances of co-operation with members of other churches. I explained that if we helped one another in times of crisis; times of sickness and death; times of childbirth, there would be co-operation between the churches. We should not only help our own, but others, even if they were not Christians. I was teaching them nothing. They already had a much deeper sense of community than I. We do these things already, they told me.

"Good", I said lamely, "excellent, splendid. Well, then, that is what the Bishops at Rome are saying we should do." I retired somewhat deflated. I really hadn't needed the Bishops at Rome to tell me all this, I could have got the same ideas from my own parishioners.

Cos told me his news. The main item was that Lionel now felt a bit redundant. Neil and Creina were working well with the co-operative, and his consultant job as vet was hardly full time. He had quietly applied some months ago for a job with the newly independent Lesotho Government as a District Extension Officer and had just accepted the post. He could still check the livestock at the farm on his trips to South Africa. He still had no contract with the Bishop to detain him.

This naturally called for a party of our crowd and a date was proposed for a fortnight hence. It was a much quieter party than the previous one, partly because it was the end of the winter and still cold at night with frost in the air. We sat inside. There was no heating, so we wrapped ourselves in coats and blankets. Pro was sat next to me, principally because I had manipulated things that way. She did not like the cold and snuggled into a blanket against me, to which I did not object. We ate and drank and we talked and reminisced into the early hours of the morning. Pro announced that she too was moving. I started in surprise. She laughed and said that she was not going as far as Lionel but only to the nearby provincial hospital at Dundee. I was secretly relieved.

Before I went home that night Cos called me to his office.

"Torkington", he said sharply, "I don't know whether you are aware of it, but you gaze at Pro as if you have been badly smitten."

"Good lord, does it look like that?" I asked concerned.

"Yes, it does".

"Do you think anyone else has noticed?"

"Everyone else has noticed, you great fool. What do you think you're doing? You are going to get yourself entangled if you're not careful, which might just be a bit unfair on her, don't you think?"

"Yes, you're right", I admitted. "But she is very pretty, don't you think?"

"I know she is pretty, you buffoon, but she is not for you. Apart from your being a priest, you may also have noticed that she is black and you are white, which might raise one or two problems, too."

"Oh, yes, I suppose I am behaving badly," I said miserably.

"Oh, go home, you lunatic", he said in exasperation. I went.

****

Both Cos and I got invitations from William Williams to attend a T- group course at a place in central Natal. Before we went we tried to find out exactly what we were letting ourselves in for, but we met vagueness everywhere. All we knew was that it was an ecumenical and multi-racial course. This sounded like a good start and we thought we would give it a try.

The course was about relationships and democratic participation within groups. The odd thing was that we had short lectures on these subjects, only after we had experienced them in our course groups and not before. It was all very intense. After the best part of a week, we were all very friendly with each other, or even madly in love.

I remember two people particularly. One was a very beautiful young woman – she was in her middle-to-late twenties, and the other was an American Congregational minister. The young woman was in my group and provided a distraction, or focus of interest, for all the men in the group. Such was the frankness and intensity of the group sessions that all the men admitted their appreciation of her startling good looks. She was a calm, secure person, she took the praise gracefully and simply went on as before in the most unaffected way. The distraction had been somehow defused and we got on with the business of the week.

The congregational minister introduced me to Bob Dylan and to his idea of the law for man. I had been taught to have an almost overwhelming respect for the law, looking on the commandments as the absolutes, upon which our moral code was based. Lon, the American minister, did not see it that way. He viewed the commandments as 'useful'. Looking back, I am surprised that I was surprised. I suppose I vaguely believed that the law was made for man and not man for the law. It took Lon to bring things home to me. The law, any law is for a purpose and to be used; it should not be allowed in Procrustean fashion to mould people into regimented uniformity.

I remember being very impressed at the time by the week's experience. On the way home Cos was, predictably, more cynical. He suspected that the warm glow of the close, almost shipboard, relationships we had formed would die down and leave the week in a clearer perspective.

It was Saturday evening as we drove slowly back to north Natal. We bought fish and chips – so prosaic after the high plateau we had

176

been living on all week – and made our way back to Cos's mission at Washbank.

As we arrived there, Cos enquired if I was going straight back to Newcastle. I needed to get back fairly soon but I had hoped to stay for a little.

"I only ask", he said, "because I understand that Miss Mayeza has invited herself here for her first weekend off since she started work at the Provincial Hospital. I thought, all things considered, especially the fact that you are a renowned fathead when it comes to being in Pro's company, it would be better if you beat it now, before she gets here."

"She might just be disappointed if I go without seeing her", I said.

"I have to admit she did ask if you might be around this weekend. I feigned surprise and said why. She said she thinks you are a nice person. I tried to put her straight on that point, but it seems this absurdity is fixed in her head."

"Cos, you don't seem to understand the meeting of like minds and the spiritual links that are forged between them."

He snorted derisively and went inside, I followed.

Pro came about ten o'clock. She was not displeased with her new job, at least she could be sure of the hours she was working. Looking mischievously at Cos, she pointed out that now she was nearer to Washbank it enabled her to visit the holy mission more often, as if it were a kind of pilgrimage. Cos gave her a severely disapproving look over the top of his glasses. And what a lovely surprise to find Fr Sam here, she exclaimed.

"Torkington," muttered Cos, "go home".

I laughed. "Pro, your favourite parish priest is chasing me away. He happens to be right on this occasion. I only stayed to greet you and to say good-bye in the same breath. I have been away for a whole week and I ought to get back."

****

As spring came in, Rupert and myself made a plan to visit as many as possible of our parishioners in the town location and the out-stations before Christmas. There were one or two mines in areas which had small compounds for the workers attached to them, though most of the workers were able to live with their families in the hills around the mines. From the point of view of visiting this was most agreeable, we enjoyed roaming the hills in the newly greened fields after the first summer rains. The mine compounds in most mines deteriorated into slums, they were roughly built and lacked the basic facilities of roads or rubbish disposal. There was nothing to encourage the residents to have any home pride in them. One day I met an

177

African wandering much as I was. He had a large book in his hand and after greeting him I asked him what it was. It was, he said, God's book, the Bible. He was a minister of the Jehovah's Witnesses. In the spirit of ecumenism I chatted to him, asking him what he was doing up in the hills. He was visiting as I was, wandering and ready to talk to anyone who would listen.

"I will talk to you" he declared. He was probably about thirty to thirty five years old, but had the eagerness and cheerfulness of a schoolboy. I laughed and told him I was listening. We sat on two great stones on the top of a hill in the midday sun and he talked; he quoted all the time from the Bible, to prove any and every point. I noticed that the pages he opened had sentences underlined and these he quoted. After a while, I called a halt having listened to him for about ten minutes, during which time he hardly paused to take breath.

"Wait, wait", I told him, "you can't do that. You can't just pick sentences from here, there and everywhere in the Bible and lump them together and hope to make coherent sense of them." He would jump from Genesis to the New Testament, taking a half sentence here and a phrase there in order to prove some point. "Some of the passages you are using are taken out of context and don't really mean what you are trying to make them mean."

"Why not?" he was astonished. "They are all God's words and they say what he says. He does not say everything at once in the one place – we must search for his meanings. I am finding them", he told me triumphantly with a happy smile.

We talked and argued for two hours in the most amiable way. I was surprised at myself. To my mind it was a flagrant misuse of the Bible, but his manner was so sincere, without any aggression or intolerance, that in the end he had me making mental concessions to his mode of operation. I could go through the missal and the breviary and point to quite blatant text-picking out of context – who was I to criticise anyone else? His tolerance was the sort of virtue needed in the leaders of all churches convinced of their own total rectitude. We parted in high good humour.

Chapter Fifteen

Round about the time of my third Christmas in Newcastle I heard that Joe O'Grady had decided to leave the priesthood to get married. I was very surprised at his decision. He must have kept it a very close secret, for when I rang Cos to ask him about it, he too had only just heard. We still neither of us knew whether it was a rumour or not. Cos said he would get in touch with Joe. He rang me back later that day. Joe was asking for a dispensation from Rome which would allow him to marry within the church. Neither Cos nor myself had heard of this possibility and even Joe said he himself had merely heard about some priests in the Free State who had made such applications to Rome. It was not yet known if they had been granted dispensations, nor indeed whether they ever would be.

By the time we gathered at Washbank after Christmas it had been established by Joe that some priests had already been granted dispensations. There was no dispensation from celibacy for a priest, which was a disappointment. We had hoped, for the sake of the Church in Africa and parts of Asia, that permission would be given for married clergy; and for that matter for the whole Church. None of us believed that the two vocations of a priest and being a celibate necessarily had to be linked together.

Pro had arrived at Washbank before me and had already been discussing the news about Joe with Cos. At the end of the discussion Cos, blunt as ever, asked her if she thought I would ever consider asking for dispensation.

"Well, I suppose he would need to have someone in mind to marry", she told him.

He gave her a disgusted look. "You know very well I mean you, you clot," he told her rudely. "Would you marry him?"

"I don't know, I don't think he'd want to. I like him a lot, of course, but I have only allowed myself to think of him as good company and fun to be with. I suppose I've been surprised to find such companionship among white men, like you and Sam."

By the time I arrived, Cos had the bit between his teeth. He began the conversation by asking if I would now be thinking of taking a wife and looked round meaningfully at Pro. Embarrassed, I pointed out I understood that Pro had been promised to a chief in marriage and was hardly for the likes of me, a mere commoner. Later, we were alone, I nervously asked Pro what she thought about such things and Joe in particular. As an African, she believed that celibacy could do more harm than good in her country. Among the priests she had met there was a high percentage of, to say the least, eccentrics. There were some quite evidently neurotics who substituted their lack of a love life for expensive toys or took to drink. We both kept the conversation unusually theoretical.

Cos came in and interrupted. He wanted to talk about another issue. Just before Christmas a final notice to get out had been given to Africans living on an area of land among the white farms, opposite the furthest point of the mission to the East. The campaign to get Africans off the so-called 'black spots' had been gathering momentum recently. Now Cos thought they might actually be serious when they said that they intended forcibly to move the Africans by the end of January, if they had not moved themselves before that. Cos had not had time to investigate, because he had been busy over Christmas, but he had heard that a place was being staked out in plots to receive the people moved from the 'black spots' in north Natal. Cos and myself had been in the country for eight years and this sort of threat had been hanging over Africans for all that time and often longer. We had all begun to think that if we took no notice maybe the threats would go away. It appeared the Government meant business this time, as an actual date had been given - January 20th. Cos said he would follow it up and see how real the threat was.

We went to see Neil later and he was sick at the thought that just as the co-operative was beginning to take shape, after all their work, it might be destroyed. He was busy trying to play it the Government way, putting himself forward as the white farmer in charge of the place and involving as many families as possible by diversifying his farming – chickens, pigs, cattle for milk and beef, plus arable farming of as many different kinds as could seem feasible on their land. When we got to the Alcock's place, Neil and Creina were sitting with some of the committee members. They were all arguing as to whether they could reasonably put down ostrich farming as an acceptable industry in that area. Creina had been organising different kinds of craftwork and these were all going down as demanding labour to keep them going. There was a fair amount of hilarity in the meeting, with outlandish suggestions being considered to justify the need for labour at the mission and after all it was the Christmas season. It was evident that there was a serious worry in many of the Africans' minds that they would be forcibly evicted. There was no right of appeal and no compensation. Not that money could ever pay for the wrecking of their whole life style.

****

About a week later Cosmas called, he was very worried, I had been surprised when I first arrived in South Africa to find there was a great deal of concern about measles among the Africans. My English conditioning led me to suppose it was a disease every young child caught at some time and it was simply a nuisance. For the Africans, the disease could be a killer because of the nutritional deficiencies they suffered. At about the same time the previous year there had been two deaths due to the disease on Cos's mission. Determined this should

180

not happen again, he had taken some of the sick children to the hospital where Pro worked. The inadequate children's ward was very full and they had been able to offer only two places. Anyway, Pro warned, all the children were put together in the same ward because of lack of space. Cosmas's charges could well end up catching something else as well as measles. Isolation facilities for black patients were unknown. She advised him to take them back to the mission. After much discussion of the alternatives, Cos decided to take her advice. He would take them all back and bed them down in the sitting room and another large spare room. This would at least confine the disease to some extent. Pro said she would come over and stay the night to keep an eye on the children and advise if any severe cases needed further attention.

I went over to help for one day but it was all so well organised that I wasn't much use. There were many helpers, mainly the parents of the children, plus Pro at night of course. She was working twenty four hours a day and was understandably very tired but she knew how serious the situation might become. Happily, and hopefully because of this prompt action, there were no deaths. In fact the children had been so well fed that week they were almost loath to go back home.

Since my visit to Washbank at Christmas, Cos had been investigating the proposed removal of the Africans living near the mission. It now appeared very likely that the longstanding threats would soon become reality. He had been to see the place set aside for their new home – part of the 'homelands' as they were called by the authorities. The name was bitterly ironic to the Africans. It sounded to anyone not aware of the implications as if the authorities were graciously permitting them to return to the land of their fathers and even providing the land at no cost. It was far from so. There was no enthusiasm at all among the Africans who regarded the idea with loathing and yet had to stand by impotently while the policy was imposed upon them. Cos had discovered the main reason for the delay in implementing the policy in the last few years. An area had been designated to receive the 'squatters' living in the 'black spots' but there was very little water there. They had been boring for water for three years with minimal success. Only latterly, after a summer of heavy rains had they found water underground in any reasonable quantity. Cos had visited the area. It was bascially an open piece of veldt, sweeping down to a dry valley area. Plots had been pegged out and tracks had been made though purely by the passage of vehicles around the area. There were no facilities like toilets, no schools or shops. There were infrequent water points and that was all.

Cos became increasingly angry as he told me about it. He had been in touch with the Bantu Affairs Commissioner in the nearest town who had reassured him that all these facilities were planned and would be provided. He should not fuss. Cos demanded to know when, since it was already early January and the people were scheduled to be moved on the twentieth. "Please, Reverend", the commissioner had blandly assured him, "we know what we are doing; we are the experts at this sort of thing." He even dared to suggest that the people would be happier and grateful in the long run. Cos had thrown down the phone in disgust at this point. He said the man spoke as if they were merely herding cattle to a new and better pasture. In Cos's mind there was no way in which the pasture would be better. The plots were only about twice the size of a semi-detached house and small garden in England. The people would have to get rid of all their livestock – cattle, goats and sheep – and would be allowed to retain only a few chickens. The whole rural economy that supplemented their meagre wages was to be swept away. The nearest town was more distant which would mean increased bus fares, assuming there was any work available in the town. Anyway it was ludicrous to suppose a small country town could cope with the increase of landless labour that would be created in the next months as people were 'resettled'.

By the twentieth Cos had spread the word to all the nearby missions and about fifteen priests appeared at the 'black spot' threatened with removal. The Rand Daily Mail and several other papers had sent representatives. When the first trucks rolled up at about nine o'clock cameras began to click. The Government organisers were a little taken aback by the assembled audience – there must have been about thirty five to forty observers. They paused and had a discussion. About half an hour later the police arrived and the enforced moves began. The contents of houses were loaded onto lorries, the residents followed their belongings, often perched precariously on top of them. The trucks set off for the new area, while bull-dozers set about knocking down the empty houses. The cameras clicked furiously. The police moved across to an African photographer from the Rand Daily Mail and informed him it was not permitted to take photos without the express and written permission of the Bantu Affairs Commissioner. The African journalist listened gravely, nodded agreement courteously and moved away. He stood at some distance, fitted a zoom-lens and continued to take pictures. We laughed. The police realised they were going to have to confiscate everybody's cameras if they were going to make the ban effective. In those days they shrank from such open confrontation.

About lunch time a local Senator arrived on the scene. He lived close by and had met Cos before. He came up and asked how things were going. As badly as we had feared was our answer. He appeared embarrassed. He stood in silence viewing the proceedings for a few moments and then pointed to a truck which was being driven slowly over the uneven ground of a previously cultivated mealie field. There were cries from the people on the back of the truck who were terrified they would be thrown off and then as the truck reached the smoother road, they laughed in relief. The Senator drew our attention to the happy laughter of the people enjoying their adventure, he ventured to suggest. They waved to us and called out in Zulu. The Senator waved back and asked what they had said.

"Actually", said Cos with his best dead-pan face, "they said 'Please pray for us'." He spaced the words out carefully so that the Senator would understand. The Senator said 'Oh', and smiled weakly. He drove off in his car after a few minutes. He later reported that the moves were taking place smoothly in a spirit of co-operation.

In the early afternoon when many people had already been moved and the last ones for that day were being loaded onto the trucks, we got into cars and went over to Limehill, the new settlement area. The trucks had simply dumped their family loads, one on each plot. The family belongings were in most cases lying in a heap in the middle of the plot; often the mother of the family – many fathers were away at work in the big cities – was seated among her family belongings. Some were in tears, most dejected, not knowing what would happen next. It had been recognised by some far-sighted official that it took time to build a new house. Even the white South African Government could hardly leave people in the open for several weeks while building took place, even if those people were only Africans. So they had decided to provide tents. These had not been erected yet – in fact they only arrived as we did – the first comers had been presented with a bare terrain, broken only by the odd thorn bush. They were understandably distraught. We had decided amongst ourselves that we should take no part in the removals. Even helping people we knew could be interpreted by Government propaganda as the local clergy sensibly helping in the resettlement. When we got to Limehill and saw the distress of the people, we could hardly stand by and watch. We angrily seized the tents being unloaded from Government trucks and started to help the Africans to erect them. The feeble and rather frightened protests of officials were brushed aside. All the new arrivals eventually got cover for the night.

The removals went on for many months until Limehill was filled with thousands of people trying to build a new life. The local mission station worked overtime providing what help it could: a soup kitchen, blankets and clothing for the children. Cos's researches had revealed that other moves had been going on quietly and gradually elsewhere. The Government were clearly nervous of too much outside attention. He discovered that in another such move, with the usual lack of facilities, enteritis and typhoid had broken out and there had been a number of deaths. He warned through the newspapers that the same was likely to happen in Limehill.

During one of the breaks in the government resettlements Cos, Pro and I decided to take up an invitation from Lionel to visit him in Lesotho. On reflection, my resolve to keep my affection for Pro in check must have been crumbling fast. We travelled through the Free State in a small beetle Volkswagen, Cos at the wheel – he professed extreme apprehension at my driving – myself by his side in the front of the car and Pro in the back. This was the accepted custom for African servants travelling with their masters. In fact if they were travelling in their master's truck -common in the farm areas – the Africans always travelled in the back of the truck whatever the weather. After the border post on the Lesotho side, Cos pulled up and asked Pro if she wanted to travel in the front. She declined, the change had not yet hit her. At first Cos and myself were also just a trifle apprehensive. How would a newly independent African state welcome white men from across the border?

We drove into Maseru and pulled up outside a hotel. We went into the bar and approached the man behind the bar, an African we took to be the landlord.

"Gentlemen, good afternoon", he greeted us, "Can I help you?" he asked courteously. We were relieved at our first reception. He was most glad to give us directions and we found Lionel's house easily.

Lionel was not in. It was about four o'clock on a Monday afternoon and he was still at work according to his housekeeper. The house was a very new bungalow in South African style, gleaming white and sparkling in the afternoon sun.

At about five as the sun was going down, Lionel came in full of smiles at the sight of his visitors.

"Torkington, how good of you to come", he laughed, "I suppose there was no way you could leave Cos behind – but never mind", he said retreating as Cos threatened him with physical violence. "And Pro", he said, his voice softening, "how wonderful to see you". His eyes stayed with her for a moment. Lionel had always been very fond of Pro, ever since she came to work for him at the clinic at Pomeroy. "Wonderful to see you all, of course", he bellowed, returning to his boisterous good humour.

"Now, listen", he said, "Have you had a drink?"

"We've had tea", we told him.

"Oh, yes, but we must celebrate". He brought out a bottle of brandy. Cos viewed it mournfully over his glasses. Lionel was quietly watching him as he poured out drinks and as he came to the last one, he stopped.

"It just so happens that I have here", he said, going to the cupboard, "a bottle of whisky, if anyone would rather..."

"Well", said Cos with a modest little cough, "Perhaps, I might..."

His housekeeper had prepared a chicken meal for us; Lionel was inordinately fond of chicken. Over the meal Lionel outlined the programme for the week. It seemed very full, with a visit somewhere every evening. The high point of the week was not for the likes of Cos or myself. Lionel was friendly with King Moshoeshoe and had been invited, with partner, to a reception given by the King. He had known that we would be staying and had put down Pro's name as his partner, when replying to the invitation.

"Sorry, Cos, Sam; there was really only one choice in the circumstances. No hope of changing it now. I have spoken to the King of the charms of Miss Mayeza, and he is very eager to meet her".

Cos was disgusted. "This – mere slip of a girl to meet the King? Her job is here at home preparing food for us, not gallivanting about in circles to which she doesn't belong." He brooded a moment. "Tell me, Steel, isn't this King a Catholic?"

"Yes, he is".

"Then you can rest assured he will welcome two Catholic priests who are here on holiday – no need of an invitation."

Lionel laughed at him. "The King has more than enough priests in Lesotho, I can assure you. He does not see eye to eye with many of them. I don't think that your clerical state will buy you any favours".

"Funny country," remarked Cos and retired to his whisky.

The next morning Lionel was gone before we roused ourselves. About mid-morning, after chatting for some time, we got dressed and had breakfast. We decided to take a stroll down to the town. Cos and myself were soon aware that Pro was not totally at ease. We guessed why."

"Miss Mayeza, do you feel, now that you are in a black-ruled country some shame at walking with us?", teased Cos.

Pro smiled nervously.

"Remember that I have never been out of South Africa before. I only know my own country. I see people looking at us and wonder if they are plain clothes policemen who disapprove of our being together. I have to keep telling myself it's alright and that no one is going to come and worry us."

We felt a little ashamed of not having realised that Pro had never experienced the freedom to walk anywhere and with anyone. We were so used to her easily socialising with us, we had forgotten how untypical this was. We explained that the looks were more likely to be meant for us and any possible hostility directed at us as white men. Many of the whites from South Africa who frequented Maseru came for a little entertainment from black girls – a thing that they would not dare in their own country and hence were resented by the Africans who saw them with black girls. As Pro became more accustomed to being in a free country and as she began to lord it over us we were almost sorry that we'd told her. Cos tried to keep the edge whispering that the policeman approaching us was going to ask to see her pass-book, but it was too late.

It was a hectic week, with parties every night – except the night when Cos and myself were left at home while Lionel and Pro went to the royal reception. Pro generally wore her hair in tight plaits on top of her head, but on the morning of the reception she undid the plaits and combed out her hair. We spent some hours creating hair styles; discussing which jewellery she should wear; telling her how to offer her hand to the King and how in all probability he would stoop and kiss it. By the time Lionel came home she was in a state of high excitement and went off with him wearing a dazzling smile and looking exceedingly pretty.

When they came back in the evening, we were compelled to hear of how the King had greeted her, spoken to her, admired her and generally lavished his time and attention upon her to the virtual exclusion of everyone else.

"Do you think he fancied you?" asked Cos bluntly. "We could leave you here when we go."

But nothing he could say would take away from Pro the delight and excitement of the whole evening and especially having been presented to the King.

Being together with Pro all week was having a profound affect on me, and on her. In Maseru we could relax without any fear of being accused of contravening some wretched apartheid regulation. We talked and we walked about the town, sometimes with Cos, though often he declined to walk any more. When faced with the necessity of moving from one place to another, his ideal was to do it by car. Walking for pleasure he viewed as a somewhat bizarre idea. When Pro and I were by ourselves we talked about life outside South Africa and as the week went by we found ourselves personalising this discussion, more and more. We both knew it was now possible to obtain a dispensation from the priesthood. The wish to do just that had been getting stronger in me for some months now. I admitted as much to Pro. I think that being in Lesotho had given her a new dimension, one without apartheid, in which to look at the possibility of our living together. I told her I should like to apply for such a dispensation – which was really a contorted way of proposing marriage. I wanted to know what her reaction might be before taking things any further. I need not have worried. Pro's emotions came spilling out. Her happiness at finally being certain that we shared the same feelings was radiant. We had spent a very long time flirting but pretending ours was purely a friendship, with no romantic content. A long time indulging in secret fantasies about each other but with no real hope that the barriers between us might ever disappear. It was like taking the lid off a pressure cooker.But it was early days. Rome might refuse, we might decide the obstacles were too great and scrap the whole idea. However, I thought that given my feelings, I must in all fairness tell the Bishop. For Pro there were a different set of problems. After all I was a white man and she would certainly have to contend with many members of her family who would very strongly disapprove. She was also aware that she would be cast as the "scarlet woman", in cases like ours the woman was always thought to have seduced the priest from the paths of righteousness. So it was in a qualified way that we admitted our love for each other, hoping that at some time in the future we could live together as man and wife.

On our last day in Maseru, after we had been for a walk without Cos, we came back to find him, lying, on the settee, reading and having a drink. He gazed at us as we came in and smiled a little guiltily.

"Just having a little drinkees, you know".

"So we see. As soon as my back is turned you are at that whisky bottle. I know that this is a holiday, but the sun is not yet down, Carstairs. Dammit man, one does have standards."

"This is my standard", said Cos, raising his glass aloft.

"Can you ever be serious?" asked Pro.

"Me?" asked Cos, "I'm never anything but. What is it my child?"

"It's about Sam and me."

"Oh, yes," he said smirking.

"We have just been talking about the possibility of getting married."

"Good God", said Cos, "you mean to tell me you have only just got round to that? I assumed that you had all that settled months ago. Everybody else had."

Pro screamed in mock anger and looked not a little embarrassed.

"Well, it's not as simple as that", I told him, "there are so many ifs and buts."

"Well", Cos fell back, losing interest and picking up his book again, "if that's all you have to tell me...."

"But then again", he said, picking up his glass and making a half-hearted effort to rise, "this does call for a celebratory drink, what?" He had learned the 'what?' from close association with the Bishop. He lay back pretending exhaustion from the effort of getting up. "Perhaps, Miss Mayeza, before you give yourself entirely to this man, you could see your way to getting me another drink." He turned to me, "Have one yourself, Torkington, you probably need it. Must have been a harrowing day for you."

"Well, it has a bit", I admitted, "I find that after several parties like the ones we have been attending this week, I do wake up with the tiniest little head-ache".

"Oh, a hang-over, you mean," said Cos, "I never have those. If you can't take your drink, you ought not to indulge. Perhaps you ought only to have a small one now, don't you think? Actually, I meant 'harrowing day' because of the momentous decisions you have been reaching. Mind you I should have thought, the inevitability of it all, would have obviated the need to make any explicit declarations. However, I suppose the pair of you think you're adult and able to formulate some sort of thought processes."

It was at this point that Pro hit him with a heavy cushion, he screamed in real terror as his glass of precious scotch nearly went over.

We had a small party with a few of Lionel's quieter friends on our last evening. We were in more sombre and reflective mood, reminiscing about the times we had all spent together over the years. Pro and I had decided not to tell Lionel just yet, we felt that I ought to see the Bishop first before telling anyone else. Telling Cos did not really count. Obviously he had been so close to us in the past few months it was hardly necessary to tell him at all.

I arrived back on Saturday and went up to see the Bishop on Monday morning. Delay would only make the task harder I decided.

"Hello, old boy, what brings you this way?" he asked in suprise.

He was living at that time in Ermelo, which was not on any direct routes I might have been expected to take.

I smiled a little weakly and then blurted it out.

"I'm thinking of applying for dispensation to get married", I told him in a rush of words.

"Oh, are you, dear boy?" he said quietly and reflected a moment. "I always thought that you, Joe and Cos might do that sort of thing",

I was a little surprised at that. "Cos?" I said, "when did he ever mention taking a step in that direction?"

"No, no, he didn't", the Bishop replied, "but he talks about married clergy and that sort of thing. Well, Sam, what are we going to do about you?" he asked, but not unkindly. "I suppose that I shall have to shift you out of Newcastle. Probably better, don't you think?"

"Entirely up to you, of course, Monsignor", I told him.

"Can I ask who she is?" he asked. He saw my expression, "no? Well, that's alright, old boy."

"Sorry, I don't mean to be snooty. I'd just rather not tell you yet. You never know what might happen. If nothing comes of this, I probably wouldn't want people to know. Do you mind?"

"Not at all, not at all. I understand perfectly. But at least this – Does she come from Newcastle?"

"No."

"Ah well I still think that I shall ask you to move. Why not take a bit of a holiday and think things over. After the build-up to telling people things might look different. D'you see, dear boy?"

"O.K. Perhaps you're right."

"Sam, we shall be very sorry to lose you; you have done sterling work. I am very grateful for all you did in setting up the seminary, and all the other things for that matter. Oh, dear, never mind", he tailed off a little sadly.

"Well, let's be practical. Can you hold on till next week. John is back from leave then and he can take on Newcastle, O.K.?"

I moved within a fortnight and went to stay with Cos at Washbank prior to taking my holiday. The time before going away had to be spent in making out an application to Rome. Cos and I treated it like a campaign document. We wanted it to embody all our thoughts about issues of married clergy, the non-essential linkage between priesthood and celibacy etc. etc. We ended up with an application for dispensation from celibacy and a request to continue as an active priest. Right at the very end I asked for dispensation from both priesthood and celibacy if they would not consider splitting the two things. It took several pages. We thought it summed up rather well our thinking about the future course of the priesthood. I sent it off to my superiors with a cocktail of feelings; equal parts of relief, regrets and elation.

While I was at it I sent off a letter home explaining what I was doing. I knew it would hurt my parents very much, but I couldn't keep it from them any longer. It took a long time to write that letter.

I decided to go on holiday to Swaziland, where I thought I might make my future home, if the prospects were favourable. I secretly intended to try to find a job there. Cos told me he would drive me over and stay with me for a couple of days, as he had not seen the country either. Pro came over to Washbank the Sunday before we went. We held each other in a close embrace and hoped.

Chapter Sixteen

On a clear winter morning, with a crispness still in the air, Cos and I set off for Swaziland. We arrived at Mbabane by late afternoon and booked in at the Central Hotel. We were lucky to get a room. There was a public holiday in the Republic and the hotel was full of visitors from the Transvaal. After the journey we felt we deserved a drink and went downstairs into one of the bars. We had barely entered the bar when we were approached by two young Swazi ladies, who greeted us extremely affably, slipping their arms through ours and leading us to the bar. They seemed grateful for the drink Cos courteously offered them, and each had half pint of beer. My escort then made her business very clear by assuring me she was clean. She certainly appeared clean and well-dressed, so I assumed that she meant 'clean' in more than the superficial sense. During the conversation over drinks it became apparent that business was not very good as the British army had withdrawn from Swaziland now that independence was imminent. They recognised from our accents that we were British and not South African. They told us that the young white men further up the bar were Afrikaner farmers over for the holiday. The young men seemed to have left their apartheid convictions at the border.

Our two young ladies had decided that we were Britons far from home – perhaps attached to the contingent which had just arrived to help with the transition to independence – and therefore we needed a few home comforts. It was only when Cos hit on the idea of telling them we had to go back to our rooms to rejoin our wives that they desisted – in a most understanding manner. They even wanted to know if we had any children. Cos was well into his role by now, he credited me with five and claimed a modest four for himself. They understood and said "Ah, that's nice", and made no further efforts to claim our custom. It seemed kinder than telling them they had been chatting up a pair of priests.

The next morning we wandered round the town. It was only about the size of a South African veldt town, but the easy mixing of races made it strikingly different. It was something of the same atmosphere we had experienced at Maseru in Lesotho. However, the whole feel and aspect of Swaziland was softer, I think because the terrain was so different. Maseru was in the plain dominated by the huge Drakensberg mountains, stark and rocky, whereas the Swaziland hills in the north of the country were gently rounded and clothed in velvet green. In the afternoon we ran down through the beautiful lush and wooded hills to Manzini. We passed along the road by a hotel and gambling casino which was beginning to entice customers from South Africa and further afield. It was set in the most glorious countryside, facing hills, of which only the tips showed any outcrops of rock. The road fell gradually over the thirty-five mile drive into Manzini and as it did so the temperature rose.At the lower altitude we began to pass through acres of orange and grapefruit trees, and to the west of Manzini, vast fields of pineapples. I mused to Cos that perhaps the garden of Eden had been this sort of fertile paradise. He has little poetic soul and the magic of the glorious countryside failed to reach him. The usual cynical and acerbic response came back.

"As I remember it, they grew apples there. And the woman Eve, tempted Adam with forbidden fruit and he succumbed. Think about it, Torkington."

"You don't miss a chance, do you?"

"I feel it my duty", he told me, assuming an expression of sickening virtue.

We drove back to Mbabane in the cool of the evening. I was instantly attracted to Swaziland in much the same way as I had been to Pomeroy. Everyone appeared to live at a relaxed pace and the country did not have the harshness of the more rugged parts of South Africa. It was generally lower in altitude than the south eastern Transvaal or the places I had known recently in northern Natal. It was now winter, but even at night there was no sign of frost. The days had the same totally clear blue skies I had known in the northern South African winter.

The next morning Cos left. I had admitted to him that I was going to try to find a job and that, if all went well, I should not be returning after my holiday. I felt isolated and a little afraid after he had gone. For quite some time I had not been wearing either my habit or clerical dress except when performing in church. Both Cos and I had changed our earlier conformist ideas. We felt our uniform did not so much proclaim our witness to a faith and way of life as followers of Christ, as set us apart, and in some instances placed us in an uncomfortably privileged category. So often do the clergy receive preferential treatment, that they learn to expect it. Now in this place nobody knew who I was or what I was. I could enjoy myself on holiday – I tried to fill my head with positive, cheerful thoughts. However, thinking about a new way of life left me apprehensive, if not a little frightened, even in so gentle a place as Swaziland. Maybe it was not as gentle when you were looking for a job, one in the crowd with little useful training.

I decided to make a start looking for work the next morning. I had no introductions and no idea what I might do. Some sort of social work, perhaps? There must be offices of the voluntary agencies in Swaziland. Or the Government service, I thought. The British were still here; there must be jobs with all the extra work coming up to independence. If I could get in now, maybe I could continue after independence.

For two days I trailed round the different departments of Government. Most were strangely uncurious as to where I had come from, they were even eager to help. At first I was impressed by the way they would give serious consideration to the possibility of fitting me in somewhere. One department would say, they had not got anything now – just beginning to draw in our horns, really, with independence

191

coming up shortly – but you might try Brown, down at Personnel. Brown didn't know of anything himself, but that didn't mean there was nothing. Why not try Green over at the Health Department – I know that they wanted an ambulance attendant recently – ever been involved in the medical field? Well, it doesn't matter really; I knew nothing about Personnel until I joined this outfit. Green hadn't got anything either, but what about Finance? He called over a colleague and they had a long think. Yes, try White at Finance; tell him we sent you, O.K.? White was somewhat more efficient and wanted to know what qualifications and experience I had, and when he learned I had none, told me I had unfortunately been misinformed about possible openings; but what about Education – done any teaching? I said that I had. Well, then, go and see Black in Education -tell him I sent you. Black was much less rigid in his demands. He thought old Nobby Clark at the school on the hill might help. It's a college actually, he told me, raising it in status. It was for failed Junior Certificate candidates who were given a three month intensive course and then jobs in the local civil service. Go and see Nobby, tell him I sent you. He doesn't really care about qualifications, because he hasn't got any himself. Used to be a District Officer, but those jobs are being Africanised now and we had to find old Nobby a job. A call to Nobby Clark at his school told me that he, regrettably, had no jobs to offer at the moment, but I could try.... At the end of two days I had nothing except sore feet.

I was discouraged. Priests are used to full employment. I began to understand what it was like trudging the streets in search of work. I was getting consideration and advice, rather than blank refusals, probably because I was a white man and because I was speaking to fellow Englishmen. I had one last hope after trailing round all the departments. An American doctor at the health department had suggested I come back in two days and he would sound out the possibilities in other parts of the country. The magic of the country seemed to be wearing a little thin. My reservation at the hotel was coming to an end the next morning and to book in for a further week at the cheaper weekly rate would eat into the small amount of money I had for my holiday. I wanted to preserve that as long as possible. I was now worrying about just how long I would have to wait before finding a job.

I went back to see Dr Muldoon who spread his hands wide in apology as he saw me. He had failed to come up with anything, he said. He stood, aware of my disappointment. He asked me what I had been doing before. I told him I was a Catholic priest. Really, he said, he was himself a Catholic. One of the problems I had anticipated facing was the attitude of lay people in the Church when they discovered they were talking to a priest who had left or whose intention was to leave the priesthood. I expected horror from a few and from the majority some disgust that I had ratted on my special calling. Dr Muldoon smiled with interest, and the fact seemed to increase his determination to be

192

of help.

"Must you stay in Mbabane?" he asked.

"Oh, no", I told him, "I am ready to move anywhere, though I would prefer not to go back to the Republic for a job."

"Oh, yes, I can understand that," agreed Dr Muldoon. "I have to go there sometimes, but I get out as soon as I can after conducting my business. Now, I know a man in Manzini who runs a company. He is an Irishman and a Catholic. I think he might be able to help you. I'll write his name and address down for you. It should be easy for you to get to Manzini."

He gave me the piece of paper with a name and address on it and wished me luck as we parted.

I had not yet thought of trying Manzini for a job but I decided that I should do so now, even if the job suggested by Dr Muldoon did not materialise. I gave myself the rest of the day off and determined to leave the next morning, after my hotel reservation had run out. That way I got breakfast which would keep me going until I arrived at Manzini.

I took to the road early the next day. I had not walked very far when a big Mercedes Benz pulled up as I tried to thumb a lift. It was driven by an African man who offered to take me all the way to Manzini. In consequence I arrived by mid-morning. It did not take long to locate the business of Mr Brogan. I asked the receptionist if I could see Mr Brogan and told her that I had been sent by Dr Muldoon. His name seemed to open doors miraculously. I was immediately ushered into Mr Brogan's office.

"Any friend of Paddy Muldoon is welcome here", he smiled, coming forward with out-stretched hand. "Sit down, sit down."

"Actually, I have only met Dr Muldoon this week", I told him, "He advised me to come and see you, I am looking for a job".

"Oh, I see", said Mr Brogan, becoming a little more formal. He sat down behind his desk and pulled a pad towards him.

"I don't know whether I can help you, young man, but we shall see".

He took a pencil in his hand and looked expectantly at me.

"Your name, then?"

"Sam Torkington".

"And what sort of experience have you had in business and in the builder's merchants trade, then?"

"Actually, none at all. I think perhaps I ought to say that I am a Catholic priest."

"Aaaahh," he said slowly, and put down his pencil. "Well, we shall have to find something for you."

I was delighted, but restrained myself from falling all over Mr Brogan with gratitude.

"You probably know that this country is about to become independent. The building trade is expanding because there are a lot of

193

new buildings going up. I'm looking for young men to manage my different branches throughout the country, but the devil is getting men you can trust. Now in your case, I don't know you, but my bet is that as a priest you'll have a fair amount of honesty about you, and you won't cheat on me. But you will have to learn the business first, right from the bottom up. And how does that look to you?"

"I'm very grateful to you, Mr Brogan and I hope I won't let you down."

"I'm going to leave it to you as to how quickly you learn things," he told me. "You can start in the yard where you will get a good idea of all the lines we sell; the different kinds of timber and roofing. Then move into the shop and so on. See the whole works. Now, accommodation. You have nowhere to stay, I suppose?"

"No, I don't yet," I admitted.

"Well, the company owns some houses – only small but alright for a start. And you can have a bed out of stock which you can pay for out of your monthly salary. Alright, Mr Torkington, you leave all that to me. Go off and get yourself some lunch and by the time you get back I shall have a few things sorted out. "And" – he called me back as I started for the door – "if you find that you are without money, come and see me. Are you alright at the moment?"

"I am, thank you, Mr Brogan." I went.

I found a little cafe on the main street called Sam's Place. This put the finishing touch to my sense of achievement and delight. It had to be a good omen. It was bright and clean and, more importantly, it sold cheap meals.

By evening I was installed in a small four roomed bungalow. The houses on the estate were like superior location houses though they were larger in size and had electricity laid on. I had a bed, and nothing else apart from the luggage and the blanket I had brought with me. I went out before the shops closed and bought myself a primus stove, a frying pan, a kettle and a few items of food. I had set up home. Another employee of Mr Brogan came across to see that I had all I needed and offered me a candle for lighting. I tried the lights and found that the electricity had been turned on, so I thanked him and declined his offer. I went into the kitchen and saw a thick cable hanging from the wall. It was obvious that an electric stove had been removed from there, and the cable would be useful if I at some stage managed to acquire a cooker. I gave the cable a casual kick. The end of it skidded along the concrete floor giving off a fine cascade of sparks and then all the lights went out. I was alarmed. The cable had been carrying what might well have been a lethal load of electricity. I went across the road and said that I would like to take up the offer of the candle after all.

The next morning I turned up for work at the building contractors' yard. I spent the day mainly observing and trying to understand what the orders from the inside shop meant. There were four African men working in the yard and they knew the job backwards. After a few days, as the signs and symbols on the invoices began to make some sense I started learning where items were stored and, by having a quick look round first thing in the morning, whether we needed to replace any stock. But even when I thought I had learned to be quick in filling a customer's order, I was never quicker than the African men. Mr Brogan's idea was that I should move through the different departments as fast as possible. He had left me to decide at what point I had sufficient grasp to be able to move on. I feared I should take a long time.

I found a laundry in the town that would wash shirts for me in two days; I found a bakery that baked new bread every day and of course there was plenty of fruit in this other Eden. In the mornings I boiled an egg in the kettle and then used the water to make coffee. I had a sandwich and a cup of tea at the yard for lunch. In the evening I went to Sam's Place, where I would sit for an hour over my meal and read the paper as I ate. Within a week I had this routine worked out and felt remarkably settled as if I had been there for longer than a mere seven days.

I saw Mr Brogan from time to time in the first three weeks and he asked how I was progressing. It was apparent from the urgency of his enquiry that he was expecting great things of me and I began to be haunted that I should prove a disappointment to him. I was frankly content for the moment to accustom myself to this new life and to think through all the implications of the change I was proposing. My house was quite adequate, my domestic arrangements satisfied me. I came to the awful conclusion after three weeks that I lacked the drive and initiative that Mr Brogan was seeking. Of course, I tried to tell myself, it was early days, I was in a period of transition. I should shortly take off with enthusiasm and ambition in the field of builders' supplies. But I didn't really believe myself.

I wrote to Pro as I had promised. I knew that she would be going to her home for a holiday, and there had been a suggestion that for the final week of her holiday she would come over to Swaziland, if I had found somewhere she could stay. She did have friends who lived near Manzini, but at the time I had left Washbank we had supposed that I should be staying in Mbabane. I asked her to come over and see the place, to see what might be a future home for us. I still had a little of my holiday money left, with it I bought some cheap, colourful material and a needle and thread. I made a pair of curtains. I was tired of having to put out the light when I wanted to undress at night. In the second week I had succumbed to great extravagance and bought a large woven grass mat which covered most of the floor of the one room I was using to live and sleep in. I surveyed my efforts at home-making and felt smug as I viewed the beginnings of a new home. There were no chairs, there was no table, but in time....

At the end of the third week and just before Pro was due to come to Manzini, I had a letter from Fr Paschal, my religious superior, telling me that to comply with regulations as devised by Rome, I had to be interviewed by a religious superior from another area. He proposed I should fulfil this regulation in ten days time. He would call for me and take me to Durban for the interview.

Pro arrived the next day, but not until about ten o'clock at night. She had taken a bus in South Africa which had visited just about everywhere imaginable before arriving in Manzini a long time behind schedule. I had been hoping that we should be able to have a meal at Sam's Place before going to see my little house. But the cafe had closed by the time she arrived. I did not know if she had made arrangements to go and stay at her friend's house on the outskirts of the town. For a moment these matters could wait. We were meeting in a free country that might become our home. It was a strange experience. I no longer felt like a priest; mainly because no one knew me as a priest except Mr Brogan and he was certainly not going to tell anyone. I was a man meeting the woman he loved off a bus and we were walking home. It was a very new feeling, not wild ecstasy, but contentment, as if we had already achieved something. We had started walking towards my house, when it occurred to me I should ask Pro, where she would be staying for the night. We stopped and she looked at me. I mean, I stammered, was she going to stay with the friends she had mentioned, I hadn't meant to presume she would stay with me. She asked me what I thought she ought to do. I said that I thought it was a bit late – to be intruding on friends who might already have gone to bed. She giggled and agreed. We walked on, my arm around her.

It was hardly possible for her to be impressed with the house, there was after all only one room even half furnished. I pointed out there was only one bed, but assured her I would sleep on the fine mat I had bought. We sat on the bed and talked. We lay on the bed together. It was an electrifying new dimension and I knew in that one week that there would be no more doubts about marrying Pro. I knew then I would have no regrets. The best time was at the weekend when we walked the town without any fears or inhibitions. We ate at Sam's Place, we bought some very new bread and I was very ill. But what matter, I had my own personal nurse to care for me.

We talked all week of our future and my job. At first Pro had been extremely amused when I told her about my work. As I spoke of it in more depth, she told me she felt that I would never be really happy at Brogans. Her words reinforced my own feelings. I needed time to reflect and consolidate. I was also very concerned about the economics not just of Mr Brogan's company, but of the whole country, it seemed. The African was treated virtually the same as his counterpart in South Africa in terms of wages and job prospects. Admittedly there was no discrimination in public places or legally in the employment field, but in actuality the black man was being exploited just as he was in South Africa. The African workers in the yard could do the job without the slightest difficulty, while I struggled to understand its complexities, but they were paid one fifth of my wages. I was aghast when I discovered this and told my fellow African workers so. Inevitably if I continued like that I should not last very long in any job.

By the end of the week we had decided that I must rethink my position. But where and when? Fr Paschal was coming for me the next day. Perhaps if I asked to stay in South Africa while I reconsidered in the light of my experiences in Swaziland. We agreed that I should do so, even if the reconsideration might mean we would never marry. Perhaps I ought to make sure that I was not simply being carried forward on a huge emotional wave that would inevitably come crashing down.

I saw Mr Brogan that day and explained my thoughts, omitting any reference to Pro. He understood. It was, he said, a risk he had taken before with priests who thought that they wanted to leave the priesthood and then suddenly found how attractive their former life was. I said that I didn't know whether that was the case with me, but it might well be. It ended up with a curious reversal of roles – Mr Brogan implicitly giving me his blessing in a patriarchal way and advising me to think hard before coming to any final decision. He undertook to make sure that my bed was taken back into stock. He embarrassed me by saying that my wages up to date would be waiting for me first thing the next morning. I protested that I could not take them, his kindness and help had been more than enough. But he insisted, saying that I had earned the money. I have always remembered his warmth and sense of fair play.

That evening Pro and I went to Sam's Place for a last meal feeling rather sad. It might be the end of our relationship and anyway we were leaving the unrestricted life of Swaziland for South Africa where segregation forbade this easy way of life. As Pro put it our love might be strong and passionate but it was also filled with uncertainties. With apartheid on top of all that, any relationship might be expected to break down under such pressure. We were afraid that emotional death was close at hand and frightened to hope for too much.

I ran from work at midday to escort Pro to a taxi which would take her to her friends about two miles away so as to avoid Paschal meeting her. The middle of town was no place for lovers' fond farewells, especially when those lovers were black and white even in Swaziland.

At five o'clock I sped from the builders' yard for the last time and made for the George Hotel to see if Paschal had arrived. His tall, husky figure was waiting for me in the foyer. He grinned and his big hands grasped my hand and pumped it up and down enthusiastically.

"Good to see you, Sam", he said. And for me it was good to see him. As a religious superior he had been worried but understanding about my decision but had never given the slightest hint of rejecting me out of disapproval. We had a meal and he cautiously tried to sound me out about the future. I told him that I had decided to give up my job

197

in Swaziland and to come back if that was alright with him and the Bishop.

"You know it is, Sam. There is no need to ask."

"I don't mean that I have changed my mind about leaving, Paschal", I explained, "I just don't know yet. What I am asking for is time to think things over. Being here has helped enormously to clear my head, but it has also raised other problems and I want to think about those. I have seen things a lot more clearly from the layman's point of view. I have seen what at least some lay people think of priests, and very often it is not how we think that they see us. Still it's early days to be boring you with all this."

"You're not boring me", said Paschal kindly. "Anyway, eat. I say with all due respect, Sam, that you look as if you could do with a good meal."

I suppose that I had hardly been overeating and I was tired. Paschal drove me home at about nine-thirty and arranged to meet me at six the next morning.

I had hoped that Paschal might be a little later than the proposed time of six o'clock, but he was prompt. I couldn't really object to the time. He had outlined his plan which was to get to Durban by two for my appointment with the religious superior and then to try to get back to north Natal that same evening. It was a long haul and demanded an early start. However, I knew Pro would be in the centre of the town about six in order to catch her bus back to South Africa. I did not want to risk a meeting between Paschal and herself. They already knew each other and he would draw the inevitable conclusion. Cos was still the only one who knew the identity of the lady with whom I was involved. I saw Pro as we approached the town centre. She drew into a shop doorway and I eschewed any sign of recognition. It was a painful moment, I felt both deceiptful and cruel.

As we drove the enormous yellow ball of sun rising through the early morning mist was an awesome sight in the quiet stillness before the bustle of the day. As the morning advanced the sun burned away the mist and defied us to look at it any longer.

We just made my appointment on time. I had made no preparations; in the event it was not necessary. The meeting was very low key, almost a formality. I told the big man who was interviewing me that I still wanted to leave in order to get married. He seemed to find this of little significance, since all priests at some time or another, and often many times, feel that way. The answer to the urge was to pray and to renew pristine resolve. His main worry seemed to be my relations with my Bishop and religious superior, Fr. Paschal. He was a little disconcerted when I told him that I liked, admired and trusted both the Bishop and my religious superior. He had seen many cases, he admitted, where a request for a dispensation was the result of poor relations between Bishop or religious superior and the priest who wanted to leave. His summing up was to the effect that there seemed to be little reason for my wanting to leave. I was the sort of young man we wanted to keep, he said. There had been those applying, he told me, that they were glad to be rid of. All my pleas about having made my decision and expecting to be taken seriously were gently set aside as just a passing desire to taste the greener grass on the other side of the fence. He eased me out with a kindly smile and advised me to go back to my mission, get on with my work and think about what he had said. He did not reveal what he intended to write to Rome but I feared he was going to advise against giving me a dispensation. I left feeling I'd been given a very casual brush off.

We arrived at Washbank by late evening. I was pleased because I thought this would give me an opportunity to talk to Cos. But he had gone, I was told. Paschal had assumed that I knew there had been some personnel changes, partly due to my withdrawal from Newcastle. Cos had gone to join the Bishop at Ermelo, as his secretary. I learnt later, that he had engineered himself a job which would leave him free of parish commitments so that he could chase about investigating the semi-secret activity of the Goverment clearances of the so-called 'black spots'. This he did, first of all in north Natal, but his searches widened until he was covering most of the Republic. The title of secretary to the Bishop was really little more than a courtesy allowed by the Bishop who supported Cos's campaign. It was pleasant to be back in familiar surroundings, though sad. I associated the mission with meetings of our group in past years and now even Cos had left. We sat and had tea. Then without any previous warning, Paschal who had obviously been in touch with the Bishop, asked if I was prepared to take a small parish over towards the Swaziland border. I told him I would naturally do anything they wished. It would, he said, entail living by myself, but perhaps that was a good idea if I wanted peace and quiet in order to think out my future. I agreed and asked when I should be moving. Tomorrow, came the answer, and we both laughed, knowing how typical of the Bishop this was. Yesterday would have been better, but granting the impossibility of that, tomorrow would have to do.

I had never been to Piet Retief before. I knew that it was only a small town with a large parish about three to four miles from the Swaziland border in the far south-east of Transvaal. It was surrounded by pine forests which fed a wood-processing plant, and that was basically the reason for the town's existence. Not surprisingly the church was small. The priest's house, set by the church, was quite old, it had three bedrooms, a sitting room, a dining room and a kitchen. The walls inside had been plastered with a type of clay mud which dries hard, but leaves a rough surface. After some weeks I became aware that in the crevices of the old walls lived a colony of bugs which came out at night and dined off me. During my stay at Piet Retief I waged war on these creatures. I smoked them out about once a month with a fumigating smoke insecticide. To no avail, in three weeks they were almost back to full strength as the eggs, unaffected by the fumigation, hatched out and went in search of blood.

The enforcement of the group areas legislation and the consequent resettlements had not yet reached border towns like Piet Retief. The Africans had been segregated into a location, but immediately opposite the house lived a family of Coloureds, while twenty yards to the right was the home of an Indian family. There were many more Afrikaners than I had met in the towns of Natal and the predominant language was Afrikaans.

There was an African in his late teens at the house to greet me when I arrived. He was supposed to be the cook and general factotum about the house. I was embarrassed by his presence which demonstrated two uncritically accepted principles. One, that white people have servants, and two, that priests have housekeepers. I found that neither of these principles stood up to any close examination. The parish was very small and the income hardly justified the employment of a servant and it was a small congregation so I was not overtaxed with work. In these circumstances I saw no reason why I could not cook my own food, but that would put an African out of work. I was trapped. The matter was resolved, not very satisfactorily, but irrevocably. After about two months the young cook took the car without asking and left it at Vryheid in north Natal, about a hundred miles away. I never saw him again. Thereafter I cooked for myself and anyone else, like Cos, who was foolish enough to come and stay with me.

On my second day I was visited by a Mrs Mockey, mother to a large Catholic family who lived on a vast farm, involved with both cattle breeding and the timber industry. The farm spilled over the border into Swaziland and had its own informal border gate, to which the authorities on both sides turned a blind eye. There was an implicit understanding that if ever any naughtiness was discovered, they would make life difficult for the Mockeys. Mr Mockey was also a Catholic, though mainly because his wife wanted him to be. They had had eight children of whom one son still lived on the farm and ran it as manager for his father, though Mr Mockey was still actively involved. Mrs Mockey refused to speak Afrikaans. There are two official languages, she told me, and I speak one of them; that's enough. She had lived in Swaziland after coming from England as a young woman and had learned to speak Swazi, which is like a dialect of Zulu, very well indeed. She told me all this within the first quarter of an hour of our meeting. She insisted that I come to dinner that evening. I obeyed.

During the first couple of weeks at Piet Retief I wrote to Lionel, still in Lesotho, telling him about my excursion to Swaziland and my move to Piet Retief. I did not want to tell him any more on paper, but I wanted to know when he was likely to be coming to South Africa so I could canvass his opinion about my proposed course of action.

It was about six weeks before I received a reply from Lionel. He

200

was surprised that I had wound up at an out-of-the-way place like Piet Retief but he was interested because it was so close to Swaziland. He was due to come to Swaziland as a kind of appendage to King Moshoeshoe's party at the forthcoming Independence celebrations. In view of my location he would call on me, stay a few days and then go to Swaziland for the celebrations. I was delighted. By the time I received his letter I had been at Piet Retief for about two months and there were times when it was lonely. I wrote back immediately telling him he was most welcome and that I planned to accompany him to at least some of the celebrations. Cos had telephoned me a couple of times. He professed to be very busy, travelling a great deal and staying in Johannesburg otherwise. He was collecting more and more information about the uprooting of African peoples in pursuance of the separate development policy and was working virtually full time on that. He rarely went to Ermelo, but the Bishop didn't seem to mind. He told me he had tried to get the Bishop's conference to make a strong statement about the Government's inhumane resettlement policies. He had been enraged by one cautious reply which suggested that we should be careful in case we lost privileges from the Government. What privileges? Cos had stormed and the priest-assistant of the Bishop's conference had scuttled away, unable to persuade Cos that suave diplomacy was the appropriate course of action.

My contact with Pro had to be by letter, we corresponded frequently. The train from Natal came three times a week to Piet Retief and went back to Natal the following day. That meant that we both received three letters a week. There seemed a great deal to write about, although we were careful to be cryptic about our plans in case the letters were opened and used as evidence against us. After two months without seeing Pro, I longed to do so. We cautiously arranged that I should drive the 150 miles and pick her up outside the town where the hospital was situated. It would be inviting inspection to meet her at the gates of the hospital, though I did do that on one occasion. About a half mile before the town I came upon Pro walking to meet me. She jumped into the car and for three hours we travelled very slowly along country roads discussing our future together, and wondering if our dreams could or would ever achieve fulfilment. In South Africa there was nowhere to go now Cos was no longer at Washbank. So we drove. We felt that though there was danger in being together, at least in a moving car there was less likelihood that we could be accused of contravening the Immorality Act which forbade sexual relations across the colour line. In fact we were far from immune. The Act empowered the police to arrest people when they judged there was a conspiracy to commit an act; it was not necessary to be caught in flagrante delicto. Our hand holding, thigh pressing and stolen kisses would have been more than enough evidence.

Pro had made enquiries about nursing in Swaziland and discovered that, not unnaturally, the Swazis favoured giving jobs to their own nationals first. At that time there was no shortage of Swazi nurses and as I had no intention of trying my former job again, we decided we should go to England and make a new start there. Neither of us wanted to leave Africa, but earning a living appeared well nigh impossible. However, even this plan had problems. To get out of the country Pro needed a passport. To get a passport she needed a good reason. It was possible to get an exit permit, but that meant giving up all hope of returning to see her family. She did not wish to do that, nor could I advise such a course. It was estimated at that time that about seventy-five percent of passport applications from Africans were turned down by a Government fearful that contact with the outside world would make the subject peoples dissatisfied with their lot. It was necessary, therefore, to devise a sound reason. Pro knew of one through her nursing. She had already applied to do courses in children's nursing at South African colleges. She had been told that there would be no places for several years. She thought that requesting to attend an overseas course might be an acceptable reason. We decided that she should try it.

After all these practicalities, Pro finally plucked up courage to ask what my present feelings were and how my rethinking was progressing. I laughed at her coyness. But she was right – very easy to make practical arrangements, but she might find herself alone and abandoned in a strange country. I told her that I still felt I should let the application for dispensation continue its course. We held hands and sat quietly, as I drove very slowly along a little used road. I dropped Pro back at the spot I had picked her up three hours earlier.

Chapter Seventeen

A formal letter arrived asking me if I still intended to go ahead with my application to Rome. I suspected that this request for confirmation was a direct result of the interview with the priest in Durban. I wrote back immediately saying that I still intended to proceed. After a further four or five weeks a letter arrived telling me that I should arrange to be interviewed again. I was given a choice between a Bishop and a psychiatrist. There was doubtless a body of opinion among my brethren which considered I must be crazy. Out of curiosity I chose the psychiatrist. I got in touch with Cos to see if he knew any good shrinks in Johannesburg. He didn't personally, he assured me, but friends of his did, he would get a name for me. An appointment was arranged and I went to Johannesburg to join Cos, who had arranged a place for me to stay with one of his friends. We were both intrigued by the idea of church authorities suggesting that I should see a psychiatrist. In the recent past the church had demonstrated a guarded suspicion of psychiatrists and we wondered why they appeared to be more accepting now.

Dr Wolfe was a cheerful young man, I guessed him to be under forty. I sat before his desk in a very comfortable high backed leather chair. He looked at me with eye-brows raised and pencil in hand. I explained the reason for my visit and he took notes as I spoke. By the time I got to the Swaziland experience he had put down his pencil and was just listening. I had not gone into any great detail, but skimmed briefly across the last two years, thinking that he would ask questions afterwards. When I had finished, he sighed and scratched his head for a minute.

"I am not a believer myself, Father", he told me, "but that does not mean that I don't have any sympathy with believers; please accept that. I cannot for the life of me see why you have been sent to me. There is nothing in what you say or in your manner that suggests you are suffering from any loss of mental equilibrium, no evidence of neurosis, and certainly no hint of a psychotic condition. Pfoof, it would be ridiculous to suggest anything of the kind. I admire your courage. I suppose in your world it must take some guts to do what you are planning. And as for the cross race marriage – well, I can speak freely with you. It would be the saving of this country if mixed marriages were widespread. But of course you won't be able to stay here will you?"

"No", I told him, "we plan to go to England".

"Well, as far as I am concerned, Father, the interview is at an end. Unless you want to..."

"No, I don't want to tempt providence by talking too much. You have just told me that I am sane. I don't want you to change your mind." We both laughed. "Will you send a report to this address, please", I handed him the Bishop's name and address.

"I most certainly will, Father. It has been a pleasure to meet you", he said, standing up. We shook hands and I left.

I told Cos about the interview. He feigned astonishment and wondered about the competency of a psychiatrist who could have missed so many obvious signs of my unfortunate mental state. I refused to let him dampen my exultation at being declared sane.

I suggested I should perhaps be making my way to Piet Retief soon, principally because I did not want to inflict myself on his friends for too long. He would have none of this, insisting that his friends were only too delighted to have a house guest. Anyway he would like me to stay until at least the next day because he needed me to carry a banner.

"A banner"? I enquired.

"Yes, a banner with something written on it. We are trying to let people know about the resettlements in Natal, and elsewhere. We are going to stand on one of the main roads out of the city tomorrow afternoon and evening to make sure people see that there are some people who are concerned about these inhuman moves in this benighted country."

"I see. I suppose I shall end up in jail."

"For a very good cause, Torkington, just think of that."

Our demonstration provoked interest of different forms the next afternoon. The particular wooden board I held proclaimed the example of Government cruelty in the Natal, moves of Africans to Limehill, and about twenty five to thirty other placards drew attention to similar incidents. We stood on the central reservation of a dual carriageway leading to the salubrious northern suburbs as the cars started to pour out of the city at the end of the day's work. On the pavement opposite us stood a small group of special branch police, one of whom carefully photographed us. The reaction from passing motorists was varied. Many haughtily ignored us, some were openly abusive, and a few were supportive, showing solidarity by blowing their horns. I was lucky. I escaped the eggs and tomatoes which were thrown at us from nearby buildings, other protesters were not so fortunate. But that was the extent of any counter protest on that occasion. There was no attempt by anyone to pull the placards from our hands and the police made no move towards us. Not one word was exchanged with the police. When the early evening traffic had diminished to a trickle we moved away. I went back to Piet Retief that night.

****

A week later Lionel arrived looking rather tired. His work was arduous, including stretches away from Maseru in the high mountains where in winter it was extremely cold.

When I told him I had applied for a dispensation his first reaction was surprise, then he smiled,

"Well, Torkington, it will be nice for you to return to the human race". After some thought he admitted it was a huge step for anyone to take, with no guarantees for the future. What really stopped him in his tracks was telling him that Pro and I wanted to get married. He was stunned for a moment, amazed that, knowing both of us so well, he had still failed to notice our relationship. But then he had been so far away latterly. Slowly, as it sank in, he smiled and said with great sincerity:

"Sam, I hope you will both be very happy". He paused and looked at me. Then he continued: "But if you make her unhappy, Torkington, I'll come and break your neck." He had always been half in love with Pro himself.

Lionel had arrived clutching a new record of Beethoven's Emperor Piano Concerto, to which he was addicted. For two days we listened to pratically nothing else while Lionel recouped his strength. He would lie on a settee looking soulful and when the first movement was finished he would call out to me to turn it over. He was fondest of the slow movement on the second side and he would demand that I put on 'the backside of the Emperor'. After two days of relaxation we crossed to Swaziland. Lionel knew of a school where there would be accommodation for lesser hangers-on to official parties. We headed for the school on the outskirts of Manzini. After a great deal of haggling we did get beds, but not in the school. While arguing with the official in charge of accommodation, waiting as he consulted interminable lists and spoke to his superiors, we fell into conversation with a teacher at the school who had been a friend of Daniel Makhaya, our colleague at Pomeroy. He said we were most welcome to stay at his house which was nearby. When eventually the school official came back, he was shaking his head and telling us that there were all sorts of problems. He could offer no positive suggestions so we left and took up the offer of our new teacher friend. In fact for our few days stay we hardly saw him, using his house for sleeping only.

Lionel had been given the itinerary of King Moshoeshoe. By late afternoon we had found the house where the King and his entourage were supposed to be staying. It was obviously a very new house, so new that there were two men on the roof still fixing tiles. The front area had been cleared but around the sides and back of the house there were still piles of bricks and old timber which had been used for walks across the scaffolding. The programme had said "to be welcomed at his new residence by King Sobhuze". This seemed unlikely but we waited for about half an hour, having nowhere else to go. Then we saw three big black limousines gliding up in a stately line, reminiscent of a funeral procession. They drew up outside the house and an aide of the King jumped out of the leading car with the air of one certain of his role in life. He stopped dead in his tracks as he caught sight of the state of the

205

house which looked so impressive at a distance. Peering through the front door, which was wide open, it was only too clear that the house was unfurnished. It seemed unlikely that King Sobhuza would emerge to greet his royal guest. Nor did he. There was some consternation, then consultation; the King remained within the second car. For twenty minutes the King's entourage indulged in gestures of helplessness, looking at watches, throwing their hands in the air and pacing the forecourt. The men on the roof showed some brief interest before carrying on with their job, which appeared to be somewhat behind schedule. We decided to maintain a low profile.

Suddenly a small Volkswagen like ours appeared travelling at great speed. It screeched to a halt in a cloud of dust. A figure, dressed in an expensive, dark grey suit, got out and started to make elaborate gestures of apology and requested that the King and his party follow him. He set off again at a more sedate pace followed by the three black limousines from Lesotho. We brought up the rear of the procession. Lionel thought we should tag along, if only to discover where his royal employer was going to stay. After about three miles the Volkswagen stopped in front of a large bungalow set in trees by a small lake. They all got out and entered the bungalow. After a decent interval of about five minutes Lionel, being familiar with some of the aides, went to enquire about plans for the rest of the evening. It was already starting to get dark and it seemed unlikely that there would be anything of great interest happening in the rest of the day. Lionel's programme gave the first royal appointment for the next morning but he was beginning to lose faith in the itinerary after the afternoon's events.

Lionel returned in about ten minutes. The King was going to rest for a while but we were welcome to visit later. We went to find food. We were situated midway between Manzini and Mbabane and I suggested Sam's Place, knowing the food to be clean and wholesome. When we arrived it was impossible to get near the cafe it was so crowded. We found it was the same all over the town and we ended up with snacks at a bar. Lionel murmured resentfully about having had no solid food that day. We each had a long brandy and coke to revive our drooping spirits.

An hour and a half later we were back at the King's temporary residence. Lionel took me in. There were several well-dressed Lesotho gentlemen sitting talking in a sitting room. They said that the King was outside on the verandah. We went round to the back of the house and came upon him just as he appeared to be coming inside.

"Your Majesty", said Lionel, "may I present Fr Sam Torkington."

In the dim light on the verandah I saw before me a tall African, covered from neck to feet in the highly coloured traditional Basotho blanket. He wore glasses and looked sensitive and intelligent.

"How d'you do?" said the King, in a British public school accent.

"How d'you do, your Majesty?" I replied, with a slight inclination of the head.

"Lionel has spoken of you and his other friends in the Republic. I wonder if you would excuse me, gentlemen, I have the most awful headache from the long journey. I think that I shall retire with two aspirins. Father, I hope that we shall see you again while we are here. Good-night."

It was no longer possible for Pro to boast that she alone had met the King; I should enjoy telling her of my introduction. We found that the rest of the King's party were similarly afflicted after the long journey and we decided to recommence our search for solid food, convinced that the casino hotel would be able to provide for our needs. Doubtless it was expensive, but we were very hungry. When we got back to the main road we found that we were very near the Swazi Inn and made our way there with eager anticipation. It was now after nine and the dining room appeared to be closed. We asked about food and were told that we could get sandwiches and snacks inside the casino, but we first had to pay about two pounds entrance fee. Despite our hunger this price seemed too high for just sandwiches. We turned away, got into the car and went back to our lodgings and to bed.

King Sobhuza was about sixty eight or sixty nine at the time of the independence celebrations and had as many wives as his years. He was a wily, wise old man, his face seemed ever creased with a watchful smile as he went about from ceremony to ceremony and met different people. A detailed and carefully-timed programme had been drawn up for the celebrations, but it seemed that when this entailed the two Kings attending functions together, Sobhuza changed the programme at will only bothering to tell his chauffeur and King Moshoeshoe about any alterations. We spent many hours attending at the wrong place because the Swazi King had changed the plans and gone elsewhere with his royal guest. In consequence we missed a lot of the official ceremonies, but there was so much going on in the two towns that it did not really matter. We finally hit on the best clue for tracing the royal party. When police cars were seen to be driving about in a frantic hurry it was almost invariably because King Sobhuza had changed plans and the police found themselves in the wrong place. All we had to do was pursue the police. We jumped a road block on one occasion when we saw the black limousines being escorted along an adjacent road. We were shouted at and chased by policemen on foot as we sped through a gap in their defences, but they gave up the pursuit as they saw us slow down to a sedate pace at the back of the royal procession.

After three days of such games we were weary and made our way slowly back to Piet Retief. We fell into easy chairs and Lionel demanded the 'backside of the Emperor', and a stiff brandy.

Sipping my drink, I reflected on time keeping in Africa. At the end of two years at Besters I had put my watch in a drawer and forgotten about it. I was making appointments for eleven in the morning or two-thirty in the afternoon, and getting ulcers worrying about arriving late, and then cross that everyone else was late. (Of course they didn't have watches). I soon began to get the hang of estimating time by the position of the sun. In European terms the matter of King Sobhuza's unfinished house would have been interpretted as typical of the doziness of Africans and something of a national disgrace. In Swaziland all that an uncompleted house meant is that a house is not yet finished so please use this other one which is both adequate and complete. Of course, it all gets a bit more complicated when white cultural standards have been imbibed by Africans and they assume that white standards are signs of being more civilised, more modern and just generally better.

"I was very impressed by Sobhuze, I must say", said Lionel. "Did you notice that all of the time he wore national costume. I am sure he is not just reverting back to some past ideal of tribalism. He knows his economic onions but he is also asserting national identity".

"I'm a bit worried about my identity, you know, Lionel. I shall miss Africa when I go overseas. This continent gets into the blood. Either that or it could just be the fascination of the sun. Remember we're only used to occasional glimpses of sunshine in England."

We went to bed early that night and slept very soundly. Lionel left for Natal the next day to see some of his family. I promised to keep him informed about my plans.

****

The beauty of being in charge of a small parish is that you can spend more time with individuals and get to know them well. My house was quite near the town location and I started doing what I had tried in Newcastle – walking instead of going by car. We needed cars to cover the distances to the out-stations, but cars can be a mixed blessing if part of your job is to meet people. If you walk, you stop and talk and get to know many more people. By this time I was not so much concerned with visiting my parishioners, as meeting Africans, whatever their religious persuasion. I thought that it might just be useful for them to meet a white man, who did not zoom by in a car and ignore them as if they were beneath notice. It was a small gesture but it had some immediate impact – people stopped, expressed surprise at my walking and inquired if the car was broken. I told them that it deserved a day off like everyone else.

I became friendly with several families in the African location, especially one which I visited at least once a week. Joseph and Veronica Msibi had two most delightful little daughters who had just started school. They were always beautifully dressed, in sharp contrast to so many children in the location but then their father had a reasonable job, whereas many had no job, or jobs paying the most miserable wages. I recall being shocked by another friend telling me that he got only nine rand, then about four pounds fifty pence. Nine rand a week, I exclaimed. 'Oh, no, Father', he corrected me, 'a month; a month'. This, he told me, was the standard rate in the town for manual helpers in the stores.

Joseph's house was always clean and comfortable, in spite of being very small. I would go there in the evenings and talk to Joseph, he wanted to be a Catholic like his wife and children. He had a small lamp – of course there was no electricity for the Africans – and this would be set in the middle of the table. I was supposed to be instructing Joseph but he would speak at least as much as I did and I suspect a great deal more. It was apparent that what he was seeking was explanations of what life was about and not just in narrow religious terms. He had many ideas himself and wondered constantly why all the theory and ideals that appeared in the Gospels, in the words of Jesus, did not seem to be reaching fulfilment. The Africans were dispossessed, meek and lowly, but they did not get the land or receive justice. I did not dare tell him that the Gospels only spoke in heavenly terms and he would have to wait until death for such perfection. I did not want to believe that myself anyway. In such circumstances we inevitably spoke of politics. I could only agree with him that by Christian or any other rational standard there was no justice in this country. Therefore, by those same standards, efforts must be made to change the system. We were not planning a revolution. We had neither the means nor the organisation for that, but to Joseph, and the friends who joined us on occasion, there was at least a glimmer of hope and some slight consolation in just being able to talk about it. They didn't need me to do that and I am sure that they did it at many other times when I was not there. I suppose I was flattered that they should feel able to speak so freely about these matters in front of me.

Always, after the conversation had slipped round to such topics, (having begun with the next lesson in the catechism), Veronica sent one of the little girls to ask shyly if we would like a cup of tea. The meetings always ended with the whole family sitting round the table with tea and biscuits and ordinary social conversation. I rather suspect that Veronica was a little worried about political talk though not because she thought Joseph would take to throwing bombs at the police. Rather because a careless word from one of their friends might let a white man know that they talked this way with the white priest. That could bring inspection from the Special Branch.

I always went to see the Msibi's on Tuesday evenings. One Saturday Mrs Mockey rang and invited me to go to dinner the following Tuesday. I explained that I had a catechism about eight in the evening. It was agreed that they should go ahead without me and I would join them as soon as I could.

After I had visited the Msibi's and cut my visit a little short, I raced out to the Mockey's house. The half dozen guests, Mr and Mrs Mockey and their son, Stephan with his wife, Nina, were all seated in the sitting room waiting for me. I was cross with Mrs Mockey for waiting -it was already past eight. I felt ashamed and embarrassed. I tried to explain to the rest of the company that I had been out visiting and instructing in the location. They had seemed amused by my embarrassment but suddenly the amusement ceased. There was silence for a full minute, while the guests looked at each in consternation. Then Stephan, never slow to express his feelings, said:

"You went into the location at night? You must be crazy, man. Do you realise the kind of danger you could be in?"

I admit that I had a deliberate policy of mentioning my work with the Africans as much as possible in the company of whites, but I had not expected to produce such a conversation-stopper.

"Well no, Stephan, actually I don't realise what sort of danger I might be in. Perhaps you could explain it to me." I tried to keep it as pleasant as I could, but there must have been an edge to my voice, because nobody carried on any other conversation.

"You can't trust the natives", he told me, "they'd as soon cut your throat as look at you, you must know that." He could hardly believe that he needed to explain it to me.

"But, Stephan, I've been here for nearly a year now and while I don't say that I go into the location every day, it is certainly very nearly every day, sometimes several times a day for different reasons. From my point of view there are a lot of parishioners there."

"Well, O.K., perhaps in the day time, you have to go", he conceded, "but at night is really tempting providence. We know these people, Father, they are unpredictable; they get a bit of drink in them and they go wild."

"Stephan, how often have you been in the location?"

"I'm not allowed in there, you know that. But even if I was, I wouldn't go."

I turned to the company. "Have any of you ever been there"?

There were shakes of the head from the tense and glum gathering – it looked as if I had wrecked the dinner party – and one woman shuddered at the idea.

"I'm sorry I've brought gloom upon this evening but let me say this and then I'll shut up. I have been going into the location here for nearly a year, I did the same in Newcastle when I stayed there for a few weeks. I was never threatened, I have never been accosted, never accorded anything but courtesy. I know that Africans assume that a white man in the location is either an official or a clergyman, but I never wear clerical dress as you know, I don't advertise my status. I am not in the least afraid, I don't nerve myself to do an odious task every time I go there. I visit there as I visit here – I am pleased to see my friends and I hope that they are pleased to see me. Stephan, you know I am very fond of your two kiddies and they like to play with me if I come in the daytime. I have been visiting a family tonight, they have two little girls and I am also very fond of them. To me it is exactly the same as visiting you and your children. I make no distinctions. All I am saying is that given an open mind, there need be no fear and there can be affection and friendship."

I had said my piece and slowly conversation broke out again as we sat down to dinner. By the time we had finished the soup, aided by the application of a little wine, the atmosphere was fairly normal. I heard a conversation at the other end of the table which was obviously a counter-argument to what I had been saying. It was being carried on by two ladies in voices designed not to reach me. I pretended to be listening politely to another, nearer conversation, while eavesdropping on the two ladies.

"We've got two Dobermann Pinschers", one was saying, "and I keep them loose in the back garden when Ted is at work. I get so frightened when I am alone there". I was intrigued, she was one of my parishioners and I happened to know that she lived on an estate where there were other houses all around her. "And Ted's got a gun by his bed", she continued to her approving neighbour, "the other day I ran up and got it when I saw two huge buck niggers outside the house." The drama was getting to me, she was telling it all so graphically, but then the end fell ludicrously flat. It turned out that the Africans were the dustmen. The bathos failed to affect the two ladies, who relaxed at the end of the story as if the narrator had narrowly escaped a nasty experience.

"I know they were only the dustmen", she said, "but you can't be too careful." I wiped my mouth with my napkin to hide a smile. Of course, there may well come a time .... but not yet.

Mr Mockey beckoned me closer at the end of the meal and while general conversation carried on around the table, he asked me what I thought was going to happen in South Africa. I played my usual foreigner role.

"Well, I don't really know, Mr Mockey. What do you think?"

"Going to be a blood-bath", he assured me grimly.

"You think so? What are you going to do about it then?" I asked.

He shook his head sadly. "Nothing. What can we do? The government won't change its policies."

"But surely if you feel like that, there must be others who feel the same way? Why don't you get together and form some sort of pressure group to change the policy?"

"Father, man, it's too late, it's too late. We just have to put off the evil day as long as we can".

"But that means that you leave a hell of a legacy for your children", I was aghast at his acceptance of the inevitable in this supine way.

He shrugged, and said no more. If he represented strength of the white opposition, the Government stood to keep power for a long time to come.

****

Another example of the fearful acceptance of Government policy depressed me further the following week. For some time a few of the white parishioners had been pressing me to do something about the singing in church – form a choir or at least have practices so that the quality of singing and the extent of the repertoire could be improved. I agreed and about a dozen parishioners started to gather on Wednesday evenings after mass to practise hymns. There were always some Africans attending the mass in the town church and among them were two or three nurses who came off duty at about that time. They asked to join the singing practices. I said of course they could. They knew English well and would have no problems in following what we were doing. I felt that they would be a definite asset. They came for a couple of weeks and the white parishioners seemed to accept their presence.

After the third such practice, however, a nervous, pink-faced lady came to see me.

"Father, I don't want you to misunderstand what I have to say. So let me take it slowly and let me finish. It's about the native nurses at the singing practices. I don't mind them being there at all, please believe me. I have spoken to them and I like them; they are nice girls. But what my husband and I, and some of the others, fear is that word will get around that you are having multi-racial gatherings in your house. I know they are quite innocent, but the police might come and make enquiries. Father, we don't want that. Once the police brand you as a certain type of person, you are finished. They harass you, they watch you and for the sake of the children we don't want that. So Jim and myself will not be attending again, I'm afraid, Father. I'm not asking that you stop the practices, or tell the Africans not to come, but just to understand why we shall not be attending. I'm so sorry, Father." She finished and there were tears in her eyes from the emotion that had been building up inside her.

We sat in silence. I had no answer. I was again the outsider. I could make exhortations to others to take risks, or suggest that they were exaggerating the risks, but I was in little or no danger. For a white family, police intervention might threaten not only a quiet home and a secure job, but also all their social relations within the white community. For instance, I knew the statistics about arrests under the Immorality Act which forbade sexual relations across the colour lines – at least half those arrested were acquitted or later released from custody. However, by that time the accused's life had been ruined and

212

their chances of employment had been reduced to virtually nil.

"Joan", I said, "I understand what you say. I can't argue with you or plead with you to reconsider."

The practices slowly died away as less and less people came each week – there were excuses made – until after six more weeks the practices ceased.

****

Towards the end of August letters from Pro were expressing concern at the non-arrival of her passport. It was now a year since she had applied. Her latest letter told me she had been along to the Bantu Affairs office in her area and complained. She found them unrepentant. It became clear that until they had a date, even a provisional one from her, they were unlikely to make any great efforts towards issuing a passport. She was able to tell them that she would be starting a course at the Children's Hospital in Liverpool, on the fifth of January.They noted down the date. Pro was still not satisfied and went out and booked herself on a flight to England at the beginning of December, she then went back to the Bantu Affairs department and gave them that date as well. I smiled. That was Pro – as tenacious as ever. I had continued to see Pro about once a month for our ride around the country roads, but we were getting more and more fearful that we would be spotted and stopped. The mere suspicion engendered by our being together would prevent the issue of a passport. Maybe we should be even more careful. Neither of us could bear the thought of our plans being thwarted at the eleventh hour.

****

So departure seemed more and more imminent. With Pro's leaving date now fixed, it was time I put my own house in order before leaving the parish. I thought of Joseph Msibi, whom I had been instructing in the catechism for almost as long as I had been there. If he was ready to be baptised and received into the Church I felt I wanted to be the one to do it. I had also a scheme I hoped would bring pleasure to another family I visited regularly in the location. Mr and Mrs Zikalala were elderly and for all practical purposes house-bound. They were very poor as neither was able to work. Their daughter and two grand-children lived with them; their son-in-law had been killed three years earlier in a mining accident and the whole family now relied on their daughter's work as a domestic servant. I thought that, as Mr and Mrs Zikalala lived very near to the Msibi house, we could arrange a meeting for mass and the ceremonies at the Zikalala's house, so that

213

the old people could take part in a church service and play host on a special occasion. They had all their lives been faithful church goers and I knew they would be thrilled at the prospect. I asked Joseph and he agreed readily. He was in daily contact with the Zikalalas to make sure that they were well and that the strain of looking after their two grandchildren did not get too much of a burden for them. Joseph suggested we should have a little party there afterwards. I promised to get some things from the town to make sure that the old people and their grandchildren had a good meal, they usually managed on so little. We decided to hold the ceremony nearer to Christmas. I saw the two African nurses after mass and invited them to join the party. They said they too would bring a contribution to the meal for they understood only too well that few Africans ever had surplus food.

****

The practice in my Order was for an outside visitator to visit and interview each member every six years. This gave a priest the opportunity to voice his feelings confidentially about the way his particular province was being run. I learnt that a visitator planned to call on me in about mid-October. When the time came I drove to Ermelo to collect him.

On the way I passed a general store belonging to a Mr Laing, whose daughter was attending the state school at Piet Retief. As Sandra had grown up she developed features which suggested she had some African blood. The good citizens of Piet Retief had noticed this and began to object to their children going to school with a coloured girl. There was a great deal of fuss and it became a cause célèbre, with feelings running high on both sides. The strict segregationists wanted her out of the school in spite of the fact that both her parents were undeniably white in appearance. The opposing side were appalled that a teenager should be put through the horrors of a witch-hunt and fearful that such actions might create a precedent and spread throughout the country. I called at Mr Laing's store. It was a bedlam of noise as customers jostled to finish their buying and catch the bus outside. I waited until the worst of the clamour had subsided. I presumed the imperturbable man behind the counter was Mr Laing, he was the only other white man present. He was courteous and thanked me for calling, though his expression did not change. I offered him accommodation for his daughter if he thought that it would help. Sandra had been excluded from the boarding hostel, but not from the school. What bizarre piece of reasoning allowed this to happen I could not say. Mr Laing thanked me but said that alternative arrangements had been made for Sandra, and they would not need to take up my offer. I told him that I was pleased to hear it and withdrew. He must have been as harassed by kindly offers of help as by nasty phone calls and news-hungry reporters from the newspapers. I know now that this incident was the thin end of the wedge.

My visitor, Fr Daniel, was the Father Provincial of the Australian Province. He told me he was fifty, but he looked younger. He was very easy to talk to and I looked forward to the two days he would be spending with me.

It was not until the next morning that any note of formality appeared. He brought out his note book and said he was going to put me through the threatened interview, but his broad smile banished any idea I might have had about an inquisition.

"Right, name – Fr Samuel Torkington," he muttered to himself as he wrote at the top of a clean page. "Now", he said, as he looked up, "you realise that I know your thoughts about your continuance in the order. I have read your application for a dispensation. You must know very well there could never be a dispensation that allowed you to stay within the Order and get married – you're no idiot. Even so, just supposing that it were possible, would you want to remain in this diocese?"

"I don't suppose they would allow that, I have some clue about the way the Roman mind works. But anyway no, for other reasons."

"One of which could be", Fr Daniel speculated, "that you want to marry someone who is black?"

I laughed out loud. "Who told you that?" I asked.

He held up his hands in protest. "No one. No one appears to know anything of your lady friend".

"Alright, you are correct, of course, but that please, is only for you".

"Sure", he agreed. "If you can't expect discretion from a visitator the whole thing's a waste of time. O.K. we have cleared that. Now, are you still of the same mind?"

"Yes, I am", I told him.

"Well, what's keeping you?"

"One thing is the dispensation."

"Ah well, as I told you I have read your application. It is long and presents certain arguments. Do you know what will happen when they read it in Rome? Well, I'll tell you", he said without waiting for a reply. "They will say to themselves: here is a chap with particular difficulties and problems. What he needs is to talk to a reputable and approved theologian who will put him straight about these matters and then all will be well again. Send him off to a secluded monastery to think about it all. See? If you really want to get married, tell them just that, without all the frills, or you will never get a dispensation."

"Excuse my asking, but whose side are you on? Everyone, or nearly everyone tries to dissuade me from taking this course, but you actually seem to be helping me."

"I asked you if you really intend to go ahead with it and you said 'yes'. After that, what can I do? I believe you. You have been thinking about it for long enough in all conscience. I just want you to go about it in the right way and get it done as quickly as possible, rather than get frustrated and leave the Church. Does that make sense?"

"I suppose so, yes," I agreed.

"Right. If I thought I could dissuade you, I should try. But you are an adult and quite able to make up your own mind. You see I don't assume, as some of our brethren do, that leaving priesthood means that you are a failure or a traitor or any of the other nasty names you might get called. I can't say that I agree with you, otherwise I might do the same myself. But I don't say either that you are wrong. It's your life and you must live it as you see best. And leaving the priesthood does not, I hope, mean that you will reject all your values."

"How would you like a drink of tea, Father?"

"I'd love one, Sam. I talk too much, I'm parched."

"Incidentally, is there a lot of talk about me in the diocese?"

"Confidentiality forbids that I name names, but yes, of course there is. It ranges from being a pity that you plan to leave, to it's being a disgrace you are still here, living, as one charitable soul put it, a lie".

"Do you take that line, or shouldn't I ask?" I inquired as I gave him a mug of tea.

"No, you ask away. But tell me your answer first."

"Well, my attitude is that I am doing a job, one that I was trained, badly of course, to do. I have nearly ten years experience and, that I suspect, counts for something. I happen to believe that married clergy should be an option, thus I also believe in a courting clergy"

"Well, sounds logical", Fr Daniel conceded, smiling ruefully.

"I know that legally and according to the rule and moral theology I am living a sin inasmuch as I continue to have a relationship with the lady, but the alternative is ludicrous, isn't it? I don't want to marry an abstract ideal, I want to marry a particular person. I write to her and see her occasionally. If I didn't want to marry her I wouldn't want to leave. I have not ceased to believe in what I preach – though there are those who would worry about the orthodoxy of what I say"

"Listen, Sam, you have made your decision. I know that we could go on talking about it, all day but where would that get us? I'm not going to fight you over it. Also I don't really want to go through all the usual rigmarole of complaints and your observance of the rule. I have seen Cos and he tells me of the work that you both feel ought to be done here. So unless you want to elaborate further, I shall declare the formalities of your visitation at an end and demand a beer from you."

"That's it then", I said, "I might have been prepared to carry on longer, but seeing as we can't have a beer during the formalities, I accept the meeting is closed. I will go to the fridge."

Chapter Eighteen

In the second week of November Pro wrote to say that just as she was about to panic, her passport had arrived. I wrote off to the Bishop asking to be relieved of my post. I assured him that I would remain until he could conveniently arrange a replacement. I also wrote to Fr Paschal, asking for my travelling home to be sanctioned. The day after I had written these two letters, I received a letter from the Bishop. I could hardly believe that the postal services had managed to carry a reply that quickly. Of course, it was nothing of the sort. Some months before I had requested Jack's services, as we had decided to renew the ceiling in the church. It was made of hardboard, and was bellying down under pressure from above. The weight came from bat dung and dead bats. There would inevitably come a time when the whole lot would collapse. I had already inquired about someone to poison the creatures, but I wanted to know that Jack was coming before being stuck with dozens of decomposing bats in the roof. The Bishop told me that Jack could start with us next Monday, I went immediately and asked for the municipal disinfestation squad to come and put in poison.

Jack arrived with a great clatter of rattling vehicle and pipping of horn on Monday morning.

"O.K. Father", he yelled, amid his laughter, "We together again, eh? Big works going to be done here. I hope you got everything ready. Anyway cup of tea first", he demanded.

Over tea he went serious for a minute.

Jack had brought with him old Thembu, his African lieutenant, and they both needed written permission to be in the Transvaal.

"Father, you got to get this thing signed, or get permission or something. We are in Transvaal now, not in Natal where we are O.K." I promised to go down to the municipal offices and sort it out. I left Jack and Thembu viewing the church and deciding what to do first. I had spoken with easy confidence to Jack and Thembu about getting permission, but I knew it would take patience. The officials wanted to know why I had to get someone from Natal to do the job I had outlined to them. I explained about the diocese crossing provincial boundaries, but it was difficult because no one could think of a precedent to follow. I had to wait while interminable conferences took place. Officials would appear periodically to ask for information they had already been given and disappear again. Eventually they knew they had me.

"You should have got permission before they came", I was told.

"Indeed that may be so, but I was not sure of dates and now they are here," I prevaricated.

"Well, you should have got permission", my informant continued doggedly.

This was where patience had to come in.

"Yes", I agreed, restraining myself, "But they are here now. I presume that you do not seriously demand that they go back while I seek permission".

"Well, that would be better", said one of the clerks brightening visibly.

"Look", I said, "I think I shall take the matter to Pretoria. Could you give me back the forms I have already filled in. I have colleagues in Pretoria and I can ring through to them and ask them to go to the relevant department there."

"No, man, just a minute", they said hastily, "Perhaps we can do something". Local offices are notoriously unwilling to have their stupidity revealed to head office. "If we put today's date on the forms that will be O.K. because the workers only arrived today, isn't that right?"

"Yes, I told you that two hours ago", my patience was wearing thin, "all I need is your stamp now on these two forms, O.K.?"

With misgivings they did it and I fled.

Jack went to work with the same old zest. It would take him two weeks he said.

On the Saturday I had a call from a faraway-sounding Lionel in Lesotho. He was coming through next Monday with a friend and would call on me. I told him my news, and Pro's. This would probably be our last meeting. I promised to try to get Cos and Pro down as well so we could all spend a day together.

After much phoning I managed to arrange for both Cos and Pro to be at Piet Retief on the Wednesday. Pro was going home the next week to spend some time with her family before leaving for England. They were sad at her going. I told her that she must promise she would visit them. Their real fear was that she would not wish to return. Pro hated to see their upset and she suffered as much as them. It reminded me that however tough things were for me at least I wasn't leaving my birthplace, my family and all of my friends.

Lionel arrived late on Monday with his friend, Kenneth, who was a Msuthu and a Lecturer at Roma University near Maseru. We had visited his house when we were in Maseru. They were exhausted from the long journey and went to bed after a quick snack. However, they had little opportunity to sleep late in the morning, Jack wanted to greet them. He had already been in bed when they arrived. He burst into the bedroom they were sharing.

"Doctor, what are you doing in bed at this hour", he thundered at Lionel, and laughed amiably.

"Oh, my God, Jack, you don't change, do you?" groaned Lionel wearily.

"I really had hoped for a lie-in today. How are you Jack?"

"I am fine and working hard as ever."

"Listen, Jack, man, you must be here for our get-together on Wednesday, eh?"

"I'll be here. I hear Fr Cos and Staff nurse Pro are coming too. Sounds like the old parties at Pomeroy". He laughed and left the visitors to have a little more sleep.

When they did arise, the day was spent in reminiscing, with a brief break while we went to the church to criticise Jack's work – repayment for his having disturbed Lionel and Kenneth. It did not last long, for as usual Jack drove us out because he wanted to get on with his work.

On the Wednesday I could hardly contain myself. Pro had agreed to come by the afternoon train – the one that usually brought her letter to me. I could see the station from my office window and as soon as I saw the train arrive I leapt into the car and sped to the station. Pro was just coming along the road from the station when I drew alongside her. Looking ahead and in my mirror to see that no one was watching I threw open the door. She jumped in and we were away again in seconds. As ever, our kisses had to wait until we were back at the house.

Cos arrived about five, looking more like a businessman in a dark suit, white shirt and navy blue tie.

"Who are you impressing?" I demanded.

"I don't have to impress anyone, Torkington. Tell me, have you whisky in the house? Ah, Miss Mayeza and Dr Steel."

"Cos, the big city has changed your sartorial style", commented Lionel. "You might almost pass for a human being. You remember Kenneth?"

"Yes, of course; after that party who could forget Kenneth, how are you?"

"I'm delighted to see that you are still alive, Cos. There was a point towards the end of the party when I thought you might not survive".

"Nonsense, Kenneth. I may have been a little sleepy, perfectly natural at two in the morning."

"Cos", interrupted Pro, "I am going to your wonderful country".

"Yes, well, stick to London if you can, because there is really nowhere else worth living. Pity you are going because I rather fancy that Torkington will miss you a bit. Still, he'll soon get over you."

"Oh, you don't know? He has promised faithfully that soon he will follow me."

"You surely don't still believe that, do you? He has privately assured me that this is his way of breaking the whole thing off, you poor credulous girl."

Pro fumed with anger and laughed at the same time.

They all intended to stay the night and after an evening of rowdy good humour, we all slept, some in beds, Cos on the settee. I gave my bed to Pro while I slept on an old mattress I had thrown down in the little office adjoining my bedroom. Pro and I talked for some time as the house settled into silence for the night. There was a tap on the door after five minutes and Cos's head appeared. He gazed at us gravely over his glasses.

"I'm in the next room, Torkington", he told us in a whisper. "I can hear all, so just behave yourself". We threw things at his head and it disappeared.

The next afternoon I was to drive Pro back to Natal. We had made plans with Cos about her departure. From her parents she would take a flight from Durban as early as possible and we should all meet in Johannesburg before her flight to Britain which took off in the evening. She gave me the address and telephone number of the hospital in Liverpool so that I could keep her informed of developments and especially the date of my leaving South Africa.

Just after we had passed Vryheid, I became conscious that there was a three-quarter ton truck behind me. I was doing no more than forty-five miles per hour and yet the powerful truck made no attempt to overtake for about two miles. I looked straight ahead and told Pro to discontinue any conversation, put her head down and look submissive. She was in the wrong place. She ought to have been in the back seat. I assumed the hard, dogged expression of a white man having no conversation with a black person. Pro dropped her head and gazed at the floor in the manner of one not expecting any conversation. After two miles the truck slowly over-took us, looking closely at us as it passed; I affected not to notice their intense interest. As the truck pulled ahead of us I could see there was a white driver with a black man by his side. The truck roared ahead and went to the brow of a hill about a mile further on and stopped. It then reversed off the road and stood facing the road. We passed it again, and I could see out of the corner of my eye we were under close scrutiny. By this time we were convinced it must be the plain clothes police or the Special Branch who had come upon us by chance. Or maybe someone had phoned ahead to tell them that a white man and a black girl were approaching Vryheid and appeared to be on very good terms. We continued our act, terrified that at the eleventh hour our plans were going to be wrecked. The truck pulled out and followed us. Very slowly I built up speed until we were travelling at about sixty miles an hour. We expected every minute to be flagged into the side of the road, but after three miles the truck turned off the road into a side-road and disappeared into wooded country.

We both breathed a sigh of relief. I dropped Pro off for the last time. There could be no protracted farewells in the public gaze. She got out of the car and walked away without a backward glance, and I drove off immediately.

****

A week before Christmas I baptised Joseph Msibi at the Zikalala's

220

house. Thirteen of us squeezed into the tiny house which was only possible because the Zikalalas had very little furniture and most of us sat on mats on the floor. The old people were delighted and declared that Christmas would be nothing after this. Joseph was uncharacteristically solemn during the ceremony and the mass, but immediately afterwards his face broke into its usual beaming smile. We spent about three hours together that evening and the old Zikalala's appeared rejuvenated as the burdens of their poor life were lifted for a few hours. At the end of the evening I told them I would shortly be returning overseas and that a new priest would be coming. They expressed disappointment, but hoped that I should have a good holiday. I decided not to disillusion them.

In my Christmas letter home I told my parents I would be back soon. They were naturally grieved over my plans, but I hoped to be able to explain myself better face to face and receive some sort of acceptance. It was a great sadness to me that they disapproved so strongly. I suppose it was understandable. They had been so proud that all three of their sons had trained for the priesthood. My younger brother had died before ordination and now with my leaving it would mean only one of the original three would remain a priest. It was one of the things that caused me to have so many doubts about my plans to marry. I was now aware of the ambiguity my delay had brought about. The longer I did not go ahead and get married, hoping they would get used to the idea, the more they hoped I would realise that it was all a frivolous notion, a temptation to be resisted. I knew my letter might well spell out for them that I had made a final decision and was coming home to marry. But this was all my speculation, I should have to go home to verify it. I was not looking forward to our first discussion of the subject.

At the beginning of December, on the eighth, I went up to Johannesburg and met Cos. He had a whimsical smile on his face as he told me he had found a place for me to stay the night. Some friends of his, he said. The next day we could collect Pro off the early morning plane from Durban and spend the day at this house.

The door was opened by a young blonde woman, who seemed vaguely familiar. She and Cos were evidently enjoying a private joke and made remarks about my age having affected my memory. Eventually Tricia had pity on me.

"Do you ever remember a girl at the school at Emerlo, who showed you a picture of yourself from the diocesan magazine and told you that you were her pin-up?"

"Good grief," I exclaimed, "You?"

"Yes, me. But you're safe," she assured me, "I'm married now."

We went to Jan Smuts airport the next morning and discreetly picked Pro up. She had brought new clothes for her overseas journey and looked very much the part in an international airport. We drove back to Tricia's house and spent the afternoon there, but we were tense and on edge, almost wanting the time for departure to come. We had said all that had to be said. Now we just wanted it to happen. The waiting was made harder – or perhaps easier; I don't know – by the whimsical exhortations of Cos to Pro to think hard, after all there was still time to cancel the whole thing.

After all that we left it until almost too late for the check-in deadline. Cos had decided to calm our restless spirits by insisting that we were panicking unnecessarily about time. He knew Johannesburg, he would get us there on time, he told us in a lordly manner. We were about five minutes late, but it did not really matter. Pro went quickly into the departure lounge; Cos gave her a quick kiss, but I didn't dare. For all I knew her passport could still be withdrawn.

"Now, Torkington", said Cos as we walked away, "I should like to talk to you seriously about reconsidering your lunatic plans, now that girl is out of the way. Or" he said hastily, seeing I was threatening violence, "would you care for a double whisky, which I may say you look as if you need?"

I agreed and we sought a bar at the airport. We watched the plane leave and then so did we.

Christmas came. There was a Polish family in the parish and I was invited to a party on Christmas Eve. It was apparently a Polish custom to start celebrations on Christmas Eve. I protested. I would be saying a midnight mass and perhaps ought not to come. They demanded my presence, shocked that I should think of not coming. They were going to midnight mass themselves after all. I had been so plied with wine at the party that by eleven in the evening I felt like sleeping and not staying up for midnight mass. I was advised to have a sharp vodka at about eleven thirty to get me in trim for the service. Indeed it did wake me up to some extent. Afterwards I was told they had regretted giving me the vodka, I was so awake I went on with my sermon until most of the congregation were on the verge of sleeping on the benches.

****

Immediately after Christmas a letter from England told me that Pro had arrived safely though she was cold and miserable, and very, very lonely. As soon as the New Year had passed I got in touch with Paschal and asked if there was any news about a flight reservation for me. He told me it was pratically certain that a flight had been booked for two weeks hence, he would confirm it in the next couple of days. He had told the Bishop and they were arranging for a replacement. Paschal said he would take me up to Johannesburg on the appointed day.

I told Mrs Mockey I was due to go home very shortly and she expressed dismay and disappointment. I smiled at her and pointed out not everyone would be sorry to see the back of me, in view of my remarks about race matters in and out of church. She said she didn't give a damn about what others thought, she was sorry I was going and intended to give me a party before I went. She asked if I was coming back and I hesitated a very brief moment before saying that I thought it very unlikely. She sensed some hesitation and in her usual blunt way came straight out with her question.

"Why, are you going to get married?"

I burst out laughing at her frankness.

"I might at that, Mrs Mockey", I admitted still laughing. She did not know whether I was being serious or not.

"Good looking fellow like you, you jolly well ought to." And then having decided that I had made a serious remark. "Who is she, anyway".

"I never said for one moment...."

"I know all about that, and if you don't want to tell me, you don't have to."

Pro was safely in England, I thought, and I don't really mind Mrs. Mockey knowing now. Of all the whites in the parish she would be the one most able to accept the idea of a mixed marriage.

"Alright", I said, "but you don't know her and anyway she is black".

"Good God, man", she said, "you are in for some problems. Not that it isn't a good idea and the more that do the same, the sooner we might have an end to this idiotic regime. So, you have hidden things well, haven't you?"

"What else?" I asked, "I hardly wanted to shout it from the roof-tops and needless to say this is between the two of us."

"Of course, it is, you silly boy. You don't imagine that I should go making noises about it over town, do you?" She thought for a minute "Now, I shall keep the next two weeks clear of dates with visitors until I hear from you about the exact date. I want the party to be on your last evening."

At the door she turned and smiled. "You young devil," she said, and went.

Two days later I got a date from Paschal – January the nineteenth, an evening flight on South African Airways. I rang up Mrs Mockey and she immediately insisted that the evening of the eighteenth was booked for my farewell party.

The party at the Mockey's turned out to be attended by many of the white parishioners, but not all. There were some who found Mrs. Mockey's forthright manner difficult to accept and found her views on race matters over-liberal. I wondered that her son's views were so different. I had met Stephan in town one day in my last week at Piet Retief, he had made a remark which obliquely suggested that I was getting out before the Special Branch caught up with me. It was said as a joke, but there was always a barbed element in Stephan's jokes to me.

At the party Stephan had a lot to drink. With so many people there we had a buffet supper and stood about in groups drinking and talking. Towards ten o'clock Stephan started making remarks about my racial stance in an offensively loud voice. His mother went to him and tried to keep him quiet, but Stephan was not to be gainsaid.

"Right, Father, isn't it? I was just telling these good people how you will be telling them in England what bastards we are out here, how we oppress the poor black man, eh?" There was an appalled silence in the large room. "Well, that's right, isn't it, Father, man?" he insisted.

"You've lived here for years and enjoyed our hospitality, but now you can live off the stories about the terrible way we treat the Kaffirs, and the coloureds and the coolies." He was at least three-quarters drunk, I tried to be patient and say nothing, but I felt the blood rising to my cheeks. "You know", he continued, "It's people like you who come in and stir up trouble where none exists. I'm damn glad that you are going, and hope to hell you don't come back."

I suppose that I didn't need to blow up, because however much some of the other guests agreed with him, they did not agree with his manners and he had succeeded in embarrassing everyone in the room. His wife was tugging at his sleeve, but to no effect. But I blew up and told him that if he was typical of the manners and opinions of white South Africans, then I would have a lot to dine out on in England, fortunately I didn't consider him typical. I accused him of having a personal feud with me for months, niggling at me and trying to make me lose my temper. I was about to launch into more of the same when Mrs Mockey appeared at my elbow, shaking her head gravely and asking me to desist. I did and apologised, but the party had been soured. I wondered how many actually thought much as Stephan did but feared to say it to me. I suspected there were many. I was saddened that ten years in South Africa had ended in such a confrontation.

The party made a brave effort to get back on course and later I was presented with a travelling case they had bought for me. I made a more temperate speech of thanks and gratitude for their patience and tolerance towards me. I even made a brave effort and shook hands with Stephan at the end of the evening. He reluctantly apologised; but we were still cool to each other.

Very early the next morning I ran out to the Mockey's to see Mrs Mockey and apologise for the previous night's altercation. She brushed it aside saying Stephan had been drunk and suggesting what I ought to have done was to have kicked him up the pants. I kissed her good-bye and left and with a softness in her eyes she wished me good luck.

I went straight from the Mockey's to the Ermelo road. Where I was due to meet Paschal who was driving me up to Johannesburg. We met Cos and all had a meal together. Cos insisted we had to have a last drink at the airport, at my expense of course. I left them sadly and went into the departure lounge.

The plane was very empty and I was able to lie across three seats during the night and get at least a little sleep. I was wearing a suit but no vest or pullover as it had been very hot in Johannesburg. The stewardess gave me a blanket for the night and I dozed fitfully.

"We are now coming into land at Luanda airport, and the ground temperature is sixty nine degrees...." I awoke to hear the announcement.

"We are now approaching Grand Canary and the ground temperature is fifty seven degrees......

"We are now approaching London airport and the ground temperature is one degree....." One degree I was horrified. I had forgotten it would be winter in Britain. There was an easterly wind blowing across the tarmac as I got out of the plane and an odd snowflake hit me in the face. I shivered and made for the airport buildings. I saw my brother David and with him the Father Provincial and another priest I did not know. I greeted them and went to get my luggage. Everything was so unreal, so strange, even my name, for my brother naturally called me Tony which was my real, pre-priesthood name.

We drove from Heathrow under threatening skies and through, or around, London – I didn't know which – we made for the East End where one of our parishes was situated. It seemed an interminable journey, the small talk was about anything and everything but my reason for coming home. Among themselves they talked about things and people in the news, but it was all foreign to me. I felt like an alien. From hot summer to lowering winter skies, from an environment I knew and understood to my own country where I felt lost.

Eventually we arrived and some of the priests looked strangely at this man in their midst wearing a collar and tie, instead of the approved clerical collar and in whispers asked who I was. I went through the day in a sort of daze, as I met new people and was plunged once again into the dark and dismal interior of a Victorian built religious house in the middle of a dreary British winter. Things improved a little when a few of my fellow students appeared in the evening and, together with my brother David, insisted we go out for a meal at a nearby Chinese restaurant. I begged a minute's indulgence and rushed upstairs to where I had located a phone. I dialed a number I had been learning by heart.

"Can I speak to Nurse Mayeza, please?" I asked, and waited.

"Hello?" a voice I recognised said faintly.

"Me," I said, "I'm here".

A little gasp, and then "Oh".

"I am just going out. Listen", I whispered, "I'll come on Monday but when?"

"I'm off at three." A pause. "My darling, I can't wait."

"I know, but we have the rest of our lives. Till Monday, my love."

Epilogue

"Are you going to open the car?" I heard Pro's voice asking.

I looked round a little startled and she laughed.

"Where were you?" she asked.

"Oh," I admitted, smiling, "I was back in South Africa – in Besters and Pomeroy, in Newcastle and Piet Retief. I suppose the sunshine set off old memories."

"What, all those places in three minutes reverie?"

"Well, not everything – just fleeting recollections and some things I did not know were still there in my memory."

I unlocked the car.

"Where are the boys?" I asked.

"Hiding round the corner, as usual after church. You had better go and chase them out."

I walked towards the corner of the street with an elaborately nonchalant air, then I plunged suddenly into the side-street and made a grab for two small boys who fled shrieking with laughter towards their mother in the car.

I got back to the car to find them claiming sanctuary with their mother. This was a regular feature of Sunday mornings, my weekly fifty yards dash.

I got into the car and Pro took up the theme of my reverie again.

"You know, Tony, you will forget all those events, places and people. You ought to write it all down, if only for the sake of the boys later in life."

So I did.

POSTSCRIPT

The story in this book ends in February 1969 with a phone call to Nurse Mayeza in Alder Hey Children's Hospital in Liverpool. Later that year Tony received his dispensation from the priesthood. We got married and had two sons, Mark (1970) and Simon (1971).

In 1970 Tony began work for the Liverpool City Council in the Social Services Department. Then in 1979 he left to take a degree in Sociology at the University of Liverpool. After obtaining his degree he went on to do a part-time M.A. Course in Latin American Studies where he sucessfully completed a thesis in Liberation Theology.

What had been a happy, secure and contented family life was shattered when suddenly on the 7th March, 1985, Tony suddenly died of a heart attack. we were devastated. The very fabric of our family life was shattered. Our loss was shared by many friends and relatives, but their love and support sustained us through it all. I clung to our two sons from whom I drew the strength which enabled me to maintain some form of sanity.

The first draft of this book was written in 1984, in an attempt to provide a record to enable our sons to trace their roots. It is about Tony's experiences in South Africa. Some of the events which are mentioned in passing are discussed in more detail in a forthcoming publication by Cosmas Desmond, a close friend and colleague of Tony.

After Tony died I re-read his manuscript and became more convinced that it had wider relevance than just a record for our two sons. The book gives an account of the effect of apartheid on the everyday life of black people in South Africa and this situation is not far removed from the experiences of black people in Britain, America and in other European Countries. I, therefore, decided to publish the manuscript.

I had already set up Spennithorne publications. In conversation with David (Fr. Rayner), Tony's brother, I decided I needed something specific to do in order to cope with my early days of bereavement. He suggested I published as a trial run "Peter Calvay – Prophet" the second book in his trilogy.

My involvement with Spennithorne helped to maintain my strength and sanity. But that strength and sanity was put to further test when suddenly on the 30th of June 1987, Mark, our 17 year old son, died of an undiagnosed heart condition known as Congenital Obstructive Cardiomyopathy.

As a family, we had experienced the warmth and the love of many of our friends in Liverpool. The real depth and sincerity of that love was perhaps best revealed when we lost Tony, then Mark. We were also absolutely overwhelmed by the love, the care and the genuine concern showed by many people in Liverpool who had not been previously known to us who have since become friends. The fact that I have been able to publish this book is a real tribute to the people of Liverpool. Without their generous love, support and encouragement I would have myself found it difficult to survive let alone be able to publish this book.

Finally, I wish to thank those who have contributed in the production of this book. My many thanks to Viv Tyler who edited the manuscript and was a most helpful consultant in the production of the book; to Sister Paula Margaret for her superb artistic creation of the book cover; to Cosmas Desmond for providing some details needed in the editing of the manuscript; to Tricia McMillan for her untiring patience in typing and editing the initial manuscript; to Bobby Howes for her initial proof reading, Elsie Cliff and Nigel Mellor for the final proof reading; to Diane Murgatroyd and Lorraine Campbell with helping to prepare the publicity material; to David Torkington for his unwavering support and encouragement. To our son, Simon, I give my thanks for remaining my source of strength and giving meaning to my life.

PROTASIA TORKINGTON

WHAT HAPPENED TO THE MAIN CHARACTERS

Jack Ramana

Died in a car crash on his way to a building job in one of the missions in 1969.

Lionel Steele

Died of a heart attack on his way to the Airport to visit the Torkingtons in Liverpool in 1970.

Bishop Christopher Ulyatt

Came back to England in the early 1970's. Died of a heart attack on the 12th October 1974 at the age of 69.

Fr. Paschal Rowland

Still in South Africa – is now the Bishop.

Fr. Neil McGovern (Fred)

Still in South Africa in the Franciscan Order.

Fr. Marius (Joe Banks)

In South Africa and is still in the Franciscan Order.

Fr. Cosmas Desmond

Cosmas completed his researches on the moves of people from "black spots" and in 1970 published in South Africa his findings in his book "The Discarded People". In 1971 Penguin printed and published the book. Granada television picked up the theme in their programme "World in Action" and revealed in a graphic form the inhumanity afflicted on black people in the course of the moves. Soon after the South African Government put Cosmas under house arrest for 5 years (1971-1975) during which period he was not allowed to talk to more than one person at a time. After his release from banning Cos got married and the family moved to England in 1978. Between 1979 and 1981 Cos was the Director of the British Amnesty. He now lives with his family in the East End of London.

Fr. Cormac	Left South Africa and joined the Holy Land Missionary Action Group. He is now based in Jaffa in Israel.
Seminarians	In 1971 the Seminary in Pomeroy closed down and all the students were transferred to another Seminary in Hammerskraal in Pretoria. Only one of the semanarians eventually became a priest.

A CALENDAR OF EVENTS

	Tony Torkington	South Africa
1931 30th Aug.	Born in Didsbury – Manchester	1936 – Land Act: 13.7 Removed Voting Rights
1936	Started School in the Convent School – Heaton Mersey	1948 – Nationalist Party wins the election Jan Smuts defeated in Standerton
1942	St. Bedes Grammar School	
1949	Manchester University Studying Law	1949 – Durban Riots v. Indians
1951	Ushaw College – Durham Studying philsophy	1950 – Group Areas Act
1953	Chilworth Novitiate – Surrey	1952 – Defiance Campaign
1954	East Bergholt House of Studies	1955 – ANC Freedom Charter
1959	South Africa	
1960	Set up a seminary in Besters	1960 – Sharpeville Massacre – Banning of ANC and PAC
1963	Moves with the Seminary to Pomeroy	1961 – South Africa leaves the Commonwealth and becomes Republic
1964	On Leave in England	1964 – Rivonia trial Nelson Mandela is sentenced, to life imprisonment
1964	Back in South Africa	1966 – Assassination of Verwoerd
1969	Back in England – gets married	1967 – Beginning of the Black Consciousness Movement

1970	Employed by City Council Social Services, Liverpool	1972-3 – Durban Strikes 1975 – Independence of Angola and Mozambique 1976 – Soweto uprising
1979	B.A. Degree in Sociology	1977 – Death of Steve Biko
1983	Part time M.A./Part-time Catholic Social Services	1977 – Banning of BCM (Black Consciousness Movement) Organisations and Christian Institute
1985	Died of a heart attack	1978 – Murder of Rick Turner 1980 – Trade Union's legalised 1983 – United Democratic Front Formed 1984 – New Constitution – tri-cameral parliament 1985 Langa Massacre State of Emergency